Representation and Behavior

Representation and Behavior

Fred Keijzer

A Bradford Book
The MIT Press
Cambridge, Massachusetts
London, England

This book was set in Sabon by The MIT Press and was printed and bound in the United States of America.

First printing, 2001

Library of Congress Cataloging-in-Publication Data

Keijzer, Fred A., 1960–
Representation and behavior / Fred Keijzer.
p. cm.
"A Bradford book."
Includes bibliographical references and index.
ISBN 0-262-11259-0 (alk. paper)
1. Cognitive science. 2. Human behavior. 3. Mental representation. I. Title.
BF311 .K45 2001
150.19'43—dc21 00-064593

For Frans Keijzer and Alie van Klink

Contents

Acknowledgments

I am indebted to many people for helpful discussions, comments, or feedback on the text. Of those, I want to name explicitly Bram Bakker, Bill Bechtel, Sacha Bem, Margriet Boekenoogen, Rob Bongaardt, Jan Willem de Graaf, Tanny Dobbelaar, Inman Harvey, Pim Haselager, Jan Heemskerk, Ronald Lemmen, Onno Meijer, Tim Smithers, Lex van der Heijden, Tim van Gelder, René van Hezewijk, Paul Verschure, Reinout Wiers, and Rob Withagen.

Figures 2.2 and 2.3 are reprinted from Figure 1 and Figure 10 of E. P. Krotkov and R. G. Simmons, *International Journal of Robotics Research, 15,* 155–180 (copyright © 1996 by Sage Publications; reprinted by permission of Sage Publications, Inc.).

Figure 3.2 is reprinted with permission from Figure 7 of M. H. Raibert and J. K. Hodgins, Legged robots, in R. D. Beer, R. E. Ritzmann, and T. McKenna (eds.), *Biological neural networks in invertebrate neuroethology and robotics* (pp. 319–354) (copyright 1993, Marc Raibert).

Figure 4.3 is reprinted with permission from Figure 1 of R. A. Brooks, A robot that walks: emergent behaviors from a carefully evolved network, *Neural Computation, 1,* 253–262 (copyright 1989, MIT Press).

Figures 4.4, 4.5 and 4.6 are reprinted from R. D. Beer, A dynamical systems perspective on agent-environment interaction, *Artificial Intelligence, 72,* 173–215 (copyright 1995, with permission from Elsevier Science).

Figure 5.1 is reprinted with permission from Figure 1 and Figure 2 of G. Taga, Y. Yamaguchi, and H. Shimizu, Self-organized control of bipedal locomotion by neural oscillators in unpredictable environment, *Biological Cybernetics, 65,* 147–159 (copyright 1991, Springer Verlag).

Representation and Behavior

Introduction

1 An indirect approach to representation

I often have this vision of a group of loud, little boys, somehow belonging to a Miss Marple-style England. They are pressing their noses and hands to the display window of an old-fashioned sweet-store and are fully engrossed in the displayed delights. The boys' main objective seems to be to reach these goodies as directly as possible, which explains their pressed noses. However, when I ask them why they do not try the shop's door in order to lay their hands on those sweets, they answer: "We don't want a door! We want the sweets!"

To me, this scene portrays a very general attitude toward theory development in cognitive science and the philosophy of mind. Cognitive scientists and philosophers alike are strongly drawn by the mind, loosely demarcated by characteristics such as thought, meaning, intentionality and consciousness. The mind provides the focus for theory building in these fields as cognitive theorists try to develop ideas to explain the different aspects of this most evasive and perplexing of all phenomena. Anything that does not have the proper mental 'glow' tends to remain at the sideline of theoretical interest. However, it is not at all clear that a direct approach should provide the most suitable 'access-door' to a better understanding of issues relating to the mind. Under certain circumstances, an investigation of a non-mental topic can provide insights that are hard to come by in any direct way.

This difference between a direct and a more indirect approach applies very well to the development of representational theories. Representation is a fundamental concept within cognitive science. Representations form the heart of cognitive explanations and the basis for formulating theories of cognitive functioning. Making the notion of representation as clear as possible is therefore an important project. Most of the work that has been done in this respect takes the direct approach. Representations are interpreted as *mental representations*, theoretical entities that are the bearers of meaning and the source of intentionality. Theories of representation are formulated so as to fit our intuitions concerning meaning and intentionality. The debate is about the proposed theories' relative success in fitting these intuitions. Within this procedure, a theory of representation that does not catch the mental surface structure is to be dismissed.

The direct approach of representation pushes attention to representation's sensory side. Representations are primarily seen as an internal reflection of external, environmental circumstances. In this form they act as the end station of sensory processes that translate the environmental state of affairs into a set of mental representations. However, besides this inward bound, perceptual side to representation it has also a side which is outward bound. Representations are the starting point for a set of processes that lead back to the external environment. They are seen as a source for the outwardly visible behavior of a person. This behavioral aspect of representation has received much less attention over the years than the perceptual one. In this book, I will explore cognitive science's notion of representation from a behavioral perspective. It will also be an indirect approach of representation which is in many ways independent from mind-based theorizing.

Focusing on the relation between representation and behavior is in itself not an indirect approach of representation. What makes it so is changing the topic. Instead of offering a study of representation, I offer a study of behavior. Behavior is a phenomenon which is independent from mind. Ants, for example, definitely behave even when it can be doubted whether they have minds. Consequently, behavior deserves an explanation of its own. In this book, I will only address the question how the behavior of agents is generated and I will explicitly not deal with mental issues. This topic may miss that special mental 'glow' which draws so many theorists. On the other hand, this loss is more than compensated for by the possibilities for investigating the notion of representation without putting it into the straightjacket provided by a mental interpretation. It allows a much freer theoretical treatment and conceptualization of representation as it is used within cognitive science.

To explain how behavior is generated, representation is generally thought to be indispensable. In this view, there has to be a kind of motor program which represents the behavior to be executed and which instructs the agent's motor system. Therefore, by aiming at behavior, representation is taken in as well. Only, representation now takes the role of a subsidiary concept whose very presence and conceptualization *solely* depends on their contribution to the larger goal of behavioral explanation. By focusing on behavior some very radical questions come to the fore: For what reason do we use the notion of representation in cognitive theories? What work does it do there? And which characteristics do these representations need to do the work that they are supposed to do?

In asking these questions, representations are treated as hypothetical empirical entities. Their presumed characteristics are tentative and to be adjusted to further the primary goal of explaining behavior. The notion of representation can even be discarded altogether, should it come out that it is not necessary to explain the generation of behavior. In short, rather than treating representation as an intuitively given, mental concept, I will treat representation as a concept whose theoretical merit is on the line, while its conceptualization can be rearranged as need dictates.

The focus on behavior offers a convenient paradigm for discussing a number of criticisms of representational thinking in cognitive science. While the use of representations in cognitive science went for many years unquestioned, over the last ten years or so a lot of criticism has been leveled against representational thinking. For example, cognitive science's representations were to be grounded in the environment (Harnad, 1990), they were to be interactive and tied to an agent (Clark, 1997a), or they were even to be discarded (Brooks, 1991a). In the direct approach of representation—where representations are *mental* representations—the suggestion that one might do without representations is not so much wrong, rather, it does not seem coherent. Doing without representations is an option that does not square with a conceptual framework in which representations are the fundamental entities. By turning to behavior, it becomes possible to interpret and systemize many of these criticisms and to portray the nonrepresentational position as a serious and coherent theoretical option. All of this will allow a much more specific formulation of what representation does and does not for cognitive science.

2 Basic behavior

Stalking representations via a behavioral route has some consequences that may be hard to swallow at first. One of them consists of the kind of behavior that will be used to access representation. To investigate a phenomenon, it is usually best to turn first to its most simple instances. These cases tend to be easier to observe and understand. Within the present circumstances, this general heuristic implies that it is best to look at the simplest kinds of behavior for which representation is invoked as a part of its explanation. I will call the kind of behavior which fulfills this constraint *basic behavior*.

Basic behavior is the behavior that humans have in common with all animals, horses and insects alike. Examples include moving about over natural surfaces, using sensory stimulation to initiate, guide and end ongoing behavior, and performing behavioral sequences. The claim that insect-level behavior is a good model-system for investigating representation may come as a surprise to many cognitive scientists and philosophers of mind. Whereas human cognition seems to require the manipulation of internal representations, the same is not usually said for the basic behavior of insect-like creatures. Insect behavior is typically seen as a simple matter of direct, mechanical reflexes. Such reflexes do not appear to involve mediation by internal representations.

Appearances are misleading here. Reflex-based accounts may specify which external variables trigger a specific behavior, but they do not explain how the triggered behavior comes about. For example, moving forward may be very simple when seen as an abstracted functional action, but actually performing the physical movements that are necessary to accomplish it is a challenging task. When one tries to explain how the nervous system of, for example, an insect accomplishes outward behavioral regularities, it becomes obvious that the processes involved are highly complex. Legs and other body parts have to be coordinated, disturbances of ongoing behavior have to be counteracted, sensory stimulation has to be processed so that it can be used to guide behavior, and so on. Basic behavior requires a lot of internal processing that go far beyond any 'direct' connection between sensors and effectors. It is common practice to use representations to help explain what happens here. For example, when roboticists try to build an artifact that is capable of some basic behavior, they habitually rely on representation-based models to generate the behavior. Although I will later on address the question whether this is actually a good idea, the fact remains that many roboticists would not know how to make operational robots if they did not use representation-based control architectures. Basic behavior is definitely complex enough to invoke representation-based explanations.

3 Multi-level naturalism

At this point, something more general should be said about setting up basic behavior as an important topic for cognitive science. Basic behavior is a long way from the concerns of most cognitive scientists, in particular for the philosophers of mind among them. When it comes to thinking about mind-related issues, the traditional Cartesian antagonism between mind and nature is still very much alive. Special features like meaning and consciousness set the human mind apart from the mechanical world of physics, which is often described using modifiers like 'mere', 'just', 'only', and 'brute' when it is compared to the mental realm (see, e.g., Searle, 1992). Almost all theorizing relating to the mind is built up around this central dichotomy, either as attempts to safeguard the independent position of the mind, or, the other way round, to eliminate or reduce the mental to nothing but physical processes.

From the perspective provided by the mind-nature dichotomy, basic behavior would appear to be a side issue. No one questions whether basic behavior can be explained in *merely* naturalistic terms, so it seems that with regard to the mind-nature relation nothing much will be gained by discussing basic behavior. The features that are unique to the human mind are thought of as the problematic ones and these will still have to be dealt with.

In this book, I do not go along with any deep, conceptual antagonism between mind and nature. Instead, I will work with the assumption of multi-level naturalism. In this view the world is taken to consist of multiple levels of organization, each requiring its own set of descriptions. This multi-level natural world is ontologically heterogeneous in the sense that many different phenomena do exist in the same way that physical phenomena exist. There is no single basic level. The mind is only one among many different natural phenomena. It may be special to us, but it has no intrinsically special status with respect to the rest of nature. The theoretical problem posed by mental phenomena is therefore not conceived of as reconciling two essentially incompatible domains, but as elucidating how nature diversifies itself into increasingly complex and different forms.

Multi-level naturalism diverges from the physicalist views on nature held by many philosophers (Kim, 1998; Papineau, 1993). On the other hand, it is a view that can be found in the work of many scientists nowadays, particularly those working on the notion of self-organization (Goodwin, 1994; Kauffman, 1993; Kelso, 1995; Stewart and Cohen, 1997). The idea that the natural world is at heart nothing but physics reflects the old Newtonian view of physics rather than the insights of natural sciences of the late twentieth century. Given the choice, I prefer to work with the modern ideas. In this book, I will not put up an elaborate defense of multi-level naturalism. I merely intend to show that working with this premise is highly rewarding from a theoretical point of view.

Without the deep conceptual antagonism between mind and nature, one need not focus exclusively on those aspects of mind that are most difficult to reconcile with naturalism. In turn, intermediate phenomena that are mind-like but still close to known non-mental phenomena become more interesting. Such 'half-mental' phenomena offer a way to gradually extend existing natural science explanations in the direction of increasingly mind-like phenomena. Success in this area would constitute important progress in itself, as well as providing a theoretical platform from which one can more easily approach the human mind.

The philosopher Mary Midgley said about the general, perfunctory treatment of animal intelligence, "That this attitude has lingered so long is also understandable, since a tradition *that a certain topic does not matter* is one of the hardest to get rid of—discussion of it tends to be tabooed before it starts" (1995, p. 232). With this introduction I hope to have removed this initial hurdle to the appreciation of the discussion in this book. This is my hope in particular because a behavioral focus has many interesting and far-reaching implications for the notion of representation as it functions in cognitive theorizing.

4 Preview

In the first chapter, I set out the basic premises: multi-level naturalism and a behavioral approach of representation. The study of behavior and the study of mind will be dissociated. Mind will be situated at a higher, personal level of organization, whereas the generation of behavior has to be accomplished by some mechanism operating at subpersonal levels. My concern will be with this subpersonal mechanism, not with the mind. However, talk about the mind immediately returns in a different form. Within cognitive science, the mind becomes reformulated as a subpersonal mechanism which is habitually used to account for behavior. I will call the use of a personal-level conceptual framework at this subpersonal level of organization Agent Theory or AT for short. I consider AT to be the dominant and most advanced explanation for behavior that is currently available, but also an explanation that has severe problems and is ultimately on the wrong track: The mind does not provide a good explanation for the generation of behavior.

AT is usually only an implicitly held view. Chapter 2 offers a reconstruction of this account as it can be distilled from work in cognitive science and is made operative in the field of robotics. In this way, cognitive science can shown to be dedicated to specific answers to the question why representations are necessary and what particular role they play in an account of the generation of behavior. This role puts specific demands on the notion of representation. Representations function as an internal (partial) model of the external environment. Because of their abstract similarity to the external situation, representations provide the behaving system with the guidance that is necessary to instruct the motor apparatus so that behavior comes about which is oriented toward the external situation.

Chapter 3 systemizes and discusses problems associated with AT. On the one hand, AT faces structural difficulties that derive from its basic setup. As a result of these structural difficulties AT provides a very brittle solution to the problem of behavior. In addition there are meta-theoretical, observer-related difficulties that jeopardize the basic premises of AT. I conclude that AT does not provide a good explanation for the generation of behavior. An alternative conceptual framework is sorely needed.

The next two chapters investigate a possible alternative for AT that I will call Behavioral Systems Theory (BST). BST derives from the idea that behavior can be explained as the result of the interactions between an organism and its environment. The concrete embodiment of organisms, as well as their being situated in an environment with a specific structure are held to be important determinants of behavior. In addition, it is claimed that behavior can be explained without internal models, and—under that particular interpretation of representation—without representations.

Chapter 4 discusses several ways in which BST has been developed so far: (1) Maturana and Varela's ideas on the biology of cognition set up a rough outline of BST (Maturana and Varela, 1980, 1988). (2) Autonomous Agents Research provides a very concrete version of BST by building animal-like robots, and (3) Dynamical Systems Theory gives a formal, mathematical interpretation of organism-environment interactions. BST has been successful in modeling sensory-guided basic behavior, but faces difficulties with anticipatory behavior where internal states play an important role. Anticipatory behavior is the strong point of AT, and, to be a serious competitor, BST should also be able to deal with it.

Chapter 5 offers an extension of BST that addresses anticipatory behavior. This extension is based on an analogy between behavior and morphogenesis, the process by which multicellular body-form develops. By using ideas developed to account for morphogenesis, it becomes possible to envision a mechanism that steers the short-term organism-environment interactions of BST without positing internal models. A mechanism like this provides a possible account for anticipatory behavior and forms the basis for a real alternative for AT.

5 Reading guide

The book is set up as a coherent whole that systematically builds up a case for a nonrepresentational explanation of behavior. It is best read from cover to cover. However, there are shorter ways to get at the most important ideas presented in the book. The absolute minimal reading would consist of only the first and last chapter, and every last section of the chapters in between. Chapter 1 introduces the major divisions and concepts that will be discussed. Chapter 5 is the key chapter that gives the most elaborate treatment of the nonrepresentational position as defended in this book. The remaining chapters provide the context and supporting arguments for this nonrepresentational position. These chapters are not easily put in a general order of importance and any choosing between them is best done on the basis of the readers' own background and interest.

Chapter 2 is important because it sketches cognitivism as a behavioral conceptual framework and brings to the fore a number of surprising twists to otherwise familiar ideas. Chapter 3 is a key chapter that brings home the message that AT does not suffice as an explanation of behavior and that therefore an alternative, such as BST, is needed. Chapter 4 discusses current attempts to fill in BST and gives a good overview of what has been done as well as what is still missing.

1

Behavior: Levels and Explanations

1 Behavioral science and mental science

Behavior is a fundamental psychological[1] topic. It is a phenomenon that stands out in the world. In contrast to inanimate objects, animals and humans move about without being pushed around by external causes. They initiate and maintain bodily movements on their own. In addition, these movements show a sense of purpose as they allow the organism to reach specific goal-states, often showing a lot of flexibility in overcoming obstructions on the way. These are very special properties that have drawn the attention of humans in all ages (Breland and Breland, 1966), while its systematic study can be traced back to Aristotle who wrote a book specifically about the movements of animals, now known as "De Motu Animalium." Aristotle stated: "For all animals both impart movement and are moved for the sake of something, so that this is the limit to all their movement: the thing for-the-sake-of-which" (translation in Nussbaum, 1978, p. 38). In the following, I will use the characteristics pointed out by Aristotle as a first, preliminary definition of behavior: the self-initiated, purposive movements of animals and humans. This phenomenon is definitely a topic which should receive due respect from psychologists.

For a large part of the twentieth century, psychology was dominated by behaviorists who held behavior to be of primary concern. In the early seventies, Margaret Boden wrote: "The basic question of psychology is: Why do men and animals behave as they do? On this point psychologists agree. They do not agree, however, about what type of answer would be most appropriate" (1972, p. 1). The consensus concerning the basic question of psychology has changed since then. The cognitive revolution—started in the 1950s and 1960s—changed psychology's focus on (primarily) behavior into a focus on (primarily) mind and cognition. By the 1980s, the mind had become the new central point of psychological interest. With this change came a new consensus: Modeling the cognitive system would provide the right type of answer to Boden's basic question, "Why do men and animals behave as they do?" But the question itself receded into the background. The new task for psychology was to model the cognitive system.

In the cognition-oriented view of psychology—cognitivist psychology[2] or cognitivism for short—behavior is viewed as a less important research topic. A part of this can probably be explained as a historical residue of the struggle with behaviorism. The latter's stress on behavior was countered by (overly) stressing the importance of the cognitive system instead. However, the topic of behavior is deemphasized in more ways. In comparison to the topic of mind, that of behavior looks plain. Mind-related phenomena, like intentionality and consciousness, are still science's ultimate mysteries. When the rise of cognitive modeling promised psychologists a real tack to unravel the mysteries of mind, it was no small wonder that many defected. This trend was strengthened when behavior was interpreted as a derivative—the output—of mental or cognitive processes. In this view, behavior is no more than the execution of a set of instructions computed by a cognitive system. Someone who studies this cognitive system will, supposedly, learn everything worth knowing about behavior as well. As a consequence, there is no need to study behavior separate from cognition. Behavior in which the mind does not seem to be involved tends to be interpreted as very simple, reflex-like, and mechanical. Such simple behavior is thought to be explainable by basic, physiological stimulus-response mechanisms. How it works in detail is, of course, not yet known, but it is a problem that biologists and physiologists are working on. For a psychology focused on the mind this is easily seen as a side issue.

Given these reasons, as well as the historical developments, psychology's former position as primarily a behavioral science looks definitely like something of the past. In this book, I will oppose this trend. I will stress the importance of behavior as a primary topic for psychological theorizing, independent of any bearings of this topic on mental phenomena. The psychological problem that will be addressed in this book is the question: How can we explain the generation of behavior?

Focusing on behavior will not set one free from discussing cognitive issues. Cognitivism provides the most developed and detailed explanation of behavior to date. As a consequence, this book will primarily be concerned with the cognitivist explanation for the generation of behavior. The discussion will center on the notion of representation, a notion which forms cognitivism's conceptual foundation. In contrast to a cognition-oriented discussion however, the notion of representation will play a secondary role. The notion of representation will be interpreted and evaluated for its usefulness as part of an explanation for behavior. The question that I will address is the following: *What place, if any, should representations occupy in an explanation of the generation of behavior?*

Both the professed interest in behavior, as well as the question concerning representation's role in its explanation, do not simply come out of the blue. As will be discussed later, over the last ten years, the basic assumptions of cognitivism have been increasingly questioned. One major theme in these criticisms is the accusation that cognitivist psychology neglects 'external' factors. Cognitivist psychology tends to focus almost exclusively on the internal thinking apparatus, abstracting away from the concrete circumstances in which real cognitive systems operate. It is now becoming increasingly accepted that—to understand intelligence—psychology should not only focus on processes going on inside the head. Processes that happen outside the head are at least as important. There are two key notions in this context that are often mentioned: *embodiment* and *situatedness*.

Embodiment refers to the particular bodily characteristics of an agent. These include both sensory capabilities as well as the capacity for movement made possible by the musculo-skeletal system and manipulative appendages such as beaks and claws. An agent's embodiment is a very important factor when this agent has to solve some task requiring intelligence. Its embodiment more or less defines what options an agent has available for solving a problem.

Situatedness refers to the environmental characteristics that bear on intelligence. The environment provides a lot of structure that a cognitive system can use to solve its problems. For example, steering a car along a road is a complex task under most circumstances. However, as long as the car stays on a road that has white stripes on the sides, the task becomes much simpler.

As long as the car does not cross these stripes, it will automatically remain on the road.

The critics of cognitivism claim that doing intelligent things is not only dependent on the internal cognitive system, which acts as an omnipotent intelligent power that thinks up solutions to problems beforehand and then imposes them as instructions on a motor apparatus and so achieves its goals. The critics claim that the internal cognitive system is only one element in a larger, embodied and situated, system. To achieve its goals, a cognitive system depends on its embodiment and situatedness. I will refer to this approach, critical of cognitivism, as *interactionism*, because it stresses the importance of the interactions between a bodily agent and its environment.

The raised interest in the outward aspects of cognitive systems provides a motive for looking at behavior again. The discussion between interactionists and cognitivists provides a motive for paying attention to the role played by representation within behavioral explanation.

The debate between cognitivists and interactionists sometimes becomes very fierce. An important reason for this vehemence arises because (a number of) interactionists challenge cognitivism's regular use of representations for explaining behavior. A number of interactionists argue that psychology could and should do without them (Brooks, 1991a, 1991b; Shanon, 1993; Van Gelder, 1995; Varela, Thompson, and Rosch, 1991). The cognitivist reaction to this claim is caustic. While the importance of the embodiment and situatedness of cognitive systems is increasingly accepted (Clark, 1994, 1997a, 1997b), a critique of the notion of representation is of a different stature.

The concept of representation is central to cognitivist psychology. Many would hold that without it there would be no psychology left. Consequently, the common cognitivist response is that any criticism of the use of representations is patently mistaken, not worth serious attention, and probably not seriously meant in the first place (Vera and Simon, 1993a, 1993b). In turn, a number of radical interactionists—those who think that the use of representations is unnecessary for explaining behavior—strongly object to this cognitivist verdict (Clancey, 1993; Winograd and Flores, 1994). The ensuing discussion has a tendency to expand into a wide-reaching, ideological battle over psychology's fundamental assumptions (Clancey, 1993; Vera and Simon, 1993a, 1993b; Winograd and Flores, 1986, 1994).

In this book, I will try to contain as well as discipline the issues that are raised in this discussion between cognitivists and interactionists by focusing on the concrete and straightforward question stated above: What place, if any, should representations occupy in an explanation of behavior?

2 Setting up behavior as an independent psychological topic

As said above, psychology is nowadays in the first place cast as a science of the mind, while behavior remains a comparative side issue. Given this state of affairs, targeting behavior as a psychological topic independently from mental concerns requires some justification. In this section, I will give my reasons for claiming that behavior deserves psychology's full attention in its own right.

2.1 What is behavior anyway?

The word 'behavior' is used to refer to very different things in different circumstances. Of course, given the psychological context, it should be evident that behavior is not interpreted in its physical sense: "the action, reaction, or functioning of a system under normal or specified circumstances" as Collins English Dictionary describes it. Still, the multiple meanings of behavior remain even after it is described as "the outward behavior exhibited by humans and animals" (Maturana and Varela, 1988, p. 136), and after prototypical examples are given, such as woodlice moving toward a more humid environment, ants carrying leaf cuttings for their mould garden, a tiger stalking through the forest in search of prey, or a man hurrying to catch a bus. This description and these examples exclude many other, seemingly unproblematic cases of behavior. Examples are an industrial robot welding two pipes together, a chess computer playing chess, or, the classical border example, a thermostat maintaining a constant temperature in your fridge? Are the latter cases now to be included or not?

The notion of behavior tends to provoke this kind of discussion. Behavior is still a very intuitive notion, which misses clear and definite criteria. Classifying a phenomenon as behavior or not is done merely on the basis of outward appearance and convention. The risk is that very diverse phenomena are grouped together in this way, phenomena that require different explanations rather than an identical theoretical treatment. Trying to fit dissimilar phenomena into a single theoretical framework is a sure way to get confusing results. The project of explaining the generation of behavior then has to be as specific as possible about its target—behavior. For this reason, I will aim the discussion only at *prototypical behavior.* Prototypical behavior consists of the self-initiated, purposive movements of animals and humans.

It should be pointed out explicitly that this disqualifies as prototypical behavior the self-initiated, purposive movements of human-built artifacts such as robots (robots may be used to model prototypical behavior though). Whether or not the latter has to be interpreted as behavior will be treated as an undecided issue. Pending more definite criteria for behavior, I hold that artifact cases should be kept apart, just to avoid possible confusions. To mark this limited application of the notion 'behavior' I make a distinction between movement and behavior, all behavior involving movement in one way or other, but not all movement amounting to behavior. With this distinction, the terminology will be that robots do definitely *move purposefully*, while it is an open question whether they *behave purposefully*.

This particular distinction between movement and behavior is unusual and may seem implausible to some. Why would a human welding two pipes together constitute an example of behavior while a robot doing the same task would not? Why draw a border here? There are definite and, I think, convincing reasons for this particular distinction. These reasons will eventually culminate in the claim that this possibility is actually the case: Current robots do not behave.

The relevant arguments and ideas for drawing this line will only take form in later chapters. However, let me try to provide some immediate grasp to this movement-behavior distinction. An important shift is that behavior will no longer be considered primarily as a functional but rather as a structural category. It is held that the differentiating kernel of behavior is to an important degree located in the structural, dynamical properties of a behaving system together with its environment and not in the functional regularities that arise from them. This is in contradiction with the widespread use of a functional criterion as the essential aspect of behavior (see, e.g., McFarland and Bösser, 1993). Functional regularities are present in organismal behavior, as well as in human artifacts (Wright, 1973; Boorse, 1976), and there is little or no difference between the doings of humans and machines in this respect. From this functional perspective, there is no difference between, for example, a welding robot and a welding human, so how could only one of them be considered behavior? The answer that I will give later will turn around the point that there are important structural differences in the way both systems achieve their separate tasks. I hope this short motivation suffices to make the movement-behavior distinction acceptable for now. It will receive more reinforcement later on.

Stating that behavior or movements can be purposive also needs clarification. 'Purposive behavior' is a term used in many different ways, many of them implying the presence of an intentional agent who has an internal goal-representation that directs the agent toward the goal. At present, I have a more limited and descriptive interpretation of 'purposive' in mind. I use purposive behavior strictly in the meaning of goal-achieving behavior (McFarland, 1989). Goal-achievement relates only to the outward functional or adaptive characteristics of behavior. The functionality or adaptivity resides in the fact that ongoing behavior is performed for the sake of some future goal. These goals can be specified in advance by an observer who has become familiar with the behaving organism, so that the organism can be predicted to achieve these goals in a consistent way. To stress the point, goal-achieving, or purposive behavior does not necessarily imply the presence of an internal goal-representing mechanism. On the contrary, it will be a central question whether such a mechanism is necessary for goal-achieving behavior.

Another relevant point is to stress that functionality or adaptivity as used here does not set behavior apart from the common, natural order of causality. Rather, behavior is a process that needs to be understood at multiple time-scales. Ongoing behavior is performed in order to achieve a goal, which is seemingly against simple forward causality. However, on a longer time scale, the consequences of achieving the goal feed back to the behaving system and help to maintain it over time (e.g., by bringing in nutrients or by producing offspring). In this sense, purposive behavior is causally dependent on its long-term individual and species history. As Maynard Smith said, "the functional explanation is also a causal one, but on a longer time scale" (1986, p. 8).

In line with this generally biological reading of functionality or adaptivity, I will use the term adaptivity in a slightly wider sense than is customary in the interactionist movement. Adaptivity is often read as an individual organism's capacity to learn, to modify its behavior to different circumstances. In the following, I will talk about adaptivity, even when behavior is totally instinctive. Even when an individual organism is not capable of changing its behavior, the behavior of this kind of organism can be modified on an evolutionary scale, by selection.

Finally, there is an important subset of behavior that needs mentioning. *Anticipatory behavior* is a specific kind of purposive, goal-achieving behavior. Purposive behavior in general can be guided toward a goal by the continuously updated state of its sensors as the behavior unfolds. In the case of anticipatory behavior, the environment does not offer the sensory signals that will allow the organism to achieve the goal. To overcome this problem, the organism needs some internal state as an addition to the missing sensory signals.[3] These internal states are standardly interpreted as representations, and they form a key issue in the following discussion. For the record, note also that anticipatory behavior as described here is a behavioral phenomenon. It does not include the subjective, personal-level aspects of anticipation.

2.2 Why behavior?

In a general sense, the links between cognition and behavior are very strong. Given that cognition is intrinsically related to the operation of the nervous system, behavior cannot be excluded. The whole evolutionary point of a nervous system is its capacity to coordinate behavior. Nervous systems are selected so that the organism in which it is situated does the right (adaptive) things at the right time. Human cognition and its capacity for abstract thought is no more than a late evolutionary addition. Understanding it would be greatly helped by clear ideas concerning the regular operation of a nervous system in connection with behavior. The trend toward a more interactionist psychology with its stress on embodiment and situatedness points in the same direction: Cognition is increasingly seen in terms of action and sensory-motor coordination (Beer, 1990, 1995a; Brooks, 1991a, 1991b; Bem, 1989; Clark, 1997a; Franklin, 1995; Port and Van Gelder, 1995). Finally, the overt discussion of behavior may have largely disappeared from (cognitivist) psychology, but, ultimately, psychology still aims to explain behavior (Leahey, 1992, p. 438; Van der Heijden, 1992). Since the cognitive revolution, behavior is just approached much more indirectly, via the cognitive system. The cognitive revolution also changed the kind of behavior studied. Behaviorist experiments in animal learning did not stand their ground against the promising study of cognitive tasks suddenly made possible by the new computer technology in the 1950s. In the process, behavior was trimmed down from actual sensory-motor actions to an abstract input-output function. The sentiments of the investigators also changed as they began to reinterpret behavior more and more as a mere means to study thought (Amsel, 1989). All in all, while the commitment of psychology to explain behavior may have moved to the background, it was never actually replaced.

Despite the close general links a large gap still separates the study of cognitive processes from the study of the concrete, sensory-motor aspects of behavior. Practical reasons for maintaining a division of labor abound. There is, however, a very specific reason for making the step from the study of cognition to the study of behavior. The conceptual heart of cognitivism is formed by the concept of representation. When one tries to articulate this concept and its place in psychology, a much closer look at behavior is required. The need to make this step from representation to behavior comes to the fore very clearly in a discussion between Jerry Fodor and Stephen Stich.

Fodor (1975, 1981) described the place occupied by representations within cognitive explanations as follows. Representations are both semantic and syntactic entities. The semantic aspects of representations make them meaningful entities like those that figure in the beliefs and desires with which we explain our own and each other's behavior in daily life (e.g., Mary believes that it will rain today, and therefore she takes her umbrella along when she leaves home). This commonsense version of belief-desire psychology is usually called folk psychology. The syntactic aspects of representations make them causally effective within a computational system. The semantic and syntactic characteristics are supposed to be closely, or at least sufficiently, correlated. This construction provided a way in which common sense's belief-desire psychology could be interpreted as a causally effective way of explaining people's behavior.

Stich argued against Fodor's construction (a) that the necessary correlation between syntax and semantics was not present, and (b) that the semantics did not do any causal work in this theory. Therefore the semantics might as well be skipped, leaving a purely syntactic theory (Stich, 1983). The first point has, for a long time, been a major issue within the philosophy of mind (see, e.g., Guttenplan, 1994a). However, the second point could have much wider implications. The first point merely questions *how* semantic properties could be realized in computational models, the latter opens the discussion *why* any semantic properties would be introduced in cognitive explanations at all. Cummins calls this "Stich's Challenge":

> Given that the causal and the computational impact of a data structure are tracked by its nonsemantic properties, their semantic properties need not (and hence should not) enter into any causal or computational explanations that feature them. So why treat them as representations at all? (1989, p. 124)

What becomes clear here is the supportive role played by representations within psychology. Representations should not be merely assumed, they should earn their explanatory keep. They are a part of an explanation of something else. The burden of proof thus lies with those who find that representations should be included in a cognitive theory. The main criterion is, what is the best explanation of behavior? This could be an account without any representations, or maybe involving a very specific and uncommon interpretation of representations. The lesson here is that *the concept of representation has to be a variable, dependent on the behavioral theory of which it is to be a part.* This contrasts sharply with the current practice within the philosophy of mind, where one's intuitions are taken as the ultimate touchstone for representational theorizing and where the problem is seen as finding ways in which this intuitive notion is materially realized. Stich's Challenge states that representation by assumption is not good enough. A concept of representation will only belong in cognitive theorizing if it does real work there. Understanding representation in this context thus necessarily involves approaching it from the larger context in which it has to fit and by which it is constrained. That context consists of behavior.

2.3 What kind of behavior?

If it is accepted that the study of behavior is a very basic and important topic for psychology, the next step is to ask: What kind of behavior is worth the attention of psychologists? The most commonly accepted answer is *human* behavior. After all, this is psychology, not biology. The ultimate aim of psychology is to explain how humans behave and think.

Since psychology turned into a cognitive science, it has almost exclusively focused on behavior that is specifically human—that is, behavior which involves a strong cognitive component. This is the kind of behavior which sets humans apart from animals. Whether this strict focus on human behavior has been a *real* success depends very much on who is talking. In many ways, it definitely has. A computer program is now the world's best chess player, however, computers still do not play chess in 'the same way' as humans do, nor are current cognitive models very good at other human games, such as playing tennis.

Whatever the verdict, there is definitely a niche for alternative ways that could lead to a better understanding of human behavior. I will promote an approach which looks at much more 'simple' behavior first (see also Braitenberg, 1984; Lloyd, 1989; Brooks, 1991a, 1991b). With "much more simple" I am thinking about behavior which is exhibited by insects and other invertebrates, as well as by vertebrates (including humans). Examples would consist of a capacity to move about in a natural environment, to find specific landmarks, or to execute serially ordered behavioral sequences. As the 'simple' behaviors that are exhibited by all multicellular organisms alike are actually not simple at all, I will refer to this kind of behavior as *basic behavior*.

There are many reasons for examining and modeling basic behavior, before turning to the complexities of humans. First of all, this is, generally, the most sensible procedure when dealing with a difficult problem. It is common practice in science to use a suitably simple experimental platform as a way to get at the basic principles involved in a phenomenon that relates to humans. For example, think how limited our understanding of human genetics would have been without the opportunities offered by studying the fruitfly *Drosophila melanogaster*.

Unfortunately, this basic-behavior-first approach is severely hampered by the presumed deep distinctions between automatic, reflex-like behavior on the one hand, and intentional, cognitively guided behavior on the other. Within cognitivism it is generally assumed that learning about reflex-like behavior can teach us little about intentional behavior which involves the mind. How far down the phylogenetic line the ascription of mind extends is debated (Amsel, 1989; Beckerman, 1988; Fodor, 1986a), but it is generally held that the involvement of cognitive processes makes some behavior distinctively human. And as long as it is uncertain when animal behavior does definitely involve mind, why not remain on the safe side and study human behavior?

The answer is that the behavior of insects and other invertebrates cannot be explained in terms of simple reflexes. Whether or not insects have minds, their behavior is an extremely intricate phenomenon which warrants psychologists' attention and theorizing.

Taking an interest in behavior only when it is connected to the workings of mind is a very strong force in psychological thinking. Attention is consistently shifted away from behavior which seems merely mechanical. An example will make this more concrete. It will also provide a concrete case to show that a different point of view is necessary. The following quote is from Franklin (1995). He quoted Hofstadter (1985), who quoted Wooldridge (1968).

> When the time comes for egg laying, the wasp *Sphex* builds a burrow for the purpose and seeks a cricket which she stings in such a way as to paralyze but not kill it. She drags the cricket into the burrow, lays her eggs alongside, closes the burrow, then flies away, never to return. In due course, the eggs hatch and the wasp grubs feed off the paralyzed cricket, which has not decayed, having been kept in the wasp equivalent of a deepfreeze. To the human mind, such an elaborately organized and seemingly purposeful routine conveys a convincing flavor of logic and thoughtfulness—until more details are examined. For example, the wasp's routine is to bring the paralyzed cricket to the burrow, leave it on the threshold, go inside to see that all is well, emerge, and then drag the cricket in. If the cricket is moved a few inches away while the wasp is inside making her preliminary inspection, the wasp, on emerging from the burrow, will bring the cricket back to the threshold, but not inside, and will then repeat the preparatory procedure of entering the burrow to see that everything is all right. If again the cricket is removed a few inches while the wasp is inside, once again she will move the cricket up to the threshold and re-enter the burrow for a final check. The wasp never thinks of pulling the cricket straight in. On one occasion this procedure was repeated forty times, with the same result. (Franklin, 1995, p. 49)

This anecdote provides a remarkable insight into psychology's attitude toward basic behavior. The story conveys a clear message: one should not be deceived by the seemingly intelligent and complex behavior of lower animals, as it cannot be taken at face value as evidence of real intelligence. The story provides the psychologist with an excuse not to pay close attention to basic behavior: it shows enough detail to prove that the psychologist has considered these cases, but that unfortunately they did not live up to the required psychological criteria. The frequency with which this anecdote is repeated (e.g., Dennett 1978, p. 65, uses the same quote) is interesting as well. It is not a conclusion which many people want to contradict. On the contrary, the story is accepted at face value and not examined critically. This becomes very clear when the background of this anecdote is considered. The story is more than one hundred years old. Lloyd Morgan (1900, p. 77) ascribes it to Henri Fabre. Fabre was a well-known field biologist of the later nineteenth and the early twentieth century, "whose life-long study of the insects remains a marvel of indefatigable labor and detailed observation" (Warden, 1927, p. 148; see also Pasteur, 1994). Fabre opposed the idea that animal instincts had anything in common with "the rational faculty which man alone possesses" (ibid.). His successive volumes of "Souvenirs Entomologiques" were published in the period 1879–1904 and became very popular among the general public (Boring, 1929). Since 1900, the story has not changed very much. Lloyd Morgan mentioned a grasshopper instead of a cricket and also that Fabre repeated the procedure *about* forty times, not forty times exactly. There is more to it however. Lloyd Morgan reported some follow-up research carried out by George and Elizabeth Peckham. They did the same experiment with this kind of wasp, no longer merely *Sphex* but more precisely *Sphex ichneumonea*. The first day they allowed the wasp to carry in her prey undisturbed to observe her normal methods. The next three days Fabre's procedure was carried out. The results differed markedly from those of Fabre. The wasp did not keep repeating itself on and on. During those three days, it carried the grasshopper in at, respectively, the fifth, the fourth, and the eighth trial (Lloyd Morgan, 1900, pp. 77–78). The wasp is not as stupid, or mechanical, as many would like to believe.

Fabre's anecdote, taken at face value for a century, does not stand up to a systematic test, a test, to make it worse, that was already performed a century ago! The only way to explain the survival of this fiction within psychology for so long is a chronic lack of interest in insect behavior and ignorance of the relevant literature. It betrays a willingness to believe anything that keeps basic behavior out of the scope of psychology's interests. This tendency is a good reason to be suspicious when the behavior of invertebrates, or animal behavior in general, is neglected or its importance downplayed.

Actually, the tendency to overlook the difficulties and problems involved in basic behavior runs much deeper. So far, the point has been that the implied inability of *Sphex* to deal with disturbances in a behavioral routine is not as bad as the anecdote suggests. The more important lesson that can be drawn from the survival of this anecdote is the way in which it is taken for granted that this incapacity is a matter of importance, as if it uncovers a serious flaw in what could otherwise be deemed intelligence.

This interpretation must be challenged. The stupid repetition, on which the anecdote focuses our attention, is a minor shortcoming when it is compared to the behavior that the wasp is capable of. This small quirk is no more than a small stain on a vast array of behavioral capacities. The thing that should get our attention are all those activities that the wasp has to perform before it can be made to look dumb: walking, flying, digging a burrow, catching a cricket, paralyzing it, finding the burrow again, and so on. There is nothing simple here for those who are looking. The *Sphex* story is also an example how these capacities are relegated to the background in a subtle way.

The tendency to belittle basic behavior cannot be upheld when attention is, in fact, given to it. Basic behavior is a surprisingly difficult topic. A distinction between intentional and 'merely mechanical' behavior can keep the latter out of focus, but as soon as one actually tries to explain basic behavioral capacities—also those that almost certainly do not involve mind—then an elaborate set of ideas and concepts are necessary. To mention an example: the idea that basic behavior can be explained in terms of reflexes is wrong. In the 1930s, von Holst already showed that the rhythmic flapping of a fish-tail could not be accounted for by chained reflexes (Von Holst, 1980). An indigenous neural oscillator is required to explain the data. Since then, researchers who have studied this topic have come up with a multitude of models and concepts in trying to account for basic behavioral phenomena: Central Pattern Generators to account for rhythms generated by the nervous system itself (Selverston, 1980), efference copies which are sent to the sensors when a movement is made to counteract the change of the sensor-state generated by the movement (Von Holst and Mittelstaedt, 1980), mutual entrainment of bodily and neural rhythms to explain their coordination despite environment-induced disturbances in the rhythm of the latter (Taga, 1994; Libersat, Levy, and Camhi, 1989), modulation of the reflex actions of all the legs of a crab when the load on one leg is changed (Zill and Seyfarth, 1996), cognitive maps to explain the navigation abilities of many insect species (Tolman, 1948; Gallistel, 1990a), and so on. In summary, basic behavior is a hard topic which requires elaborate theorizing and modeling to understand it.

The same lesson can be drawn from attempts to model basic behavioral capacities by building robots that should accomplish tasks of which any insect is capable. The results are sobering. For example, just traversing a rough surface in a quick and fluent way is still a major challenge, which goes beyond current cognitivist psychology's modeling capacities. For example, complex cognitive models are used to make robots put their feet at suitable supporting places (see the discussion on the Ambler, chapter 2, section 3.4). Interactionism has somewhat better cards with respect to insect-like locomotion (chapter 4). Brooks (1989) built many six-legged robots capable of moving about on an office floor. However, so far the walking capacities of these robots do also not come close to an insect-level of performance (in terms of speed, dealing with rough terrain, etc.). If basic, insect-level behavior is—in principle—so well understood why then—in practice—is it so difficult to replicate such behavior by artificial means?

To conclude, basic behavior poses deep and difficult problems for psychology. It provides a theoretically and empirically challenging topic. Basic behavior offers a more than sufficiently complex testing ground for investigating the use and the usefulness of representational explanations in psychology.

The concepts and theories necessary to deal with the problems in the area of basic behavior will provide a much-improved conceptual toolbox which will be very useful for dealing with the even more complex, human issues.

3 A mental mechanism to explain the generation of behavior

Limiting this investigation to the explanation of adaptive and anticipatory behavior is one thing. Given this position, it does not follow that issues relating to the mind or mental processes will be avoided from here on. On the contrary, when the mind is not allowed to assume its usual place of primary importance it immediately demands at least a secondary role: It provides probably the most influential explanation of behavior in existence.

Explaining behavior by means of mental entities is the stock in trade of every human being. Humans as well as animals are ascribed beliefs and desires. Their behavior is interpreted as the acting out of those desires, given what the human or animal believes to be the case. Because they have knowledge and are aware of their surroundings, they are capable of doing intelligent things, such as showing adaptive and anticipatory behavior. Ascribing mind and intentionality to an agent is a very powerful way to make sense of what an agent is doing and it offers a comprehensive conceptual framework for predicting this agent's behavior. All of this is extremely familiar and generally accepted, certainly in everyday life. This conceptual framework is usually referred to as folk psychology.

I claim that folk psychology does not offer the sort of explanation that we are searching for *here*. The goal is to formulate an explanation which does not involve any thinking or sentient agent in its premises. The explanans should involve *no one* who is acting as an intelligent, sentient force, guiding behavior in the right direction. Before the reader's aversive reflexes take over, let me qualify this statement.

3.1 Nature's levels

To understand why folk psychology does not offer the right sort of explanation for behavior, I will first discuss the context in which this claim is made. This context comes in the form of a general commitment to naturalism. There are various interpretations of naturalism, but its common denominator amounts to something like: the general acceptance of the world picture as provided by the natural sciences, both in its present form as well as in its future development. The view is sometimes, somewhat irreverently, called the "Scientific American" view of the world. The world consists of the things and processes which feature in these natural sciences. Such natural phenomena are very diverse and range as wide as trees, stones, oxidation, planets, cells, molecules, metabolism, ecosystems, and catalysis. Behavior has to be understood as one of these.

For present purposes, a key aspect of naturalism consists of the notion of levels. Nature is considered to be organized along many different spatial and temporal scales (Allen and Starr, 1982; Salthe, 1985; Weiss, 1971; see also chapter 5). At these diverging scales, different sets of processes take place, giving rise to multiple, largely independent levels of organization.

These levels provide the material studied by separate sciences, such as chemistry, biology, geology, and psychology. The characteristic phenomena of each of these levels cannot be derived from a lower level in any direct way. Of course, there are mutual constraints, but processes occurring at one specific level, regularly run their course without interference by events at different levels. The latter act merely as constants (Salthe, 1985). At higher levels—that is, on larger or longer spatio-temporal scales—new phenomena can emerge which are not present at lower levels. This gives rise to the many different natural phenomena such as those mentioned above.

In this general perspective of multiple, largely independent levels of natural organization it is not difficult to accommodate behavior and mind. Both are empirically well-established phenomena, and thus provide self-evidently an interesting topic for a special branch of the natural sciences. This does not detract from the peculiar and specifically 'mental' of the mind. For example, intentionality may be held to be a unique feature of the mind, which will not be encountered anywhere else in the physical universe. This does not make it an obstacle for the reconciliation of mind and nature. The universe abounds with unique and new properties which are somehow, at least at first, mysteriously taking shape within the world. What to think of ontogenesis or high-temperature superconductivity? These and many other findings are remarkable as well. Noticing that intentionality stands out does not set it apart from nature; it signals that it is a topic which is not well understood up to now. It presents a puzzle that could be solved by an appropriate branch of science.

Naturalism might be contrasted with physicalism. Both imply a general commitment to the natural science picture and they are often used interchangeably (Guttenplan, 1994b). The difference seems to be that physicalism, but not naturalism, has a strong tendency to read all the levels of nature in a reductive way. Naturalism has strong connotations with biological naturalism and the study of living nature in the field. The biological naturalists always had an open eye for the many different forms and structures of the living world (Wilson, 1995). Naturalism can also be affiliated with the artistic movement of that name and its respect for the patterns to be encountered in this world. Naturalism does not imply a commitment to reduce all these levels of organization, while physicalism does. In contrast to naturalism, physicalism embodies the ideology that there is some basic, physical level of organization from which all the other ones can be derived. Or, going the other way round: all other levels can be reduced ultimately to a singular most basic level, consisting of fundamental, physical events.

The ideal of reduction has fallen upon hard times, both for principled and practical reasons. The principled reason for being dissatisfied with reductionism can be nicely illustrated with the old cognitivist idea of *multiple instantiability*. This idea states that the same higher-level, computational state can be instantiated by an indefinite number of different hardware implementations. It is used to support the idea that a computer can implement a mind, just as well as a brain can. The principle of multiple instantiability has a much wider application though. Any higher-level phenomenon can be instantiated by an indefinite number of lower-level events (Garfinkel, 1991). Equating the higher-level regularity with one particular lower-level event generates a hyperconcreteness which obscures the higher-level regularity. Consider the relations between a population of foxes and a population of rabbits. In this case, it is irrelevant that an individual rabbit *r* was killed by an individual fox *f* at place *x* at time *t*. In choosing such a micro-reductive account, the "resulting explanation gives us a false picture of the sensitivity of the situation to change. It suggests that, had the specific cause not been the case, the effect would not have occurred. This is false in such cases because there is a redundant causality operating, the effect of which is to ensure that many *other* states, perturbations of the original microcause, would have produced the same result. Microreductions cannot take account of this redundancy and to that extent cannot replace upper-level explanations" (ibid., p. 451). The "explanations we want simply do not exist at the underlying level. It is not that the microreduction is an impractical ideal, too good to be true, but rather that it is, in a way, too true to be good" (ibid., p. 449).

Besides principled reasons against a strict reductive interpretation of the natural world, there are also many practical ones. Given the general heuristic that theories, and ideas in general, should be kept in accordance to the facts, the current state of physics, chemistry, molecular biology, and so on infuses the strong impression that the idea of a total reduction lacks corroboration. The idea that nature consists of many different levels which cannot be reduced to one basic level has taken root very widely. Philip Anderson's old rallying cry "more is different" (Anderson, 1972) has acquired a large following. Maintaining that all of molecular biology, neural science, and so on are ultimately 'nothing but' quantum physical events, or even more basic happenings, is a gratuitous opinion that has no practical significance. Large parts of newly developed fields such as self-organization, artificial life, and complexity are even explicitly conceptualized as being the result of interactions between several levels of organization. Reductionism would make these developments incomprehensible.

For me these are sufficient reasons to uphold naturalism rather than physicalism. With it goes an acceptance that nature is organized along multiple levels of organization, each one as real as any other. The criteria for something to be considered 'real' can be very pragmatic: acceptance by the scientific community. Of course this does not provide us with the ultimate, fundamental, and never-changing view of the 'real world' which we emotionally crave for. Still, it is the best that humanity can bring forth in this respect. The rules and practices employed within this community act as self-correcting processes, enabling science to overcome current limitations, and counteract mistakes and fraud (Latour, 1987). Going along with its opinions, or criticizing and trying to change them from within, seems the best way to delineate 'real' ontological levels at any particular moment. I conclude that, given the current state of science, there are no principled problems with interpreting behavior and mind as normal, and 'real' natural phenomena. Both consist of one more of nature's multiple levels of organization. The problems that do exist are much more practical. *How* do behavioral and mental phenomena arise within the natural world?

3.2 Transitions: explaining the generation of behavioral potentialities

The picture of the natural world sketched above is very permissive: It acknowledges the reality of multiple descriptive and ontological levels, among them the behavioral and mental. However, merely stating that behavior is a higher-level, so to say, 'emergent' property is not enough. The naturalistic view sketched above is only permissive in acknowledging it as a 'real' phenomenon. It is very strict in demanding explanations specifying how emergent, 'new', higher-level properties are generated by lower-level processes.

This approach to explaining behavior contrasts with more traditional views on explanation (Cummins, 1983). In the classical deductive-nomological explanatory model, the goal was to search for general laws which, together with a set of initial conditions, would be sufficient to predict the next set of events. The laws of physics are taken as the prototypical examples of a good explanation. Explanation and prediction are held to be equivalent, their only difference being the timing with respect to the explained or predicted event (Bechtel, 1988). This explanatory model has had a very strong influence on science in general, and on psychology in particular (Cummins, 1983). Behaviorism's search for general laws of behavior was, for example, strongly influenced by the deductive-nomological ideal. When the deductive-nomological model is brought into the context of multiple levels of organization, it can be interpreted as providing a description of the changes at a particular level (Salthe, 1985), for example, the change of the number of foxes in relation to the number of rabbits. On the other hand, talking in terms of levels also implies the need to understand the relations between those levels.

The crux here is that the lower-level processes do not have the properties of the higher-level ones. Individual molecules do not have a temperature, but many molecules together do. Similarly, individual car parts do not have automotive power, but an assembled car does. Going from one level to the next can be thought of as a transition: processes occurring at a specific ontological and descriptive level organize themselves into new phenomena at a different spatial or temporal scale, generating a new (higher) ontological and descriptive level. Such transitions do not imply any mysterious or supernatural processes. Lower-level processes just have typical higher-level counterparts which can be observed by looking at the 'same' thing over longer or larger spatio-temporal scales (Allen and Starr, 1982; Salthe, 1985). To provide a satisfactory understanding of such transitions, a theory of the transition rules between the two levels of organization is necessary (Roland, 1994), or a property theory as Cummins calls it.[4]

In the case of adaptive behavior a relation has to be established between (a) the lower-level neural, bodily and environmental processes (which together constitute an agent) and (b) the higher-level, purposive characteristics of behavior as exhibited by a whole agent. The question faced by psychology thus becomes: How does nature arrive at the higher-level characteristics of adaptive behavior when it starts out with lower-level processes which do not show the same characteristics? This particular transition will be referred to as the *cognitive transition*. Do not overinterpret the term 'cognitive transition'. It will be used as a convenient and pragmatic label to denote the generation of behavioral potentialities by means, which do not themselves exhibit these potentialities. It does not imply any single leap from the noncognitive to the cognitive; there could very well be many small transitions involved. Also, the present goal is to investigate how *behavior* can be explained. It does not aspire to a full treatment of the whole of cognition. The point is merely to stress the idea of a transition and the generation of new, behavioral properties.

Interpreting behavior as a complicated property that needs to be explained by more simple means concurs with the common practice in many natural sciences (Latour, 1987; Bechtel and Richardson, 1993). In this view, the goal is to develop mechanical models which produce and thus explain the phenomena observed. The biological, medical, and earth sciences provide many examples of the search for such models. Its success can be witnessed in the spectacular rise of molecular biology (Judson, 1979). Mechanical models allow humans to understand how a higher-level phenomenon is generated. They offer guidelines for manipulating these phenomena or even reproduce them in artificial ways. In the following, I will accept this general mechanical interpretation of explanation: Explaining behavior consists of providing a mechanical model, capable of generating behavioral phenomena.

I want to make three amendments to this general subscription to mechanical modeling, loosening it from its worst traditional connotations and implications: being 'mechanistic' and reductive.

- I will maintain the position concerning reduction as described above: Providing mechanical models is not a matter of reduction but of explaining the emergence of new properties. The notion of a mechanism refers to a specific set up of lower-level regularities. Still, 'lower-level' is relative to the particular property that has to be explained. It can be rather high-level itself, depending on what the explanandum consists of. When this is a social event, the 'mechanism' could very well involve conscious persons, whose interactions are responsible for the social setup. 'Mechanism' does not need to be interpreted in a strong mechanistic sense, such as screws, bolts, and wires. It can be anything, as long as it belongs to a more basic level than the explanandum.
- The second amendment concerns the idea of modeling and forms the reason to talk about the much looser and more general 'framework'. In

cognitivism, models are concrete. They are often implemented and running simulations of specific cognitive capacities. In this book, modeling is used in a wider sense. My concern is with the underlying *conceptual model* which lies behind the concrete, implemented models. The conceptual model provides the underlying *"Bauplan,"* or the *conceptual framework,* for the concrete solutions and models with which psychologists make sense of behavioral phenomena. In this book, I will examine aspects of this more abstract interpretation of modeling. I will argue that almost all of the concrete cognitive models are, at heart, variations of the same conceptual model (chapter 2).

• Mechanical models usually consist of clearly delineated subcomponents in which specific contributions to the operation of the whole system can be localized (Bechtel and Richardson, 1993). The operation of the total system can then be understood by analyzing the operation of its components. In certain complex systems the behavior of the total system depends not so much on the characteristics of their subcomponents but rather on their subcomponents' relations. It becomes increasingly difficult, even impossible, to disentangle the separate contributions of the system's individual components. A good example are connectionist systems where the contributions of individual neurons to the global network behavior are often diffuse. Nevertheless, it makes sense to talk about a mechanical model here. The computer provides a tool that makes it possible to model the many interactions of complex systems. It also opens up the possibility of developing clear ideas concerning the behavior of complex systems (Kauffman, 1993, 1995; Waldrop, 1992), and gives a clear physical meaning to a concept as self-organization (Haken, 1987; Prigogine and Stengers, 1984). In these cases the relations between the properties of the components and the total system can be very indirect. It is often impossible to predict beforehand what the total system will do, given knowledge of its part's states and behavior. As a consequence, the idea of a mechanism is interpreted in a broader and less 'mechanistic' sense than its traditional, seventeenth-century based connotation. Complex systems and the concept of self-organization, meant to deal with the phenomenon of many small parts coming to act together in a coherent way, will play an important role in this book.

In summary, the basic behavior on which this book focuses is to be explained as a part of the natural world. A distance is maintained to reductive interpretations. The generation of new—in this case behavioral—properties by more simple means is stressed. The goal is to develop a naturalistic conceptual framework which will explain how behavioral properties come about. This framework should provide a guideline for building more concrete models of specific behaviors. In the rest of this book, any mention of the explanation of behavior will always refer to this interpretation, unless explicitly stated otherwise. It can be contrasted with the sort of explanation provided by folk psychology.

3.3 Personal and subpersonal explanations of behavior

The aim, then, is to formulate a naturalistic framework which describes how behavioral phenomena arise within the natural world. How does the notion of 'mind' bear on this goal? Folk psychological generalizations, based on a person's beliefs and desires, can be taken as the prototypical example of a mental explanation of behavior. It should now be clear that this will not do for our purposes.

To explain how behavioral properties arise, a mechanism is necessary that is more simple than the behavior itself. Folk psychology takes behavioral properties as a given, and gives an account that explains why certain behavioral regularities arise rather than others. Folk psychology starts out at too high a level of description. It applies to persons (sentient beings) who know their environment and decide on their actions on the basis of this knowledge. In other words, folk psychology applies to systems which are already capable of behavior. When this level of organization is called the personal level, the mechanism behind behavioral properties should be sought at a *subpersonal* level, using a phrase first introduced by Dennett (Hornsby, 2000). Mind applies at a personal level and does not provide a conceptual framework which specifies how subpersonal processes operate to bring a person's behavioral capacities into being.

To explain a phenomenon, it is necessary to have a model which consists of components more simple than the phenomenon itself. Mind does not provide ingredients which are more simple than adaptive and anticipatory behavior. Mind involves features like beliefs and desires, awareness, consciousness, intentionality, feelings and qualia. Nobody knows at present how to relate this to the general naturalistic context. The present focus on behavior is partly motivated as a way to generate a more gradual ascent toward these phenomena, instead of confronting this enigma head on. Also, the cases of adaptive and anticipatory behavior are spread much wider than the cases where we would ascribe mind with confidence. Just think of our poor, maltreated *Sphex*. To conclude, for those with an interest in behavior, invoking the mind is clearly not a good way to proceed.

The reasoning is straightforward, though, no doubt many people will object to the conclusion. They can be divided into two groups: philosophers of mind and practical workers in cognitivist psychology. The first group will maintain that mind *should* play a role in an explanation of behavior to stave of a threatening reduction or elimination of the mental. The second group will claim that their practice is evidence that mind *does* play an important role in the explanation of behavior. To oppose these critics, more context is necessary. This comes in two pieces. (a) Denying the soundness of folk psychology as a naturalistic framework that explains behavioral properties does not detract from it being a sound framework in other settings. (b) Mental processes can be used as a *guideline* for a subpersonal mechanism which is used to explain behavioral properties. I will argue that this is what cognitivist psychology has been doing all along. Turning mind into a subpersonal mechanism does not detract from the argument's validity, nor from its conclusion. I will discuss these two in turn.

3.4 Philosophy of mind's stake in the explanation of behavior

Discarding mind as a suitable framework for explaining behavior does not lead to a denial of the reality of mind or cast doubt on its sheer existence within the natural world. When this proposition is accepted, a very large part of the philosophical motivation to oppose the conclusion mentioned above will vanish. The problem is that many philosophers think otherwise (Fodor, 1987; Dretske, 1988; P. M. Churchland, 1989). They are convinced that discarding mind as an explanatory entity within psychology could lead to the elimination of mind.

The starting point is the age-old dualism between mind, or soul, on the one hand and the natural world on the other. Aristotle may have connected the soul to the body, ever since they have been held in opposition to one another (Warden, 1927). In Christianity this became the opposition between the immortal soul and the material, mortal body. Later, under the influence of Descartes, it turned into dualism and its associated mind-body problem (Rorty, 1979). Mind became the seat of properties like rationality, intelligence, intentionality, consciousness, creativity, and morality. The body and the natural world became the merely mechanical and material which lacked those properties. As a way of thinking, the general antagonism of mind and nature still holds very strongly (see, e.g., Baker, 1987; Moser, 1994; MacDonald, 1989).

The interpretation of nature as a multi-level organization breaks with this long-standing dichotomy and offers a route to reconcile the two. Unfortunately, this way of deescalating the mind-nature relation seems to be much more readily accepted within the scientific community than among philosophers (Guttenplan, 1994a; Horgan, 1993; Kim, 1998; Moser, 1994; Papineau, 1993; but see also Hornsby, 1997). Many philosophers of mind are very reluctant to accept the idea that the natural world consists of multiple levels of organization. Or rather, they are reluctant to accept that these levels are as real as a (still hypothetical) most basic one, to be provided by (a branch of) physics. Papineau shows his cards very clearly when he writes:

> Like many other contemporary philosophers, I have strong physicalist intuitions. I am inclined to think that chemical phenomena, for example, are all at bottom physical, even though chemists do not describe those phenomena in physical terms. What is more, I am inclined to think the same about the phenomena studied by meteorology, biology, psychology, sociology and the other so-called 'special sciences'. (1993, p. 9)

The old eighteenth-century view of physics still seems to prevail here. Everything is seen as a combination of elementary particles. Higher levels are not taken to be 'real', but are ultimately to be reduced to physics. This sentiment can also be witnessed in the tendency to talk about a singularly physical world, not the manifold provided by the many current natural sciences (Kim, 1998; Moser, 1994; Papineau, 1993).

For those who go along with it, this strong reductionist interpretation of the natural world makes the very existence of mind extremely troublesome. Nowadays, the natural sciences have become so all embracing and well respected that mind can no longer be held in a position which remains totally outside its frame of reference. Mind would lose its credibility and become an anomalous entity. At least, that is what is feared. While most philosophers of mind have no qualms about the idea that all of nature is ultimately nothing but physics, many do try to find a way to stave off this fate for mental phenomena. These attempts have had a strong influence on cognitive theorizing.

A large group of philosophers of mind have committed themselves to the project of *naturalizing* the mind (Fodor, 1981, 1987; Dretske, 1988). They seek to reformulate the mind in a way that makes it compatible with the natural science picture, while at the same time maintaining those characteristics that make mind special and precious. Probably the most influential version of the naturalization project consists of claiming a role for mind in a fully naturalistic psychology. If mind finds a place here, it will be saved from the onslaught of a full-scale materialism. This attempt is opposed by a tough-minded bunch of eliminative materialists, or eliminativists for short (P. M. Churchland, 1989, 1990; P. S. Churchland, 1986; Stich, 1983; see also Haselager, 1997). Eliminativists deny the usefulness of folk psychological entities within cognitive science. They are also prepared to bite the bullet: they deny the very right of existence of folk psychology's principles and ontology (P. M. Churchland, 1990). For them folk psychology is an outdated and unproductive theory which should be discarded and its ontology replaced by concepts derived from neuroscience.

With these two options, finding a place for the mind within psychology as a truly explanatory entity is an urgent matter for many philosophers of mind. However, allowing for the third option of a hierarchical interpretation of the natural world, it becomes a nonissue. Mind is a solid natural phenomenon and the intentional vocabulary is well suited to describe its characteristics. The concepts associated with mind (beliefs and desires, consciousness, intentionality, feelings, qualia and rational action) do readily reflect the experiences and doings of agents with well-developed behavioral capacities (see also Hornsby, 1997). It probably goes too far to ascribe a full-scale mind to *Sphex*, but man does certainly qualify, and presumably some other animals as well. Mind can thus be held to be a higher-level property which applies to complete, acting agents. Whatever the theory explaining the generation of behavioral properties may turn out to be, folk psychology amounts to a legitimately naturalistic way of describing and explaining happenings at the personal, or agent, level. To avoid confusion, *I will refer to this personal-level 'behavior' as 'action', reserving the term 'behavior' for the result of subpersonal processes.*

For many there will still be a catch. The position defended here is similar to Dennett's intentional stance (Dennett, 1987a). Dennett maintains that it makes perfectly good sense to treat whole, acting agents as if they have beliefs and desires. Intentional descriptions often provide reasonably accurate predictions of a person's actions in a succinct way. These descriptions can be used independently from the underlying mechanisms. The catch is that Dennett leans toward instrumentalism. He talks about an intentional *stance*, a way of looking at a phenomenon which is useful and in that sense 'true', but nevertheless not literally true. For him beliefs and desires are abstracta, like a center of gravity. They are useful, but not a part of the physical furniture of the world (ibid., p. 72). Granting the reality of beliefs and desires in this way can easily be seen as a cheat, saying the proper words in a way that withholds the proper commitment. The Roman inquisition would not be fooled by such a heretic's trick.

In contrast to Dennett, the position defended here does grant that beliefs and desires can be as real as atoms and stones are. A distinction between merely useful abstractions and the real physical furniture of the world is difficult to uphold. Who could pass such ultimate judgment? A stone might look and feel pretty solid, but it disappears when looked at up close. Then it turns out that the stone really consist of empty space and subatomic particles. Beliefs and desires look like pretty solid characteristics of the people that I know. However, looking closely, the beliefs and desires disappear out of sight and a neural picture comes into focus. Which of these descriptions depicts reality? The old limiting criterion of being observable is increasingly stretched by new sensing and imaging techniques which allow the perception of previously invisible domains (Hall, 1992). It is now possible to 'see' the hole in the ozone layer, to 'see' brain activity or to 'see' atoms. There is no good reason to limit reality to only those features for which evolution has provided us with the proper sensors. As no person has a direct link to ultimate reality, it seems that the best one can do at any moment is maintain a pragmatic position and accept as 'real' those entities and phenomena that feature in the then current theories of the natural world. The scientific enterprise brings the most scrutinized and elaborated set of descriptions that anyone has come up with at any particular time in history. It seems a sensible strategy to let this consensus decide on what is 'really' there. An exception, of course, should be made when one participates in a specific domain of research and wants to differ with specific ideas. In this pragmatic view of reality, there is no a priori reason why beliefs and desires could only be taken to be real 'with a grain of salt' as Dennett has it.

There is one caveat. The message is only that folk psychology can be taken to depict real entities, even when it does not do any work in behavioral theory. There is no guarantee that the descriptions applied to personal-level phenomena will not be influenced by ideas and theoretical developments that apply to subpersonal levels. On the contrary, such influence is to be expected and even to be encouraged as it provides a way to gain insight in personal-level phenomena (Hurley, 1998; Sheets-Johnstone, 1999; Varela, Thompson, and Rosch, 1991). No guarantees for folk psychology's undisturbed future are, can, or should be given in this respect. It might turn out that there are much better ways to describe sentient agents. My point here is only that this issue does not bear on the current search for behavioral mechanisms.

In conclusion, folk psychology does not suffice as a theory of behavior but it is a perfectly good candidate as a theory of action. The project to *naturalize* mind is superfluous. Mind is a natural phenomenon from the start and does not need to be saved from any onslaught of materialism. As a consequence, the topic of behavior can be dealt with in a much more relaxed fashion. The fate of our minds does not hinge on it. Approaching the problem of behavior can be done without challenging our self-image as rational beings, even when our folk psychology is not considered to be a suitable theory of behavior.

3.5 Mind turned into a mechanism: subpersonal representations

Philosophers of mind are not the only ones who will speak up against the rejection of folk psychology as a basis for behavioral explanation. There is another group who will also protest: those cognitivist psychologists who have been working for thirty years to make the mind an acceptable explanatory force in psychology. The claim that the explanatory framework based upon mind cannot provide a basis for behavioral explanation must be wrong because it already has provided this basis for over thirty years! The idea that the mind can be modeled and is capable of explaining behavior is at the very heart of cognitivism.

The point to make here is that it is not mind itself which is used to explain behavior. This is done by *models* of mind. The explanation that is in actual use within cognitivist psychology is a dressed down and mechanized version of folk psychology. After all, cognitivism is clearly committed to the sound principle that an explanation should be simpler than the phenomenon explained (Cummins, 1983; Dennett, 1987a). Presenting a cognitive model that would incorporate a homunculus just as complex as the outward agent would not bring any explanatory progress. Cognitivism tries to develop mechanical models capable of mimicking the outward characteristics of mind, such as a capacity for behavior. Whether this is sufficient to provide models of mind itself has been a matter of controversy almost as long as the field exists. Dreyfus (1972) was maybe the first to question cognitivism's way of dealing with factors like consciousness, experience, a tolerance for ambiguity, and a potential for boredom (Gardner, 1985). Searle's Chinese room example is probably the best known attack on the idea that computational models can be said to understand what they are doing, just as humans can (Searle, 1980). Since that time the arguments for and against have never resulted in a consensus on this point. The basic theoretical problems faced by cognitivism are still sought in its potential as a science of mind and the possible vindication of folk psychology (Fodor, 1987; Stich, 1983; P. M. Churchland, 1989). In contrast, this book addresses an issue that is neutral regarding these themes. Whether and how cognitive models could capture the essence of mind will not be considered. Attention will be limited to the subject of behavior.

Cognitivist models are currently the most elaborate and most widely used for behavioral explanation. For that reason they deserve close attention. To articulate how these models deal with behavior is of primary importance. So far, relatively little attention has been paid to their adequacy as behavioral models. It is simply assumed that there are no principled problems: Sufficiently complex and well-designed cognitive systems should be capable of producing any behavior. The evident question then becomes: what are the means by which cognitivism thinks it can explain behavior? This question will be answered in chapter 2. The answer will be criticized in chapter 3. Here, I will give a short sketch of the general idea. It will enable me to introduce the central concept of this book: *subpersonal representations*.

The starting point is the folk psychological conceptual framework with which we understand our own and each other's actions. Folk psychology makes it comprehensible to us why sentient agents act as they do by referring to the beliefs and desires they entertain. Cognitivism takes this conceptual framework, out of its original context of whole, acting agents, and changes it into a form that is realizable by mechanical, computational means. Personal-level, agent-related properties are redrawn and turned into a subpersonal mechanism that can be used to explain the generation of behavior.

I will call this particular theory of the subpersonal level's makeup the *Agent Theory* (AT). AT involves the hypothesis that agent-related properties like 'perceives', 'wants', or 'thinks' or more abstract ones like 'cognitive', 'rational', or 'intentional' can be applied to describe the operation of the processes that generate agent-like properties.

The general idea behind AT may sound highly circular. However, this approach has led to the many, working computational and connectionist models within psychology. It cannot be discarded out of hand. On the contrary, AT is a widely applied conceptual framework and the fundament of the cognitivist explanation of behavior. This is how it works.

AT starts with the assumption that there is an agent and an environment. An agent acts upon this environment by means of "sense-model-plan-act cycles" (Brooks, 1991a). The agent's first operation is to sense 'what is there' in the environment and to generate internal representations of the environment. These representations provide an internal model of the external world. Of course this model can be limited to parts of the environment; there is no intrinsic need to postulate a full-scale, internal world-model. The model can be manipulated and used to make predictions as to what would happen in the real world if specific actions were produced. An action can be selected which would bring about a positive result in the modeled world. Subsequently the chosen action is translated into genuine happenings in the environment.

The notion of representation is central to AT's explanation of behavior. The way in which behavior is oriented toward the future and is relatively independent from the immediate environment is explained by supposing that a subpersonal cognitive system incorporates a set of representations of the environment which guide the system through ambiguous and insufficient sensor-readings to achieve its goals.

The notion of representation is normally used in a context involving agents. Agents, or persons, use symbols (words, pictures, signs, ciphers) to represent things which are not immediately at hand; for example, I use and manipulate representations when I write text. What AT does is to change the normal, personal-level context of representation and use it at a subpersonal level.

At a subpersonal level it makes no sense to refer to agents, or persons, or a someone. The term 'agent' applies only to complete persons, not to their constituent component or processes. My brain is not an agent, I am. A brain—or a comparable control structure—is essential for anyone to have the properties that are characteristic for being an agent, but a brain would not usually be expected to have agent-like properties. To signal that a description applies to an agent at a subpersonal level (and thus not really to the agent at all), I will use the term '*behaving system*' as a way to refer to the combination of a neural control structure and an embodiment, which provide the necessary ingredient for making up an agent.

AT consists of the hypothesis that—when viewed at a general, behavior-related level of operation—a brain (the agent's control structure) operates basically the same as a complete agent operates (as interpreted in terms of folk psychology). This hypothesis involves the idea that *the notion of representation can also be used as a part of a description of what a brain—or a comparable control structure—does at a relatively general functional level.* As the concept of representation is used here at a subpersonal level, I will call it *subpersonal representation.* The explanation of behavior and the feasibility of subpersonal representation are intimately connected.

4 Other established options for behavioral explanation

AT is the most sophisticated conceptual framework that has been formulated so far to account for the generation of behavior. AT has resulted in a large number of concrete models capable of performing cognitive tasks, and it forms the theoretical backbone of robotics, the creation of machines that perform behavioral tasks. Yet, there are also strong criticisms of the general ideas on which AT is based. The fear is that AT does not reflect the organizing principles which lie behind the behavioral capacities of biological organisms. Explaining the generation of behavior may require a different set of ideas. In the following section, I will introduce this critique of AT and the implied need for alternative explanations for the generation of behavior. In the ensuing sections, a number of these possible alternatives are discussed.

4.1 Criticisms of cognitivism and the need for alternatives

Psychology's cognitivist consensus is currently under attack (Beer, 1990; Bickhard, 1993; Bickhard and Terveen, 1995; Brooks, 1991a, 1991b; Carello et al., 1984; Clancey, 1989, 1993; De Graaf, 1999; Edelman, 1989, 1992; Globus, 1992; Harvey, 1992; Pfeifer and Verschure, 1992; Shanon, 1993; Skarda, 1986; Steels, 1991; Thelen and Smith, 1994; Van Gelder, 1995; Varela, Thompson, and Rosch, 1991; Winograd and Flores, 1986). These criticisms often challenge cognitivism's most basic assumptions. For example, it used to be a fundamental question whether representations consist of syntactic strings or neural network states (Fodor and Pylyshyn, 1988). Now the claim is made that psychology would be better off without any representations at all (Brooks, 1991a). Also, the wider conceptual context of cognitivism is being criticized. Winograd and Flores describe the cognitivist approach as being part of a "rationalistic tradition" that "can be traced back at least to Plato," and which "has been the mainspring of Western science and technology" (1986, p. 14). This rationalistic tradition is well entrenched in everyday discourse about thinking and reasoning and closely correlated with the approach of organized science. Winograd and Flores depict it as follows:

1. Characterize the situation in terms of identifiable objects with well-defined properties.
2. Find general rules that apply to situations in terms of those objects and properties.
3. Apply the rules logically to the situation of concern, drawing conclusions about what should be done. (ibid., p. 15)

They state further that the rationalistic orientation is also regarded as "the very paradigm of what it means to think and be intelligent" (ibid., p. 16). It provides the conceptual background with which cognitive scientists interpret intelligent action. Subsequently, this very general interpretation of cognitivism, as well as its 'rationalistic' home base, is deemed to "have important limitations in its scope and in its power to explain what we are and what we do" (ibid., p. 26). These limitations are held to be a result of what is often referred to as a Cartesian split of mind and body (Varela, Thompson, and Rosch, 1991; Harvey, 1992; Bem and Keijzer, 1996).

At the heart of many of those critiques is the charge that cognitivism studies mental phenomena separately from bodily and environmental factors:

It focuses almost exclusively on the internal thinking apparatus. What Howard Gardner (1985) once proudly presented as "The Mind's New Science" is now held against it. The mental should not be studied on its own, but always in conjunction with its behavioral context. Cognition is not a topic that can be properly addressed without taking into account the 'embodiment' and 'situatedness' of a cognitive system (Varela, Thompson, and Rosch, 1991).

The critique of being overly preoccupied with cognitive factors does not apply only to so-called 'classical', computational psychology. It is directed to connectionist approaches as well when these remain within a cognition oriented framework (Pfeifer and Verschure, 1992; Thelen and Smith, 1994). At issue is not *how* the thinking apparatus is modeled—either neural, computational, or otherwise—but *that* the thinking apparatus is modeled, while its behavioral context is neglected. Intelligence is no longer thought to reside in disembodied thought but rather to consist of successful, task-accomplishing action in an environment (Bem and Keijzer, 1996). It is claimed that the problems which psychology needs to address first are not those of abstract thought (reasoning, problem solving, language) but rather those of behavior (Beer, 1990, 1995a; Brooks, 1989, 1991a, 1991b; Hintzman, 1993; Kugler et al., 1990). Behavior, in this context, is understood as the process by which humans, as well as other organisms, manipulate their environment through movement in ways which, under many different circumstances, regularly result in the continued existence of the organism or in the production of offspring.

These strong criticisms have not gone unchallenged (Bechtel, 1998; Clark, 1997a, 1997b; Clark and Toribio, 1994; Kirsh, 1991; Stefik and Bobrow, 1994; Vellino, 1994; Vera and Simon, 1993a). The main tenor of these reactions is two-sided. On the one hand the reactions tend to be rather positive as far as the incorporation of embodiment and situatedness into psychology is concerned. On the other hand, the interactionist analysis of the cognitivist position itself is strongly opposed as being caricatural and not applicable to research done within cognitivist psychology. Stefik and Bobrow, in reaction to Winograd and Flores's description of the "rationalist tradition" state: "It is a strange composite that includes one rendition of the scientific method, some out-of-favor notions about how sentences convey meaning, the physical symbol system hypothesis in AI, and various kinds of reductionism. . . . it is not clear to whom they ascribe this mess" (1994, p. 182). However, in a reply, Winograd and Flores interpret this as "a basic failure to recognize how traditions are manifested" (1994, p. 212). Varela, Thompson, and Rosch stated: "Our point is not to caricature a sophisticated research program but simply to render explicit some tacit epistemological assumptions" (1991, p. 136). A similar disagreement is fought out between Vera and Simon (1993a, 1993b) and Clancey (1993) on the topic of situated action. Clancey gives a criticism of the general characteristics of cognitivist psychology (cognitive science). Vera and Simon retort that their symbol structures are "perfectly tangible systems" while "Clancey leaves us with philosophy . . . but with precious little science" (1993b, p. 118).

Whether or not Vera and Simon have the final word in this discussion about 'tacit rationalistic assumptions' in psychology, with their last remark they have a point. If the cognitivist explanation of behavior is to be rejected, then what should replace it? The critics seem to drive at a major Kuhnian paradigm shift (Kuhn, 1962). They want a reorientation or restructuring of the conceptual framework by means of which a set of phenomena is interpreted and understood. The typical example of a paradigm shift is the Copernican turn in astronomy. This 'turn' took almost a century to complete and involved many more people than Copernicus alone. Nevertheless, it all started when Copernicus came up with a crude, but new conceptual image in which the earth turned around the sun, instead of the other way round. This new image generated different questions to worry about and different interpretations for known phenomena. It set astronomy on a new course, which culminated in the modern conceptualization of the solar system (Dijksterhuis, 1950). There are remarkable differences between the Copernican turn and the current demand for a radical reorientation of psychology. In the first case, someone brings up a new idea which proves to be very successful and so inaugurates a major reorientation of the field. In the second case, it is argued that we *need* a major reorientation while it is unclear, as Vera and Simon note, with which 'bright new idea' the old framework is to be replaced. The essential question to ask is then: Do the critics of cognitivism offer, like Copernicus once did, an alternative conceptual framework with the potential for putting psychology onto a new and profitable track? Without a good replacement, even a feeble story will remain the best explanation available (Stich, 1983). Without a 'Copernican alternative' we will not have a 'Copernican turn'.

Criticizing AT should be accompanied by generating possible alternatives. What are the options? Those critical of cognitivism tend to converge on a conceptual framework which sees behavior as the interaction between an embodied agent and an environment: together these two make up a larger behavioral system. Before turning to this interactionist conceptual framework, I will briefly review some of the more conventional options for explaining behavior.

4.2 Long-term adaptationism: the evolutionary view

One very important explanation for behavioral properties is evolution. The general evolutionary model of variation and selection explains why organisms capable of adaptive and anticipatory behavior do exist in this world. In this sense it offers an explanation of the cognitive transition: how do you end up with organisms which have those properties that initially were not around. Evolution explains the existence of innate capacities for behavior such as instincts or fixed action patterns (Tinbergen, 1951), but also of a capacity for learning. Organisms with such properties could have a clear adaptive advantage and thus these properties will have been selected for. Evolution explains behavior as the result of a long-term adaptation of species to their environments.

The evolutionary view on behavior is extremely important (Alcock, 1989). Still, as a mechanism capable of explaining behavior it will not suffice. Mayr (1961) made a clear distinction between ultimate and proximate causes in biology. Ultimate causes refer to why questions (why in the sense of how come): *why* is an organism or an organ doing this or that? It has to be answered by referring to the long-term evolutionary history in which this trait or behavior has been adaptive and selected for. Proximate causes, on the other hand, concern the immediate means by which such a trait is realized: *how* is an organism or organ doing this or that? Proximate causes refer to the physiological, mechanical operation of an organ or the physical interactions in which an organism takes part at a particular moment. Ultimate causes explain why we have hearts, livers, and kidneys; proximate causes explain how these organs perform their evolutionary important functions, such as pumping or filtering (Lorenz, 1973; Edelman, 1987). An evolutionary theory might explain the origins of a certain instinct. For example, the compulsive inspection tour which *Sphex* makes of her burrow, while leaving her cricket on the doorstep, has a clear evolutionary advantage. Parasites frequently invade such burrows and there is a clear advantage for the wasp to get rid of them (Hogendoorn, personal communication). The selection pressure in favor of this behavior explains why the wasp inspects her burrow with such fervor. However, given this knowledge of its evolutionary history, it is still an open question how this 'instinct' is realized. What neural or other organization is responsible for this behavior? The quest for a mechanism of behavior should seek a reply to this latter type of question. It is here that AT would provide an answer, and it is here that any alternative should do the same.

Evolution does not suffice as a proximate explanation of behavior. But it does provide the proper context for looking at behavior. It brings home the point that behavior is not a complex but essentially arbitrary collection of mere movements. Behavior is an ongoing (and at heart a molecular) interaction between an organism and an environment which tends to involve increasingly large and long-term elements (Breland and Breland, 1966; Maturana and Varela, 1980; 1988; chapter 4). This point will become very prominent in the interactionist proposal.

4.3 Short-term adaptationism: the behaviorist view

Behaviorism was the first major psychological movement who sought to explain animal and human behavior in fully mechanistic terms, without involving any subjective and unfathomable mental processes. Watson's behaviorist manifesto of 1913 became the catalyst of psychology's rejection of the introspective method and the move toward a more objective approach centering on behavior (Herrnstein, 1967). This change made psychology a full-blown natural science (Warden, 1927). It also meant a commitment to the then current model of explanation, the deductive-nomological explanatory model as derived from Newtonian physics. Behaviorism sought to explain behavior by the formulation of general laws which would describe behavioral regularities. For about fifty years, behaviorism has been the dominant conceptual framework for psychology. Obviously, behaviorism cannot be adequately described in a few sentences. Any short treatment has to be a caricature, turning it into a particular sort of behaviorism which is relatively easy to dismiss, as Amsel (1989) rightly complains. Please bear this in mind because I am going to do this anyway.

The good thing about behaviorist psychology is that it so openly aims to explain behavior. That fits in nicely with the goal set forth in this book. The reason for this choice seems to be a negative one though. Behaviorism wants to avoid unobservable, theoretical entities, in particular mental ones, as much as possible. By starting out with externally observable behavior (responses) and tracking their relation to externally observable environmental factors (stimuli) it hopes to keep its explanations parsimonious in this respect. As a result behaviorist explanations always take the form of relations between externally visible stimuli and responses that both can be defined in an objective way. Behavior is never an internally generated output of a cognitive system, but always a response to an environmental variable. Behaviorist theory searches for outwardly visible, lawful regularities. Everything that happened inside the organism became an 'intervening variable', such as Tolman's cognitive maps, or Hull's habit strengths, while Skinner radically denied all such hypothetical, internal constructs. In all cases the outward state of affairs was taken as the basic starting point.

As a mechanism for explaining behavior, behaviorism will not do. Behaviorism never paid sufficient attention to the internal processes that would provide a mechanism for generating behavior. Behaviorism was strongly influenced by the deductive-nomological idea of science. And even though there were attempts at model building (Tolman, 1939; Cordeschi, 1991), the main push of the behaviorist movement was—and still is—toward an account centered around stimulus-response regularities.

As will be discussed in chapter 3, this is a very feeble basis for a behavioral theory. The argument presented there casts severe doubts on the presumed objectivity of the behaviorist characterization of stimuli and responses. These descriptions are not as objective or clearcut as they seem. On the contrary, stimuli and responses can vary greatly, depending on how one looks at behavior (Brunswik, 1952; Heider, 1959), and are more or less at the mercy of the investigator. One hint in this direction is given by the different interpretations of the notion of response. Watson originally thought of responses as movements. His most influential successors—Tolman, Hull, and Skinner—all turned away from Watson's complicated, so-called molecular muscle twitches and turned the response into the much more convenient, molar environmental effects such as lever pressing. Behaviorists claim the importance of objectivity, but their choice of inputs and outputs betrays the convenience and specific interests of the experimenter rather than a strict and disinterested study of behavior in all its complexity.

Another reason for being discontented with a behaviorist story is its focus on learning. Behaviorism focuses on changes in stimulus-response relations under the influence of a series of reinforcements, for example the positive (i.e., food) or negative (i.e., pain) consequences of a response. In accordance with the deductive-nomological ideal, this procedure allows the behaviorist to uncover general behavioral regularities, such as Thorndike's 'law of effect': "An animal . . . repeats actions that have gained it satisfaction and avoids actions that have cost it discomfort" (Herrnstein, 1967, p. xvii). On the other hand, the search for such laws does not lead to the development of a subpersonal mechanism capable of explaining the generation of behavioral regularities. Like the evolutionary story, behaviorism does not offer a mechanism but only adaptationism (Pribram and Robinson, 1985). Behaviorism assumes the existence of behavioral properties and only seeks for regularities in the changes that occur under the influence of specific reinforcement schedules. Rachlin (1994) states that behaviorism looks at mental life and not at mental mechanisms. In other words, behaviorism looks at a personal level of description, which is not the present interest.

The limitations of a behaviorist approach become even more prominent when species-specific behavior is considered. Behaviorism tends to interpret reinforcement learning as a generally applicable principle which determines what any organism will do, given its reinforcement history. It is clear nowadays that reinforcement alone does not suffice. Chomsky (1959) showed that language could not be dealt with in this way. Garcia and others proved the influence of species specificity on learning curves (Leahey, 1992). The basic status ascribed to learning becomes even more doubtful when it is considered that of the approximately 1,000,000 known animal species, 75 percent are insects and 20 percent are other invertebrates, leaving a mere 5 percent for all the vertebrates, ranging from fishes to mammals (see, e.g., Wilson, 1992). Most invertebrate behavior, and thus most of behavior, comes ready-made at birth (as instincts). There are relatively few animal species for whom learning is more than the basic fine tuning of evolutionary established behavior patterns. The seemingly universal applicability of the discovered learning-regularities was only maintained by studying a very limited number of species, mainly rats and pigeons (Breland and Breland, 1966; Hilgard, 1987).

The attractiveness of behaviorism rests on the general conviction that a lot of behavior can be explained in terms of reflexive stimulus-response pairings. In particular, nonhuman behavior is often thought to be reflexive. Behaviorist explanations, being based on thinking in stimulus-response terms, fit in nicely with this tendency and provide it with a theoretical framework. The limitations should be clear by now. Stimulus-response relations rest too much on the outward manifestations of behavior. These relations do clearly exist, but they do not suffice as an explanation. When the play-button of my video is pushed, the video tends to respond by showing a *Star Trek* episode. This can be construed as a clear case of a regular stimulus-response relation, but, if so, it does not teach us a lot about how a video operates. To conclude, the behaviorist explanation of behavior is not an option when one seeks for the processes that generate behavior.

4.4 Physiology and neuroscience

Probably the most obvious place to turn for an alternative explanation of behavior consists of physiology and neuroscience. Here the physical, neural events which provide the basic ingredients for any explanation of behavior are studied. In order to avoid AT it seems natural to turn to this lower level of organization which does not seem to involve the entities hypothesized by AT. By developing a general theory of the functioning of the nervous system, behavior could be explained independent of AT's conceptual framework.

What would a neurophysiological explanation of behavior look like? Examining individual neurons activating and inhibiting one another and so jointly producing external behavior will not do. This procedure is much too complicated and overly detailed; it is like explaining the movement of a ball by looking at the movements of its composing molecules. A neurophysiological theory should be much more general and involve larger-scale physiological events encompassing large parts of the nervous system. It should also involve the relations of neural happenings to external events. Such a neurophysiological explanation involves much more than an additive sum of small-scale neurophysiological features such as neurotransmitters, synapse-properties, nerve-cell morphology, and the intricate detail of neural connections. It will involve general ideas concerning the global functioning of the nervous system. These ideas cannot be directly derived from studying the nervous system at a local level. Hebb made the point in the following way:

> Even a physiologically based or "neuropsychological" theory of behavior remains a *psychological* theory. Its main features must be determined by certain constructs, theoretical conceptions, whose *raison d'être* is behavioral instead of physiological. (1982, p. 48)

Neuroscientists who work on this general, behavior-related level of brain-functioning need a different kind of concepts than the strict morphologically and physiologically based conceptualizations. When this level has been described above as subpersonal, it should now also be declared to be *superneural,* since it relates to much more global processes going on in the nervous system.

Where do the right concepts come from? Neuroscientists do not work in complete isolation of the ideas of the cognitive sciences and many do readily incorporate cognitivist concepts into their theories to make sense of global brain functioning (Jeannerod, 1997; P. M. Churchland, 1989, 1995; P. S. Churchland, 1986). A neuroscientific account of behavior does not stand in opposition to the conceptual framework provided by AT. When neuroscience is used to understand behavior it tends to rely on AT. This conceptual framework provides the neuroscientist with a set of general ideas concerning the tasks performed by the brain: neural circuits are named and interpreted with these ideas in mind. Physiology and neuroscience on their own do not provide an alternative explanation for behavior.

5 Interactionism: the idea of behavioral systems

In contrast to more well established traditions within psychology, the current critics of cognitivism seek a conceptual framework for behavior which is neither cognitivist, nor behaviorist, nor physiological. Although there is no real consensus, there is convergence on what a genuinely alternative conceptual framework might look like: Behavior is envisioned as part of a reciprocal interaction between a behaving organism and the environment in which it behaves, as an aspect of an integrated organism-environment system. Classification in terms of separable motor, sensory, neural, and environmental parts or stimulus-response relations is rejected. Instead, organization in terms of a circular, loop-like dynamical structure is emphasized. In the following, this very general idea of a circularly coupled organism-environment organization will be referred to as a *behavioral system*. Other terms that are used for the same basic idea are: System-Environment system (Verschure, 1992), Agent-Environment system (Beer, 1995a), and Agent-Environment Interaction system (Smithers, 1994).[5]

The tendency to think in terms of behavioral systems has a relatively long history, although mostly on the fringes of psychology and biology. This history can be witnessed in the works of authors such as Dewey (1896), Von Uexküll (1921, 1980), Ashby (1960), Gibson (1966, 1979), and Lorenz (1973). Reed (1982) and Kelso and Tuller (1984) spoke about 'action systems' in which the importance of the functional organization of organism-environment relations was stressed and contrasted with interpretations of a behavioral agent's organization on the basis of anatomical structure.

Nowadays, the idea of behavioral systems is popular again. There are currently two major lines of empirical research in which the idea of behavioral systems is being developed: Autonomous Agent Research (AAR) and coupled dynamical systems. AAR consists of the very practical project of building or developing robots or 'animats' capable of acting within the same world that we inhabit (Brooks, 1991a; Meyer and Wilson, 1991; Harvey, Husbands and Cliff, 1993). Successful research in this field has given a major boost to thinking in terms of behavioral systems. The concept of two coupled dynamical systems offers a formal way to describe the interactions between two changeable systems over time. It arises within the general study of dynamical systems, or Dynamical Systems Theory (DST). In contrast to AAR, this is not a specific research area but a much more general, formal way of describing physical or other temporally changing phenomena. In this role, it is also a major source of inspiration for developing the behavioral systems idea (Beer, 1995a; Thelen and Smith, 1994).

When adherence to the idea of behavioral systems is interpreted as the kernel of the constructive side of anti-cognitivism, the challenge faced by its proponents is to develop it in such a way that it provides a comprehensible and convincing explanation for the occurrence of behavior in the natural world.

For this discussion, the most notable difference between a cognitivist and an interactionist explanation of behavior consists of their attitude toward (subpersonal) representations. While representations are central to AT, the cognitivist account of behavior, interactionists—at least the radical ones—reject the use of (subpersonal) representations altogether: It is claimed that a behavioral system has no need for representations to explain the generation of behavior.

The remaining chapters will spell out this discussion between cognitivist and interactionist explanations of behavior in detail. First, the conceptual framework of AT will be explicated to make clear what the critics of AT are exactly criticizing. Subsequently, I will discuss the difficulties with this explicated conceptual framework. I conclude that AT ought to be rejected, if only there was some good alternative. The two final chapters investigate the options for turning the idea of behavioral systems into a full conceptual framework—to be called Behavioral Systems Theory—a conceptual framework that can really compete with AT and that does not rely on the notion of subpersonal representations.

2

The Agent Theory: Mind Turned into a Subpersonal Mechanism

1 AT: a reconstruction of psychology's current cognitivist explanation of behavior

How is behavior generated? In the last chapter, it was established that an answer to this question should take the form of a mechanism which itself only involves subpersonal properties, and which is capable of generating the personal-level properties of outward behavior. This chapter will discuss a conceptual framework that is thought to provide the general outlines—the *Bauplan*—for such a mechanism. This conceptual framework is the Agent Theory, or AT.

AT is the conceptual framework which lies behind cognitivist psychology's explanation of behavior. There are many other labels and acronyms which are meant to designate the general conceptual framework of (at least a large part of) psychology as cognitive science: Good Old Fashioned AI (GOFAI) (Haugeland, 1985), the Representational Theory of Mind (RTM) (Fodor, 1981), the Computational Theory of Cognition (CTC) (Cummins, 1989), the Representational-Computational View of Mind (RCVM) (Shanon, 1993), and many others. In a way, AT is one more of these, but with a difference.

Most cognitive scientists see their work primarily in relation to understanding the mind. At the same time, the proposed cognitive models are also taken to provide an explanation of behavior, even though this aspect of cognitive theorizing is often not explicitly stated. AT covers only this latter, largely implicit, behavioral component of the general, cognitivist conceptual framework. It does not address mental issues.

AT is strictly neutral with respect to possible implications of the conceptual framework for studying the mind. The only connection between mind and AT that will be acknowledged is that mind-related concepts form the origins of the set of ideas that AT embodies. Since AT is constructed as a subpersonal framework, any positive or negative evaluation of the framework does not bear (directly) on the personal-level descriptions of our commonsense folk psychology. Also, AT has no direct bearing on the phenomenon of consciousness. AT is only a conceptual framework that tries to make sense of what humans and all other animals have in common: behavior that consists of self-initiated, purposeful movements.

It must be stressed that *AT is a reconstructed position*, it is not a position that is explicitly held or defended by many cognitive scientists. Cognitive scientists are primarily concerned with mental, or at least cognitive, phenomena. Their theories and models are heavily influenced by mind-related considerations. That there is also a conceptual framework for understanding behavior enclosed within these theories and models is acknowledged, but, to see the behavioral aspects of the cognitivist framework properly, they have to be drawn out of their cognitive shell. Describing cognitivist ideas only in their bearing on behavior will thus involve a restructuring and a reordering of the theoretical positions explicitly held by many cognitivists. The changed (behavioral) criteria sometimes result in grouping together positions that are highly antagonistic in their claims concerning mental phenomena.

To summarize, AT does not describe a position which is explicitly held in cognitive science. AT is a reconstructed position that depicts cognitive science's explanation of behavior as it can be distilled from a collection of theories and models which are primarily *meant* as contributions to understanding mental phenomena.

Why go to the trouble of interpreting cognitivist psychology as providing only a behavioral theory and neglect its potential as a theory of cognition? The focus of this book is on explaining the generation of behavior. Cognitivism is looked at with that motive. Taking in cognition as well would only sidetrack us from this prime directive. Discussions of behavior are too often subordinated to, and overshadowed by, an interest in cognitive phenomena. To avoid the temptation to pay insufficient attention to behavior and move on as soon as possible to the cognitive stuff,[1] it seems wise to dissociate the two topics.

Another reason for focusing strictly on the cognitivist treatment of behavior comes from the context in which cognitivism will be discussed: the discussion between cognitivists and interactionists. The interactionists promote an explanation of behavior without much cognitive processing. An honest comparison of the two proposals should be on their respective success in accounting for behavior, not on how well they deal with higher-level cognition. Any shortcomings of cognitivist explanations for behavior should not be compensated by maintaining that it does a good job in some other area, say playing chess.

Once it is accepted that there are sufficient reasons to explicate the behavioral story of the general conceptual framework of cognitivism as AT, there are also good reasons for spelling out this AT in some detail. The discussion between cognitivists and interactionists has a tendency to expand into a very general theoretical debate. Cognitivism is criticized in a very general way (see chapter 1, section 4.1). Its representatives are accused of being part of the 'rationalistic tradition' in Western science and technology (Winograd and Flores, 1986), of making category mistakes, and of conflating first-person and third-person perspectives (Clancey, 1993). In turn, the cognitivists complain that these arguments are merely philosophical and theoretical, while it does not really bear on the practice of cognitive science research (Vera and Simon, 1993b). The defenders of cognitivism also state that the examples of an 'alternative approach' (such as Brooks's robots) are actually not alternative at all, but fall clearly within the borders of standard cognitivist psychology.

At this general level, neither side is capable of convincing the other party of the soundness, or even the contents, of its own views. A more fruitful discussion could take place if the topic were kept as constrained and specific as possible.

Limiting the topic to behavior is one step toward a more constrained discussion. The next step is to specify as precisely as possible how cognitivism seeks to explain behavior. The discussion is then no longer about a 'rationalistic tradition', but about the pros and cons of AT, the cognitivist conceptual framework for explaining behavior. AT provides a relatively specific target that can be evaluated and compared with an interactionist account.

AT also draws out into the open aspects of behavioral modeling that often remain unspecified in the cognitivist approach. For example, the physical behavior—or motor control in the cognitivist idiom—remains at the sideline of cognitivism. However, by turning to robotics, the cognitivist way of dealing with this topic can be made much more explicit and specific. Such robots also illustrate the difficulties surrounding basic behavior. Making robots that are capable of walking across rugged (in practice this often means, not absolutely flat) terrain is now possible, but insect-level performance is still a long way off.

The discussion between interactionists and cognitivists can be made even more specific because describing AT does also involve a description of the kind of representation that functions within this conceptual framework. The notion of representation is at the center of this discussion. Interactionists claim that a nonrepresentational account of behavior is possible, or even necessary (Brooks, 1991a). In the eyes of most cognitivists (and less radical interactionists) the claim that (all of) behavior can be explained without the use of representations makes no sense: The existence of representations within cognitive systems is here held as an undeniable fact. It should be obvious that the word 'representation' is used in different ways here. Describing AT will give a more specific meaning to the notion of representation as it is used in cognitivist explanations of behavior.

A nice side-effect of restricting cognitivism to behavioral issues is that it allows one to anticipate and answer a number of difficulties with the cognitivist position (see chapter 3). These difficulties primarily concern the neglect of situatedness and embodiment in cognitivism. Recasting cognitivism as a behavioral theory turns it into a form that does take account of these factors. AT provides an embodied and situated cognitivism. On one hand, this allows cognitivism to answer some of the criticisms leveled against it, but it also makes more explicit how cognitivism deals with behavioral phenomena. The result is a clearer view on the deeper differences between cognitivist and interactionist positions.

2 Which problem is AT thought to solve?

Behavior is a phenomenon open to different interpretations. In the previous chapter, I gave a rough indication of what I take as the core characteristics of behavior: Behavior exhibits but is not defined by purposive (goal-achieving) characteristics, and behavior is a subpersonal phenomenon.

Together, these characteristics result in a loose hierarchical classification of movement, behavior and action: *Movements* are just changes in spatial position as exhibited by all physical systems. Current robots do definitely move, while it is as yet uncertain whether this constitutes behavior. Prototypical *behavior* consists of the self-initiated, purposive movements of animals and humans at a subpersonal level. Behavior does not involve an intentional agent, but is part and parcel of the processes that bring intentional agents about. *Actions* on the other hand apply to a higher, personal level where the presence of behavioral regularities can be assumed. Actions describe what an intentional agent does. They involve a person to whom these acts can be ascribed, and whom can be held responsible for these actions (Bem, 1989; Moya, 1990).

However, this hierarchy, setting behavior apart from movement and action, does not describe behavior as the cognitivist sees it. Given the general heuristic that there is always a mutual adjustment between a phenomenon that is to be explained and a proposed explanation, AT has its own story to tell about behavior, a story that diverges from the proposed hierarchy. These discrepancies will be sorted out later on; first, let us turn to the cognitivist view of behavior.

2.1 Behavior as the output of an intelligent system

Probably the greatest contrast between behaviorism and cognitivism is their respective focus on the external and internal determination of behavior. While behaviorism's behavior consists of the overt responses to environmental stimuli, cognitivism sees behavior as mainly the result of an intelligent system, which is inside the organism. The cognitivist conception comes from the folk psychological view in which behavior consists of the actions of an intelligent, thinking agent who can be held responsible for its actions: The behavior originates from intelligent or rational processes, which take place somewhere inside the agent.

Before cognitive science became an established field, the view of behavior as originating from intelligent processes could only be sustained by believing in some sort of Cartesian soul, a continuing enigma for a thorough naturalistic approach and, in the first half of the twentieth century, a major reason for steering psychology toward a seemingly more objective, behaviorist approach. Starting around the 1930s, a series of discoveries leading to the development of the electronic, digital computer changed the scene. From then on it became possible to imagine in a very concrete way how thought could take place in a mechanical way (Miller, Galanter, and Pribram, 1960). The development of the computer was one of the events that helped to spark the cognitive revolution, turning psychology into a science that investigates cognition. The story is very familiar and well documented elsewhere (Gardner, 1985). Here are some of the highlights. In 1937 Alan Turing published a paper in which he showed that a machine could be built that, in principle, would carry out any computation that could be specified in clear steps. This machine later became known as the Universal Turing Machine and was one of the major inspirations for the development of the digital computer of Von Neumann. Another important contribution to setting of the cognitive revolution came from McCulloch and Pitts (1943). They showed that neural networks could instantiate logical operations, and thus that the brain could, in principle, act as a computer. Norbert Wiener developed the idea of a purposive mechanism—this was previously considered to be a contradiction in terms by most psychologists—based on feedback mechanisms and so founded the new discipline of cybernetics (Rosenblueth, Wiener, and Bigelow, 1943; Wiener, 1948; Heims, 1980, 1991).

These and other developments brought about a change in the perspective of many psychologists. It renewed, or rather it brought out into the open, an interest in the internal, mental causes of behavior. As Miller, Galanter, and Pribram somewhat ironically observe: "Once a teleological mechanism could be built out of metal and glass, psychologists recognized that it was scientifically respectable to admit they had known it all along" (1960, p. 43). Eventually, all this led to the shift of psychology's main focus from behavior to cognition. For many psychologists, the new conceptual framework made it conceivable, and later even self-evident, that machines could think. The new cognitivist framework also had a major influence on the interpretation of behavior as a scientific problem: Externally observable behavior became the 'mere' output of a computational system. The idea that probably did most to bring home this point was Alan Turing's notion of a Universal Turing Machine (Turing, 1937).

The Universal Turing Machine (UM) is a theoretical device that can compute any function that is computable at all. Turing devised the UM in the 1930s in the context of the overarching "Hilbert Program" in mathematics

(Pylyshyn, 1984). This extremely ambitious program aimed to build up mathematics by purely formal means: All mathematical theorems ought to be derived from a limited set of axioms, using a limited number of rules. This program was only partially successful. Gödel demonstrated by purely formal means that the ultimate goal of a *complete* formalization can not be achieved. On the other hand, Alan Turing, Emil Post, and Alanzo Church independently developed distinct formalisms that were shown to be powerful enough to formally generate *all* provable theorems of logic. Turing's formalism showed that a universal mechanism (UM) exists that can simulate any mechanism describable in its formalism. This is done by providing it with a suitable program which lets the UM compute the same function as a chosen target machine. The 'same function' means that the same input-output pairs—or the same extension of the function—are generated as the target machine does. A UM is completely general and plastic as it can do anything which any other mechanism can do, as far as computation is concerned.

The complete generality and plasticity of a UM is limited to those functions that can be specified by a finite set of instructions. However, the fact that a UM has complete generality and plasticity within those limits has made the larger impact on psychology. Pylyshyn makes the turn very narrow: "Thus it seems that . . . the input-output behavior of a mechanistic system is not really arbitrary plastic; if such behavior is to be described finitely, the behavior cannot be arbitrarily varied. On the other hand, it is natural to ask just how flexible such behavior can be. What sort of behavior *can* be described finitely?" (1984, p. 52). From then on he stresses the plasticity and universality of UM-equivalent computational devices, not their possible limitations. Pylyshyn's attitude in this matter is representative for cognitive science as a whole. His way of dealing with this matter is but one, relatively careful, route toward the general conviction that computers are truly universal and thus, in principle, can do anything that human beings can do.

Of course, this conviction has implications for what humans are supposed to do. As computers produce specific input-output pairings, this has also become the mold into which cognitivism fits human behavior. Instead of real, physical movements, behavior has come to be seen as the production of specific sets of bit-strings. If necessary, it is thought, these bit-strings can be used to instruct robotic devices and so generate the physical movements of actual (basic) behavior. However, for cognitivism, it is not thought to be necessary to be able to re-create these movements in order to understand the basic processes that are responsible for the generation of behavior. It is assumed that the movements are merely the execution of the instructions provided by a cognitive system. For cognitivism, finding out how a cognitive system comes up with the proper instructions provides the real challenge for psychology.

To summarize, the cognitivist view has several implications for the conceptualization of behavior. First, after the notion of a program was introduced, behavior ceased to be seen as a particularly vexing problem. Its previously difficult—because purposive and future oriented—nature could now be explained as the result of a suitable, mechanistic program. Second, behavior became very much abstracted and a matter of cognitive problem-solving: finding intelligent solutions to intellectual problems. Third, turning the solution to the cognitive problem into actual physical behavior was turned into a side-issue. The movements of behavior came to be seen as the 'mere' execution of a solved cognitive task and thus more a topic for engineers, than for psychologists.

2.2 Behavior as distal regularities overcoming proximal disturbances

Conceptualizing behavior as the output of an intelligent, possibly computational, system makes it something trackable and at heart well understood. For many psychologists the story ends here. They take a well-circumscribed aspect of behavior as the relevant output, for example, the past tense of a set of verbs or the next move in a game of chess, and subsequently focus on a cognitive model which is to produce this output. However, as the interpretation of (basic) behavior as a specific, well-circumscribed output is not easy or straightforward, and given the present aim of relating how AT explains behavior it is worthwhile to dig a little deeper here.

Behavior is a phenomenon which is difficult to analyze. This "does not arise from any lack of ways to do it but from an embarrassment of riches. We can describe an action as a set of muscle twitches, or as a sequence of movements of limbs and other parts, or as a sequence of goal-directed actions, or in even larger units" (Miller, Galanter, and Pribram, 1960, p. 13). For what reason should any of these options taken to be as *the* output? It is unusual to pursue this question. Ever since Tolman in the 1930s, all psychologists are familiar with the distinction between molecular and molar behavior—molecular behavior referring to little units and molar behavior to large ones—but this distinction does not play an important role in practical psychological research. As Van der Heijden states:

> It is not the complete behaviour that is observed and registered, but only some specific, quantifiable, aspects, such as the latency and/or correctness of the response. Other aspects, e.g. the duration and the detailed execution of the observable behaviour are simply neglected. (1992, p. 14)

Being confronted with the "embarrassment of riches" of actual behavior, psychologists deal with the situation by focusing only on specific aspects of the total behavior. The choice of these aspects is constrained by the available experimental and modeling possibilities.

Given the present interest in the totality of behavior, what should be done—ideally—is to provide a systematic description of behavior at all of its constitutive levels simultaneously. Miller, Galanter, and Pribram (1960) already stated that a hierarchical description is necessary which specifies how molecular units generate molar patterns. The obvious showcase is human language which is explicitly divided into phonemes, morphemes, phrases, sentences, utterances, and so on. Concerning language, linguists and psychologists take it for granted that a multi-level approach is necessary. Language is made up of elements from all levels and none of them is considered to be the most essential part. Miller, Galanter, and Pribram observed, however, that psychologists describe behavior in a more general sense at a single level and leave it to their colleagues to use their own common sense to infer what happens at other levels.

Since 1960, when Miller, Galanter, and Pribram published their book, the situation has not changed in any dramatic way. Multi-level descriptions of behavior are still rare, and when they are given they tend not to be well developed. Most multi-level descriptions are of animal behavior and fall outside the scope of cognition-oriented psychology (Berridge, 1990; Fentress, 1990, 1991; Golani, 1976; Jacobs et al. 1988; Vowles, 1970). I will return to this topic, in later chapters.

Given the relative lack of explicit theorizing on behavior within cognitive science, what can cognitivism tell us about behavior, beyond designating it as output? Conceptualizing behavior may not have been a hot topic for a long time, but sometimes some effort has been put in for other reasons.

Fodor and Pylyshyn (1981) criticized Gibson's ecological psychology, and in the process made some contributions to a more elaborate cognitivist view on behavior. Fodor (1986a) developed these ideas further when he sought to distinguish genuinely intentional systems from systems which are generally thought to behave but which we intuitively do not consider to be intentional, such as thermostats and bacteria (see also Beckermann, 1988). Dretske (1988) made a contribution to behavioral theory as part of a reconciliation between folk psychological reasons and naturalistic causes. I will focus mainly on Fodor's 1986 account. A good introduction and background for these ideas can be found in the older work of Fritz Heider (1959) and Egon Brunswik (1952; see also Tolman and Brunswik, 1935; Campbell, 1966).

Heider and Brunswik were both concerned with the structure of the environment as a relevant factor for the adaptive behavior of organisms. In 1926 and 1930, Heider published two important papers in German, later translated as "Thing and Medium" and "The Function of the Perceptual System" (Heider, 1959). In these papers he made a distinction between the 'near' and 'far' environments of an organism and addressed the implications of this distinction for adaptation. Brunswik, influenced by these papers, used the notions of proximal and distal to mark the distinction between distal objects or events (at some distance of the organism), and the proximal stimuli which impinge on the organism directly as a pattern of sensory stimulation. The proximal-distal distinction offers a very suitable way to organize and relate a number of important aspects of basic behavior (Brunswik, 1952; Heider, 1959).[2]

Heider and Brunswik stated that the adaptively relevant elements in an environment consist primarily of the distal objects or 'things' therein. These provide the possible nourishment, threats, or mates on which survival and reproduction depend.[3] Of course, it is only when these distal events or things come very near to the organism that they become a matter of life or death. However, at such a moment—when the tiger is already at your throat—these normally distal entities also become irrelevant as far as behavior is concerned. Nothing further can be done at such a moment (except being eaten).

The background assumption is that a certain time-frame is necessary in which an organism still has the opportunity to act. Behavior consists of bringing about (or avoiding) specific close encounters with such—most of the time—distal stimuli. As Brunswik says: "Organisms may in this sense be characterized as 'stabilizers' of [distal, FK] events or of relationships" (1952, p. 20).

The 'near' environment of an organism consists of proximal stimulation which impinges on it directly. This stimulation in itself is very often neutral as far as adaptation is concerned. The presence or absence of light, sound, or air-born particles do usually not make a dramatic impact on the life-processes of an organism. The near environment provides a relatively neutral medium in which the organism can move about. Proximal stimulation does, however, convey cues about the existence and whereabouts of distal, nonlocal features of the environment. Consequently, the organism can use these cues to guide it to those distal objects or events and so generate adaptively relevant, proximal encounters of the kind mentioned.

The problem with using proximal stimuli as cues for distal stimuli is their unreliability as signs of distal states. The relation between the proximal stimuli and distal events is not one to one.[4] Similar proximal stimulus patterns can correspond to different distal states of affairs, and, the other way round, the same distal state of affairs can give rise to very divergent proximal patterns. On the behavioral side, the same principle applies. The behavioral means available to the organism are also proximal: it can make movements. A series of 'properly' controlled movements can result in the achievement of an adaptively relevant event. However, the proximal set of movements that leads toward a similar distal event (feeding, escape) will differ every time.

Heider and Brunswik state that the problem to be solved by an organism amounts to the following: given a state in which the organism is immersed in a highly variable, proximal environment—as well at the sensory as at the effector side—how does it achieve a consistent coordination with relatively invariant distal events? This basic question can be illustrated with Brunswik's expository "lens model" (Brunswik, 1952).

The lens model conveys the general idea of proximal variability and distal stability when the organism is observed over several behavioral trials (see Figure 2.1). This particular figure displays another distinction. It consists of two 'lenses'. The first one displays how a particular distal object is, on different occasion, connected to a particular central (mental) state by different

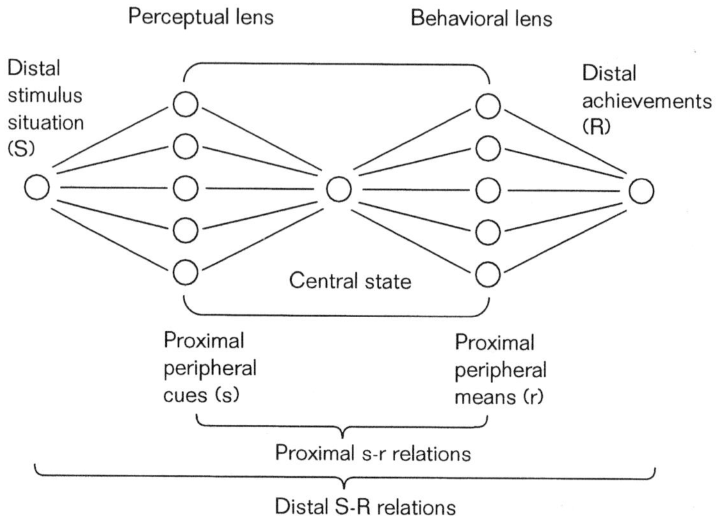

Figure 2.1
Brunswik's lens model. (Based on Brunswik, 1952.)

proximal sensor-states. The second lens portrays how the presence of a central state leads to the achievement of a distal, functional achievement through variable proximal movements on different occasions. The global picture is subsequently one in which a locally, or proximally, operating system—the s-r part can be seen as a single 'lens'—enforces stable distal S-R relations. As said above, the organism acts as a stabilizer of distal events.

The Heider-Brunswik analysis of organism-environment relations and the lens model offer a good set of conceptual tools to characterize the cognitivist view on behavior as it is sketched by Fodor (1986a). Fodor posits that in behavior a stimulus property becomes connected to a response property. Certain properties are such that the objects which have this property fall under laws because of it. For example, a left shoe has, as a property, a certain mass, and because of this mass it will behave in a lawful way when left unsupported in a gravitational field. The property of having a mass makes the shoe behave in this specific, lawful way. Fodor calls this a nomic property. However, an object will also have nonnomic properties, such as, for example, being a left shoe. 'Being a left shoe' is not a property that makes the object that possesses it, behave in a lawful way. For this reason it is a nonnomic property. In the example above, the left shoe's downfall is a consequence of its mass, not its being a left shoe.

Intentional systems are capable of responding selectively to the nonnomic properties of an object. They are capable of responding selectively to a left shoe, because it has the property of being a left shoe. An intentional system, somehow, generates regularities between nonnomic stimulus properties and behavioral responses which are not governed by natural laws. The general idea here can be restated in the vocabulary of Heider and Brunswik. While nomic laws still apply at the proximal level of stimulus and response, an intentional system succeeds in projecting much wider, nonnomic, distal regularities. Some behaving organisms succeed in producing a series of 'properly' controlled movements that will result in the achievement of physically arbitrary, but adaptively significant distal events. The big issue here is of course: How are these movements 'properly' controlled? Cognitivism proposes an answer to this very question. As Fodor formulates it:

> So there appears a puzzle: how does a property of a stimulus come to be implicated in the explanation of a property of a behavioral response if there is no law by which the two properties are connected? *It is largely this puzzle that motivates the representational theory of the mind.* Or, to put it less in the formal mode: selective response to nonnomic properties is, on the present view, the great evolutionary problem that mental representation was invented to solve. (1986a, p. 14)

I will abide by this definition of the problem that AT tries to solve. There is one complication, though, that should be kept in mind. Solving the problem of selective response to nonnomic properties generates new nomic properties. Being a left shoe might be nonnomic in a physical context. In a psychological context it makes perfect sense to base generalizations on this property (whether these are truly lawful remains to be seen). Cognitive systems are capable of generating arbitrary (from a lower-level, physical perspective) 'nomic' relations, such as those that apply to left shoes in virtue of their being a left shoe: they are put on left feet. The distinction between nomic and nonnomic is thus perhaps not as clearcut as Fodor implies. Still, the main point is that AT offers an explanation of how these arbitrary 'nomic' relations are established.

3 How is AT thought to solve this problem?

By what sort of subpersonal mechanism is anticipatory behavior realized? The answer that AT gives is simple: by means of a mechanism that acts in the same way as an aware, thinking agent would to achieve some goal. In

AT, the subpersonal mechanism is molded after a conceptual framework that is traditionally used to describe and explain the actions of whole, behaving agents: folk psychology, or belief-desire psychology. Folk psychology explains actions as the result of an aware, thinking and deliberating agent who perceives its environment, represents this environment in a set of beliefs, makes plans that will result in a new desired environmental state and subsequently executes those plans so that the goal is achieved. These are the very properties which make us speak of a *person* or an *agent* who has a mind.

The fundamental idea is that it is possible to use the agent-related conceptual framework as a guideline to construct a subpersonal mechanism capable of generating specific, distal behavioral regularities. In this process the agent-related conceptual framework is redrawn. This reconstructed conceptual framework (AT) is set to work in a subpersonal context which does not exhibit the intentionality, awareness or any other of the phenomenological properties of mind.[5] The agent-related properties are used as—and in the process transformed into—a part of a bottom up explanation of behavior. Mind is used to specify a subpersonal mechanism.

The central concept which is taken from the mental context is the notion of representation. The reliance on representations will be taken as the primary factor for turning a model into an instantiation of the Agent Theory. As AT operates on a subpersonal level, this amounts to accepting *subpersonal representations* as a part of behavioral explanation.

Using concepts that typically belong to an agent to account for the capacities of that agent at least looks like a clear case of a *circular explanation* for the emergence of behavioral regularities. The explanandum is used as its own explanans. Still, in practice it does work as the AT conceptual framework has given rise to many, widely differing and elaborate models capable of performing many different cognitive and behavioral tasks (Vera and Simon, 1993a, 1993b). AT is not just a paper story which has never been put to the test. Many people consider AT to be a great success. It is then plausible to suppose that the circularity which seems to be at the heart of AT is defeated when it is worked out in definite models. AT is thus not a necessarily false account of the generation of behavior. On the contrary, it could be seen as an extremely bold hypothesis which has so far been quite successful.

3.1 The Craikian automaton

At the heart of the Agent Theory is the very general idea that the behavior of organisms is guided by a set of representations, just as an agent's actions are guided by the beliefs and desires he or she entertains. How can this be made more specific?

The behavior of interest is under the constraint of nonlocal, distal factors. That is, it is behavior that leads predictably and repetitively to similar future events, under a wide variety of circumstances and disturbances. A paradigmatic example of this is the capacity of certain wasps, bees and ants to return to their nests after foraging (Gallistel, 1990a). However, proximal and distal are relative terms. The distal can also be drawn much closer to the organism. Take the control of a motor system in an irregular, natural environment. It is easy to claim that the direction in which an insect moves is under direct stimulus control, but much less so when all the movements that are required to actuate this behavior are also considered. These movements require internal pattern generators for fluent and reliable performance. The problems become immediately apparent when robots have to mimic such basic behavioral capacities (Thorpe, 1992). All of behavior is influenced by factors that cannot be traced to the immediate, proximal sensor-array. The problem can thus be stated as follows: By what factor can behavior be guided when this guidance is not provided by the current state of the sensors?

Someone who deserves a lot of credit in coming up with the current—artificial intelligence and cognitive science—way of dealing with this problem is Kenneth Craik. Craik stated that one of the most fundamental properties of thought is its power to predict events (1943, p. 50). He mentioned three essential processes:

> (1) 'Translation' of external process into words, numbers or other symbols,
> (2) Arrival of other symbols by a process of 'reasoning', deduction, inference, etc., and
> (3) 'Retranslation' of these symbols into external processes (as in building a bridge to design) or at least recognition of the correspondence between these symbols and external event (as in realising that a prediction is fulfilled). (ibid.)

The process of reasoning produces a final result similar to that which might have been reached by causing the actual physical processes to occur: The thought process mimics the external events and so can be used to predict these external events (on the condition that there is a time difference between the two). Thus, according to Craik, the essence of thought is that it provides a *model* of the external world.

Craik postulated that the capacity of modeling is not restricted to minds: "Surely, however, this process of prediction is not unique to minds, though no doubt it is hard to imitate the flexibility and versatility of mental prediction" (p. 51). As examples he mentioned—it was 1943—a calculating machine, an anti-aircraft predictor, and Kelvin's tidal predictor as mechanical parallels to the three stages of thought. Johnson-Laird described a simple robot, made by Christopher Longuet-Higgins. In the absence of direct sensor information the robot's behavior was guided by a model. Johnson-Laird called this a *Craikian automaton.*

> The robot moves freely on the surface of a table, but whenever it reaches an edge it rings an alarm bell to summon its human keeper to rescue it from disaster. It possesses neither pressure sensors for detecting edges, nor any sort of electronics. How then does it respond to the edge of the table? The answer turns— literally—on a model. As the robot travels around the table, its main wheels drive two small wheels that hold a piece of sandpaper up underneath its baseplate. The paper is the same shape as the table, and as the small wheels turn they move the paper around beneath the baseplate. In fact, their position on the paper at any moment corresponds exactly to the robot's position on the table. There is a ridge at the end of the paper (corresponding to the edge of the table) so that whenever one of the small wheels is deflected by it, a simple circuit is closed to ring the alarm. The large wheels in effect act as perceptual organs (as well as a means of transport) that register the robot's movement through its environment. The small wheels and the piece of sandpaper are not intrinsically a model, but they become a model in the robot because of their function as an arbitrarily selected symbolic notation that is used to register the position of the robot in the world. (1983, p. 404)

Of course, this sandpaper robot is extremely simple. Still, it incorporates the three essential properties that Craik ascribed to thought: There is a translation process from the world to an internal representational medium, subsequently a process of prediction takes place, and finally the result is retranslated into the world where it modifies the behavior of the automaton in an adaptive way.

The example illustrates how a mind-derived conceptual framework can be realized in a fully mechanical way and turned into a theory of the generation of behavior. Anticipatory behavior is thus explained by postulating the existence of an internal model which is isomorphic to the processes happening outside the organism (Rosen, 1979, 1987). The model can subsequently act as a program that instructs the motor system so that specific, distal goals are achieved. It is this very general and very coarse theory of behavior that I call *Agent Theory*.

3.2 AT taken apart

According to AT, adaptive, anticipatory behavior results from a process containing four basic components: sensing, modeling, planning, and acting (SMPA) (Brooks, 1991b, 1991c). Craik's middle stage has been differentiated into two separate stages. These components are thought to operate in a globally sequential way, one after the other, even when many local deviations from strict sequentiality occur.

Sensing The first component process translates external (proximal) signals into an internal model of the external situation. David Marr described this for vision: Vision is "the *process* of discovering from images what is present in the world, and where it is" (Marr, 1982, p. 3). The task of vision is then to translate the information which is present at the retina, consisting of the "intensity value at each point of the image" (ibid., p. 37) into a three-dimensional (3-D) model representation, which "describes shapes and spatial organization in an object-centered coordinate frame, using a modular hierarchical representation" (ibid.).

Modeling The second component is the stage where traditionally the mind would come into play. Leaving the possibility for a mental interpretation aside, a model can be described as an internal structure which is isomorphic to the external situation, like the sandpaper is to the table. In this case the sandpaper *represents* the table. A somewhat more complex example is SHRDLU, a program devised by Terry Winograd around 1970. This program could answer questions about a (simulated) blocks world consisting of blocks, pyramids, and boxes in various sizes and colors (Winston, 1977). To do this, the program incorporated a model which specifies the positions of all objects, together with knowledge concerning how these objects could be placed on top or inside of one another (e.g., a block cannot be placed on top of a pyramid). By using the modeled blocks world, the program could answer questions as to where certain blocks were, and which steps were necessary to move a block from one place to another.

Modeling depends on an isomorphism between external and internal structures. This isomorphism should not be taken in too concrete a sense (Palmer, 1978). The sandpaper and the table may have been literal lookalikes, but for AT to work in a general way, the isomorphism has to be more abstract. What is necessary is that there be a systematic correspondence between states and change of states of the isomorphic domains. The actual features that do the representing can be very different from the represented domain (Palmer, 1978). Indeed, if there has to be any modeling of complex and more abstract situations there should not be any literal resemblance. It is downright impossible to construct any literal, physical resemblance in these cases (Janlert, 1987), in particular when also considering the fact that brains do not resemble their environments.

The lack of any concrete similarity should actually be taken further. The isomorphism that is required only has to be manifest in the way in which the behaving system makes use of it to guide its behavior. Representation involves operational relations, defined by the processes that interpret the representation, rather than apparent model-world relations as witnessed by an external observer (Palmer, 1978, p. 265). Such representations don't have to be isomorphic to external situations in a way that is easily recognizable by an observer who inspects the system's operation.

The existence of representing models will be taken as the crucial feature of AT's explanation of behavior. Generating and updating such models by processes involving evolutionary and sensory feedback is, of course, essential for extending and maintaining the capacities provided by representational models. But the modeling capacity itself is the core factor of AT from which an organism's capacity to generate anticipatory behavior is derived.

Planning The modeling capacity forms the basis for a planning component. "Planning is the generation of an action sequence or action program for an agent, such as a robot, that can change its environment. The purpose of a plan is to achieve one or more explicit goals" (Vere, 1992, p. 1159). Planning has three essential inputs: an initial world state, a repertoire of actions for changing that world, and a set of goals prescribing a world state that has to be reached. The form of a plan is usually a linear sequence of actions that will connect the actual world state to the goal state.

Since Newell and Simon's first attempts at a general problem solver (GPS) around 1963, planning has been at the heart of AI (Gardner, 1985). Planning problems are solved by searching through the space of possible plans. The differences between the current state and the desired state are minimized until a sequence of steps (actions) is found that connects the two. This way of problem solving may require a search through an enormous space of possible plans. Search control is therefore one of the prime topics in AT's way of dealing with behavior.

Planning is advocated as, probably, the most reliable method for controlling the behavior of living and artificial agents (Vere, 1992). There may be faster control methods but these are thought to apply merely to stereotypical behavior. For example, stored behavior programs may suffice in standard circumstances, but can lead to inappropriate or unsuccessful behavior when these 'standard circumstances' no longer apply. When considering the problems that are addressed in robotics, it becomes clear that almost any action involving motor control is nonstandard (see section 3.4). The movements involved in behavior are highly sensitive to even small deviations in the placement of external objects and the load of the effectors. Planning thus seems to be required for almost all behaviors, at least within the AT framework.

Acting This component involves the execution of a plan. It consists of Craik's 'retranslation' of the (representational) plan into external processes. The sequence of represented actions has to be turned into external events so that the goal state is reached. As Cummins puts it: "Motor-Theory: laws relating representational states to motions" (1991, p. 97).

An interesting asymmetry appears here. It is fairly easy to study planning separate from action. For example, artificial intelligence studies problem solving—or planning—in a formalized domain where the present situation, the actions, and the goal state can be strictly defined and remain stable. However, when plans have to be executed by a motor system in the real world, this can hardly ever be done according to a predefined plan. Any natural environment abounds of unexpected events which make the actual consequences of a plan that is being executed uncertain. Plan violations are to be expected and need to be dealt with. According to AT, this requires the formulation of new plans. Doing elaborate planning without continuously accommodating for changes within the current situation, the repertoire of actions, and the goal state is unwise. The moral is that, for AT to work, it should not limit itself to the study of the separate SMPA components, but should try to weld them together into a more integrated system which is actually capable of motor behavior.

This advice brings us back to a point that should not be forgotten. AT is my own reconstruction of what cognitive science has to offer as a science of behavior. Cognitivism's interest lies with the internal cognitive system. Given this interest, problems with the actual execution of plans do not gain the urgency that they have for someone with an interest in behavior. When these problems do occur, as in robotics, they are usually 'solved' by constraining the effectors and environment sufficiently so that a reliable execution of planned movements is ensured.

Despite the relative neglect of behavior within cognitive science, when explicitly searched for, it has a story to tell in this respect. That story is AT: Behavior results from an ongoing sequence of sensing, modeling, planning, and acting. This conceptual framework stays very close to traditional intuitions concerning the mind's relation to action. It still shows the characteristic translation process in which happenings from the external, material world are translated into an internal, mental, or at least symbolic, domain, and back again. The main modern addition is that the framework has been transformed into a genuine mechanism that offers an explanation for how behavior can be anticipatory, purposive, or, in general, intelligent.

3.3 AT: a coarse model for analysis and for synthesis

AT is a remarkably crude conceptual framework. This is not a drawback. AT is no more than the general structure that can be discerned within the more detailed explanations of behavior provided by cognitive science. It is like the biological notion of a phylum which brings together a (sometimes) large group of potentially very different species which nevertheless share a common, recognizable *Bauplan*, or bodyplan (Brusca and Brusca, 1990). In the next section, I will discuss a case where this rough guide is turned into a detailed model of a behaving system. First, I will say something about the relation between AT and more detailed models.

AT shows up in two complementary ways—analysis and synthesis—and is used as a conceptual framework to analyze the operation of behaving systems. Usually this would involve naturally occurring behavior, but AT is applied to analyze artificial systems as well (see section 4.1). AT also provides a rough blueprint for the synthesis—the construction—of artificial behaving systems. It gives guidelines as to which components to use and how they should be put together in so as to create a successful artificial agent.

AT provides cognitive science with a conceptual framework that takes apart the processes involved in the behavior of an organism. AT dissects the whole acting organism into a sequence of four distinct and separable components: sense, model, plan, and act (Brooks, 1991a). AT thus predicts which basic elements a cognitive scientist will encounter in a behaving organism. It molds the expectations of the researchers, and biases them to interpret the processes occurring within a behaving organism along these lines. For example, a cognitive scientist will look for the representations used by an organism and even find them, while a behaviorist investigating the same system is much less likely to conclude that there is clear evidence for these entities. A behaving organism can be analyzed in many different ways. AT is a particular way of doing this analysis. In later chapters we will encounter different ways to carve up the behaving organism.

AT's interpretation of behavioral phenomena provides cognitivist psychology with its standard research topics. AT's components provide the right sort of well-circumscribed and manageable topics that a psychologist might choose to investigate: the translation from world to a representational model of the environment, the planning part, and finally motor control, the retranslation from the representational plan to overt behavior. These pieces can, so it is presumed, be studied relatively independently from one another without seriously disrupting (or misinterpreting) their normal operation. Most research in cognitive science is directed at one, or a small subset of these SMPA elements. Perception is studied as a separate process, and so are the problems of knowledge representation, planning and motor control (execution). In this way, AT prescribes to a large degree the research agenda that cognitivism seeks to fill in. For most of cognitivist psychology the story ends here. Still, to explain behavior—which always remained a background assumption of cognitive science—all these ingredients are necessary. Even when only a part of the total system is investigated, the other parts have to be present by default.

AT also provides a set of guidelines for synthesizing behaving systems from ingredients which do not show this property. In other words, AT is used as a guide for modeling behavior. Two different projects should be distinguished here: (a) the modeling of the SMPA elements, and (b) modeling which puts these components together into a complete, synthetic behaving system such as a robot.

The first project is the regular practice within cognitive science. For example, it involves providing models for vision along the lines outlined by Marr, or a model for speech as proposed by Levelt which describes the process that 'translates' an internal 'meaning' to the outward articulation of spoken language (Levelt, 1989). These models make concrete different ways of solving AT's subtasks and offer a way to test the feasibility and efficiency of such proposals. Except for prescribing which components to investigate, AT has not much to offer here. Its conceptual framework has little to say on the organization within these components. The exception here is the action part where the whole SMPA architecture is reiterated on a smaller scale (see chapter 3, section 2.2).

In the second project, the SMPA-components that are used to analyze existing behaving systems are used as building blocks for generating models of complete behaving systems. For the evaluation of AT, modeling complete behaving systems is of central importance. Models of subtasks can be evaluated and optimized on the basis of criteria that derive from AT itself. But ultimately this (local) evaluation on the basis of AT-based standards is subservient to a global evaluation of AT itself.

As an analogy, consider the problem of delivering clean water to as many people as possible. One general solution might consist of a number of water dispersion points from which people can carry the water home in jerry cans. Once this general solution is adopted, the system can be further optimized by developing better jerry cans—making them bigger, lighter, put wheels under them, whatever. This optimization takes place by creating new kinds of jerry cans and comparing them with one another to decide which design serves best. However, this evaluation remains within the limits set by the chosen water dispersal system. A water dispersal system can also be evaluated and optimized at a more global level when it is compared with altogether different water dispersal systems. For example, one might think of a system which delivers water to each house individually by a system of water pipes. The latter system makes the optimization of jerry can design irrelevant, and should not be judged for any neglect in this respect.

It is possible to improve on an explanation of behavior by optimizing the postulated elements within this explanation. However, the explanation as a whole should also be evaluated at a general level where it is asked how well it deals with the phenomenon of behavior itself, instead of subproblems that are derived from the explanation.

The synthesis part of AT allows its separate components to be modeled independently. But to know how well AT does as a theory of behavior, the parts will have to be put together and put to use within a model of a complete behaving system. As a consequence, one of AT's really critical testing grounds lies in the area of robotics. In robotics, all the separate units have to be assembled, to make a passable, artificial behaving system. The field of robotics is of prime interest for evaluating the merits of AT (or, for that matter, any account of the generation of behavior). In this context it is interesting to note that one of the most strong criticisms of AT has arisen within this field and that alternative approaches are being pursued (Brooks, 1991a, 1991b). In the next section, I will discuss an example of a robot which is representative of AT's dealings with behavior.

3.4 AT exemplified: a walking robot named Ambler

Robotics is the place where the conceptual framework provided by AT comes to the fore most explicitly. Here, all the different subtopics that cognitive science usually deals with one at a time are combined and integrated to create systems that actually behave. Nitzan proposes the following definition of a robot: "A robot is a general-purpose machine that, like a human, can perform a variety of different tasks under conditions that may not be known a priori" (Nitzan, 1992, p. 1375). Most robots serve in industrial plants. They consist of disconnected arms, fixed to a particular spot, and their operation is restricted to a standardized (prepared) environment, for example welding and painting robots. Such robots do not readily reflect the capacities of humans and other animals as behaving systems that move freely in a natural environment. More 'organism-like' robots can be found in some space projects where a number of mobile robots, or 'planetary rovers', have been developed to traverse the terrain of planets other than Earth, most notably Mars (Krotkov, Simmons, and Whittaker, 1995). These robots have to be capable of moving around in a natural environment without human intervention. Sometimes this is done with wheeled vehicles, others attempt the more difficult, but also more energy efficient, approach of *walking* (Raibert and Hodgins, 1993). The latter provide an excellent showcase of cognitive science's modeling of this basic and important form of behavior.

The robot that will be discussed is the Ambler (Krotkov and Hoffman, 1994; Krotkov and Simmons, 1996; Krotkov, Simmons, and Whittaker, 1995; Simmons and Krotkov, 1991). The Ambler is supposed to operate autonomously without teleoperation by humans, and it should be capable of traversing a natural, desert-like environment, without prepared surfaces and exhibiting roughness over a wide range of scales (Krotkov and Simmons, 1996, p. 155). More specifically, it must be able to climb 30 degree slopes and negotiate obstacles of up to 1 meter in size.

> The Ambler has six legs, arranged in two stacks on central shafts [see figure 2.2]. The shafts are connected to an arched body that supports four enclosures housing electronics and computing. Each leg consists of a rotational link and an extensional link that move in the horizontal plane, and an orthogonal vertical link. A six-axis force/torque sensor mounted on the base of each vertical link measures the forces acting on the feet. The height ranges from 4.1 to 6.0 m, and the width varies between 4.5 and 7.1 m. The mass of the mechanism and all equipment (excluding power generation and storage) is about 2500 kg. On top of the body structure is a scanning laser rangefinder mounted on a panning table, as well as two inclinometers that measure the body's orientation. (Krotkov, Simmons, and Whittaker, 1995, pp. 75–76).

The Ambler is primarily built for safe and energy efficient locomotion. To accomplish this it walks in a highly deliberate manner. Every single leg motion and footfall is individually planned. It does not have a fixed gait which is continuously repeated. One reason for this is the specific set up of the Ambler's legs. The three legs on each side are vertically arranged on a shaft, which allows them to move in a horizontal circle. A hind leg can be moved to the front through the cavity in the middle of its inverted U-shaped body and so become a front leg (see figure 2.3). This gait allows larger distances to be traversed with fewer steps and decreases energy consumption.

The operation of the Ambler is along the general lines prescribed by the sense-model-plan-act framework. Its primary sensor is the scanning laser rangefinder. The rangefinder measures both reflectance and range of the terrain 1 to 8 meters in front of the Ambler. A scanning laser is used because

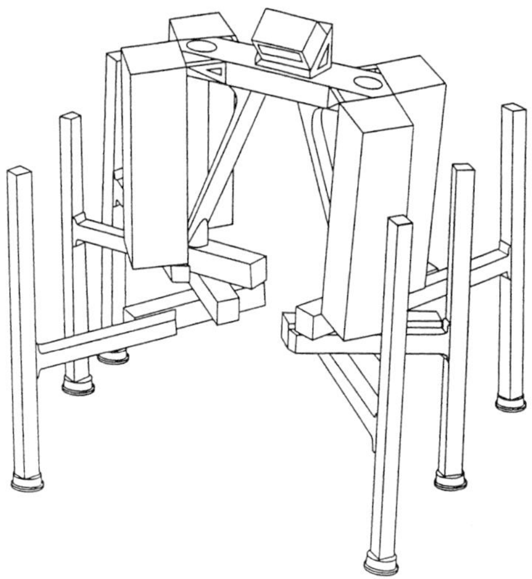

Figure 2.2
The Ambler. (From Krotkov and Simmons, 1996.)

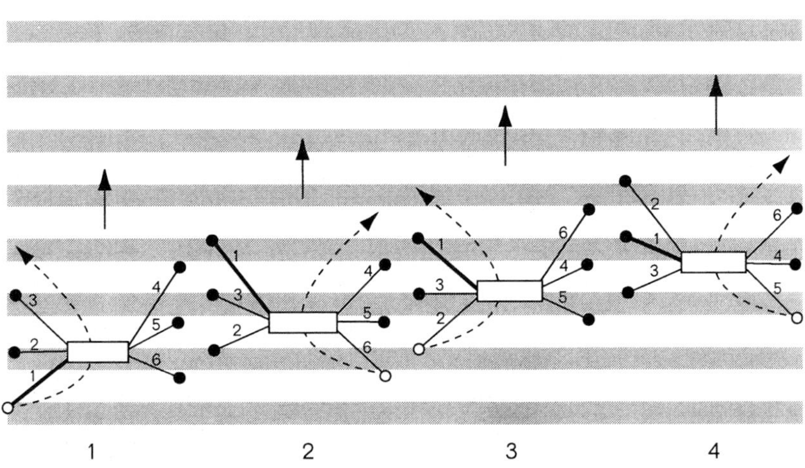

Figure 2.3
A top down perspective on the walking pattern of the Ambler. (Redrawn from Krotkov and Simmons, 1996.)

it directly recovers the environment's three-dimensional structure, supplying 3-D data more rapidly and reliably than passive vision techniques.[6] A calibration technique is used to identify the transformation between the Ambler-centered reference frame and the sensor-centered frame (basically it looks at its own feet and so relates the 'seen' leg position to its actual body position). The rangefinder data are preprocessed, tagged with relevant information concerning current body pose and world coordinates, and stored in a queue of up to 30 images. The stored images are used to construct terrain elevation maps on demand. This demand is triggered when a passable route has to be planned.

Walking is initiated by a human operator who indicates a sequence of trajectories via a graphical user interface. Each trajectory in turn is forwarded to a gait planning module. This module plans a series of leg and body moves. The gait planner first determines the leg that maximizes subsequent body motion and then finds a region in which footfall may take place, taking into account the limits of the leg's motion, the need to avoid colliding with the current leading leg, to avoid placing the leg in the path of the body, and the need to maintain support in subsequent moves.

Next, a request is send to the perception subsystem for a terrain elevation map of the prospective footfall region. The "Local Terrain Mapping" module requests subimages from the queue of stored images that contain laser range data relevant to constructing the desired terrain map. The mapping module of the perception subsystem then combines the images to construct a terrain elevation map. The map is evaluated for the goodness of the foot-sized patches it contains and the gait planner chooses the best footfall location within the specified region.

After the leg move is chosen, the gait planner finds the maximum body move along the indicated trajectory that does not violate limits on leg motion and maintains the Ambler in a stable position. Then the gait planner forwards the chosen leg move to the *leg recovery planner* which plans a fast trajectory that moves the leg to its new position without colliding with the robot or the terrain. The chosen leg and body moves are then delegated to the real-time controller module which supervises the execution of the planned moves.

The real-time controller generates leg move trajectories that are linear in joint space, coordinating the leg joints so that all motions start and end simultaneously. During execution, it monitors the force/torque sensors in the feet and also the inclinometers which measure any tilt of the Ambler. If an unexpected collision or tilt occurs, all motion is stopped and an exception is reported to the task-level controller. The latter initiates a replanning of steps after which walking is continued. Planned body moves are executed in a similar way. The motion control task is divided into two parts, a planar translation and/or rotation followed by a vertical lift or lower of the body. For the planar translation, the real-time controller computes the horizontal joint motions that simultaneously translate and rotate the body to achieve the horizontal position commanded. It executes a horizontal body move by first locking the vertical joints and then servoing the 12 horizontal joints to achieve smooth acceleration and deceleration of the body. Subsequently, the horizontal joints are locked, and the Ambler lifts or lowers by servoing the six vertical axis joints.

Once a new body position has been reached, the perception subsystem is notified to acquire a new laser range image. This allows the preprocessing of the image to occur concurrently with planning and control tasks. Typically, by the time the leg and body moves have been executed, the planners are ready with a new set of moves. In this way the Ambler achieves nearly continuous motion.

What can be learned from this example of robot behavior? (1) It illustrates how a model built along the outlines of AT's conceptual framework generates a basic form of behavior. (2) It gives an impression of how well such a model performs this task, which (3) gives an indication of the difficulties involved in generating basic behavior.

The first point is basically an existence proof. Robots, like the Ambler, show that AT provides the basic setup for robot architectures that actually work. AT may sound like a circular way of explaining behavior, but it does give rise to models that are implemented in silicon and metal. AT can not be dismissed on principled grounds alone.

Given their sheer existence and thus the possibility of AT-based models of behavior, the next question concerns their adequacy. How good is the walking behavior generated by the Ambler? This issue is more difficult to decide. What are the criteria? To what systems should the Ambler be compared? Some grip on the issue can be gained from reports on the Ambler's performance (Krotkov, Simmons, and Whittaker, 1995), both for the data reported as well as what the authors deemed relevant enough to include. At the time of the report, the Ambler had walked a total of over 2 kilometers. In one indoor trial, the Ambler walked autonomously over a boulder, 4 meters long and 1.5 meters high. In one outdoor trial, it took 1,219 steps over rolling, grassy terrain, traveling 527 meters horizontally and 25 meters vertically. The Ambler's average walking speed was 35 centimeters per minute, and each body move about 50 centimeters.

Is the performance good or bad? The Ambler may seem rather slow, but it crosses very rough terrain in a way that is safe and fairly reliable. The builders seemed satisfied enough. With respect to the boulder-strewn obstacle course they commented: "We know of no other robot that could surmount all of the obstacles in the course" (Krotkov and Simmons, 1996, p. 175). On the other hand, when the Ambler is compared to the walking capacities of biological organisms, its performance is less impressive. An average speed of 21 meters in an hour is very slow compared to biological organisms, in particular when the huge size of the robot is also taken in consideration. The Ambler is also incapable of dealing with environmental changes that take as long as minutes, let alone occurrences in the milliseconds to seconds range within which biological behaving systems can operate. The only fast response that the Ambler is capable of in the event of unforeseen circumstances is 'freezing' and relying on its static stability to ward off any danger of falling. The Ambler has a very limited sensor and motoric capabilities. Its stability depends on never raising more than one leg at a time Even the successful crossing of rugged terrain is largely a result of the Ambler's size. Its sheer size and weight allows the Ambler to step over 1 meter high boulders and crush minor ones, "many objects that are obstacles before the Ambler steps on them are planar afterwards" (Krotkov and Hoffman, 1994, p. 739).

Given the behavioral capacities that we tend to take for granted in humans and other animals, the Ambler is surely a limited behaving system. This should not be held against it. The Ambler may make a bad insect, even when it is a good robot. The fact remains that it is one of the most advanced operational machines, one that is actually capable of integrating perception and motor control to deal with a rough, nonprepared environment. Integrating sensor information and motor control at the speeds required for behavior is a huge challenge. The basic behavioral capacities that most psychologists tend to overlook are a continuous source of problems: "The most difficult aspects of robot planning arise in the lowest levels" (Thorpe, 1992, p. 1412), and "Robotic trajectory planners, which plan how the vehicle should negotiate the next few meters of terrain, must go beyond symbolic and geometric planning to consider issues of precision and control" (ibid., p. 1413). The Ambler shows the practical difficulties involved in relating a stream of sensor values with the angles of the leg's rotary joints and the lengths of the sliding joints, so that the foot ends up at a given footfall location. In order to accomplish this, many subproblems have to be solved: joint-to-world coordinate and world-to-joint coordinate transformations have to be made, motion trajectories have to be determined which allow a smooth path from the starting coordinates to the goal coordinates, the dynamics of the body and legs have to be related to the applied forces—torques to the joint motions (in both directions), the motion has to be controlled, and so on.

Basic behavior, such as walking across a natural surface, is a complex process which tends to be underestimated as a psychological topic. The Ambler provides a working model for such basic behavior along the general lines prescribed by AT. So far, such models remain very limited in comparison with animal behavior.

4 Positioning AT: connectionism, eliminativism, instinct and learning

AT is a reconstructed position. It is an interpretation of what is primarily meant as a science of mind as a science of behavior. AT involves a change of perspective which messes up the conventional way of traversing cognitive science's territory. Major topics are relegated to the background, while the relative side-issues of behavior and motor control suddenly stand up front. This different angle from which theoretical and practical issues are viewed may look confusing at first. As a way of global positioning, I will situate AT with respect to some conventional landmarks within cognitive science: (1) The discussion about classical computation and connectionism is a major issue in cognitive science. How should AT be placed within these developments? (2) The debate on eliminativism: should we get rid of our common sense psychology and replace it by neuroscience? AT has some ironic implications here. (3) The explanation of behavior provided by instinct and learning fits in nicely with AT. In section 5, I will provide a fourth landmark by discussing the question of whether AT's representations derive their meaning from (abstract) isomorphism or from a dependency on external states, which is a dominant idea within the philosophy of mind. Section 5 does double duty, as it also explicates AT's notion of representation against which interactionists react.

4.1 AT and its implementations: classic computation and connectionism

Up to now, cognitivist psychology has been treated as a unitary field, all of which is dedicated to AT. However, there are many different approaches and theories. One major division of the field is that between classical computational and connectionist approaches.

The classical computational approach interprets the brain as a device which operates in essentially the same way as digital computers. Fodor and Pylyshyn (1988) described the classical approach as being committed (1) to representations with a combinatorial (syntactic) structure, and (2) to cognitive processes that are sensitive to this combinatorial structure. For example, you can have an operation that applies to any representation of the form $P \& Q$ and transforms it into P. This operation can also be satisfied by an expression like $(A \vee B \vee C) \& (D \vee E \vee F)$ which it turns into $(A \vee B \vee C)$ (p. 13). It is hypothesized that the brain systematically manipulates such syntactical strings or symbols, and it is assumed that this higher-level computational/cognitive process can be studied and understood to a large degree independently from lower-level brain processes.

Connectionism challenges this downplaying of neural processes (McClelland and Rumelhart, 1986; Rumelhart and McClelland, 1986). Connectionists stress that cognitive processes emerge as a global phenomenon from the interactions between a large number of elements in a neural network (Smolensky, 1988). Connectionists aim to generate the characteristics of higher-level cognitive processing by modeling the lower-level, neural microstructure of cognition.

How does this relate to AT? When AT is loosely described as a commitment to a representation-based explanation of behavior (the output), there can be no doubt that classical computational models, as well as connectionist ones act as implementations of the AT framework.[7] The presence or relevance of representations was never a point of discussion between the two (Cummins, 1991; Churchland and Sejnowski, 1990; Rumelhart and McClelland, 1986; Smolensky, 1988; Fodor and Pylyshyn, 1988). Classical computationalists and connectionists only differ in their opinions on how representational structure is implemented.

Classical computational models are clearly capable of implementing AT's representation-based SMPA architecture. Connectionism's relation to AT is more complex. Connectionist models are generally held to incorporate representations. These representations are thought to be the relevant factors in explaining the output of a model. From this perspective, a connectionist network implements AT. But what if one asks whether connectionist networks implement a complete SMPA architecture? Many connectionist models are at most border cases of AT in this respect.

To model cognitive tasks, connectionism uses artificial neural networks that are highly stylized versions of the network properties of nervous systems. The most familiar networks are feedforward ones where a layer of mutually unconnected nodes—or neurons—is connected to another layer (two-layer), and so on (multi-layer), where the first and last layers are the input and output layers. The network's task consists of producing a particular pattern at the output layer when presented with a particular pattern at the input layer. The discovery that such multi-layer neural networks could learn complex input-output pairings by back-propagation (Rumelhart, Hinton, and Williams, 1986), and in this way learn to perform cognitive tasks, has been central to the rise of connectionism.

A famous, representative example is NETtalk (Rosenberg and Sejnowski, 1987; Churchland and Sejnowski, 1990). NETtalk transforms written text into phonemes. It consists of a three-layer, feedforward network, taught by back propagation. The input layer is stimulated by seven letters of input at a time. The output layer is connected to a voice synthesizer that produces speech sounds. NETtalk has 309 processing units and 18,629 weights that must be specified. The network has no built-in organization for mapping letters to sounds. All the structure emerges during the training period where the weights are set. After training, the network does a very good job at turning text into speech.

Another example of this type of network is Pomerleau's "autonomous land vehicle in a neural net" (ALVINN) (Thorpe, 1992; Touretzky and Pomerleau, 1994). ALVINN is capable of steering a car along a road. It consists of a fully connected three-layer network, trained by back-propagation. It receives video images as input and a human driver's steering wheel position serves as the target output. After approximately 200 training images, the network settles and is capable of steering the car. The features that the network learns to respond to depend on the kind of road it is trained on. Given an unimproved road, the hidden units learn to operate as large matched filters that look for the entire road or road edges. When lines or stripes are present, it learns to look for these more salient features (Thorpe, 1992).

Representations in connectionist networks consist of patterns of activation across nodes. Single nodes do not represent specific features (Hinton, McClelland, and Rumelhart, 1986). Instead, a case is made for a "type of representation that is less familiar and harder to think about than local representations" (ibid., p. 77). These are called *distributed representations.* In distributed representations, any single representation is dispersed as a pattern that involves the total set of neural nodes. Single nodes act as microfeatures, a subpart of a full-scale representation that in itself has no recognizable meaning. In comparison to the classical approach, connectionism deals with the microscopic structure of the syntactic symbols that are used there. The many contributions of individual nodes act as a large number of mutually interacting soft constraints that together shape the large-scale representation. It is argued that this provides a much more flexible way of representation than syntactical strings with their rigid forms.

How does this work in the example of NETtalk? Rosenberg and Sejnowski (1987) used cluster analysis to display the structure present at the hidden layer. It turned out that there were 79 distinctive activity patterns, each coding for one of the 79 possible letter to phoneme pairings. They interpreted this as "the network's representation for letter-to-sound correspondences [which] is neither local nor completely distributed; it is somewhere in between. The point is, each unit participates in more than one correspondence, and so the representation is not local, but since it does not participate in all correspondences, the representation is not completely distributed either" (Churchland and Sejnowsky, 1990, p. 361).

According to Sejnowski and his co-authors, NETtalk clearly incorporates representations (Churchland and Sejnowsky, 1990; Rosenberg and Sejnowski, 1987). This is also true for ALVINN (Touretzky and Pomerleau,

1994). Should NETtalk, ALVINN, and similar connectionist models now be interpreted as members of the AT phylum? It is clear that connectionists *analyze* their own models along the lines of AT, and they see the outputs produced as representation mediated. However, the representational capacities of these neural networks are very limited. When it is asked how well connectionist models do actually incorporate the SMPA components on which AT is based, the situation is less clear (Touretzky and Pomerleau, 1994; Vera and Simon, 1994).

A three-layer neural network is at most an extremely limited case of a SMPA architecture. The input and output layers and their connections form a translation and retranslation component. External processes are translated into a representational format at the hidden layer, and are retranslated into external processes at the output layer. As a representational model, it is restricted to the distinct patterns that can be discerned among the hidden layer activity values. It has no capacity to manipulate its representations independently from the current sensory situation, nor to plan and execute different actions given an identical sensory situation (after training has taken place).

The interpretation of connectionist, feedforward models as implementations of AT's conceptual framework is more a matter of willful interpretation (analysis) than a reflection of their actual characteristics. The analysis betrays the cognitivist context from which connectionist modeling springs. A behaviorist would not interpret these models in representational terms. A neural network would then simply be a way to generate stimulus-response pairings. The notion of representation doesn't do any work in this case.

The discussion between classical computationalists and connectionists about the structure of representations surfaces here (Fodor and Pylyshyn, 1988; Fodor and McLaughlin, 1990; Smolensky, 1988). The classicists argued that representations in connectionist models do not show the combinatorial structure that is necessary to create structure sensitive cognitive processes.

For AT, this implies that connectionism is thought to be incapable of providing the representational structure that is necessary to implement the complex planning and motor control components that behavior requires according to AT. It makes a lot of difference whether the output consists of an immediate response to a sensor-configuration (steer left or steer right for

ALVINN) which can be easily solved by a neural network, or the temporally extended planning and control of a walking hexapod (such as the Ambler).

In response, connectionists have put a lot of work in overcoming the present limitations by more complex network architectures. This has resulted in a great expanse of the models used, as well as their applications (Van Gelder, 1990; Elman, 1990; Pollack, 1990; Shastri and Ajjanagadde, 1993; Krakauer, 1995). For example, by introducing recurrency—which is when the network feeds its output back on its own hidden layer—networks can be made to respond to temporal relations between input patterns (Pollack, 1990; Elman, 1990). With this (and other) improvements, it is expected that the capacities of neural networks can be significantly extended.

Whether these new improvements will turn out to be a success or not is not an issue for present purposes. What counts is that connectionists use the AT conceptual framework to interpret the problems that need solving.[8] Connectionists (at least most of them) seek to overcome present limitations of connectionist networks in a way that will make neural network models better at implementing the conceptual framework provided by AT.

The debate between classical computationalists and connectionists is important for improving and extending the range of representation-based explanations of behavior. But it is not a debate in which AT itself is being discussed. Both parties in the debate work within the confines of AT. Both parties are committed to an explanation of behavior which involves some translation of the external situation into a set of representations, a set of transformations on these representations, and subsequently a retranslation into external processes. This debate between classical computationalists and connectionists bears only indirectly on the present topic: the evaluation of AT as an account of the generation of behavior.

4.2 AT and the discussion on eliminativism

Eliminative materialism, or eliminativism for short, is a radical view which has been most forcefully advocated by Paul and Patricia Churchland (P. M. Churchland, 1989; 1995; P. S. Churchland, 1986; P. S. Churchland and P. M. Churchland, 1983; P. S. Churchland and Sejnowski, 1990). Eliminativism states that our commonsense, folk psychological notions of beliefs and desires do not refer to anything real. As Ramsey, Stich, and Garon put it: "It is the claim that some category of entities, processes or properties exploited in the common sense or scientific account of the world do not exist" (1991, p. 201). Eliminativists hold that once a truly scientific explanation of mind and behavior has been achieved, there will be no more place for the psychological entities and categories that we now use in daily life. It will then become clear that such entities were never there in the first place, just like witches, phlogiston, and the flat earth. The entities of folk psychology will be replaced by those of neuroscience.

Of course, there are many who oppose this idea of a radical elimination and who defend the integration of folk psychological notions into an adult cognitive science (see chapter 1, section 3.4). Well, is AT a way in which folk psychology can find a home in cognitive science and so be saved from eliminativism? Or is AT maybe a way to eliminate folk psychology and replace it by a genuinely scientific cognitive science which does away with the folk psychological notions that it started out with? The answer to both questions is no.

In chapter 1, the task of developing a theory of behavior was dissociated from developing a theory of mind. There are two points here. (1) The current discussion revolves around explaining behavior, and is not concerned with any possible implications of this explanation for studying mind. (2) A theory of the subpersonal behavior mechanism has no straightforward implications for a theory that applies at the higher, personal level of folk psychology.

Given the dissociation of mental and behavioral theory, AT, as a theory of behavior, is neutral concerning the debate on eliminativism. The debate concerns an issue—and a level—which remains outside AT's scope.

In addition, when the different positions on eliminativism are compared in their bearing on behavior, they do not differ very much. The most striking example in this respect is that provided by the opposition between Fodor's classical, computational view on the mind and Paul and Patricia Churchland's ideas derived from neuroscience. As far as mind is concerned, their views are in firm opposition. Fodor seeks to vindicate folk psychology by means of cognitive science. The Churchlands think that folk psychology should be eliminated and replaced by neuroscience. However, as accounts of behavior their respective positions are both solid examples of AT.

Like Fodor's sentential account, the Churchlands' position is not opposed to a representational explanation of behavior (Churchland and Churchland,

1983; Churchland, 1989; Churchland and Sejnowski, 1990). They only oppose a specific implementation of such a representational account. In this sense, the debate on eliminativism is just another example of the discussion between connectionists and classic computationalists. Both sides use a version of the SMPA architecture. The differences all lie in the details of its implementation. Fodor seeks to maintain close links with agent-level concepts. The Churchlands base their representational model on neuroscience. The defining features of AT are present in both cases.

To conclude, the debate on the elimination of folk psychology has no direct bearing on the present discussion of AT. Furthermore, with respect to AT, both parties are situated in the same camp. Both parties defend cognitive science's general account of the generation of behavior.

4.3 Instinct and learning

Instinct as well as learning in the behaviorist sense are both generally accepted explanations of behavior. In the previous chapter, it was argued that both are forms of adaptationism and do not by themselves provide a subpersonal mechanism that might explain the generation of instinctive or learned behavior. Consequently, whenever instincts or learning are invoked to explain behavior, there must also be a behavioral mechanism at work that generates the observed behavioral regularities.

First, it should be stressed again that reflexes do not suffice as a mechanism for the generation of behavior. A reflex-like mechanism ties stimulus configurations to specific behavioral responses. However, stimulus configuration provides insufficient structure to provide the source of the order present in organismal behavior in all of its complexity. The example of the Ambler makes clear how very complex basic behavior is when the relations between perception and behavior are to be spelled out in sufficient detail to artificially produce behavior. Direct connections are insufficient here. In all instances of naturally occurring behavior, the stimulus-response vocabulary can only be maintained by either focusing on a single aspect of a total behavior—which can be interpreted as a single response—or by drawing the stimuli and responses in distal terms—divorcing them from the proximal physical stimuli and movements making up the total behavior. Reflexes make a suitable vocabulary for describing generated behavioral regularities; they don't give a clue how a mechanism might work that is capable of generating them.

As instinct and learning require some mechanism and reflexes are not an option, might AT step in to fulfill this role? One may expect some kind of opposition between these two explicitly nonmental forms of behavior and the mind-derived conceptual framework of AT, an opposition that makes it questionable whether AT does really apply here. In this section, I will argue that AT can very well fulfill this role. There is no antagonism between instinct and learning, and AT.

The crucial point that connects nonmental behavior and AT is that the sense-model-plan-act cycles of AT do not necessarily have to apply to all levels of a behaving system. For example, the *Sphex* wasp's behavior in chapter 1 consists of a rigid sequence at the general level of digging a burrow, finding a cricket, returning to the burrow, and so on. This rigidity seems to contradict the intelligence of AT's SMPA architecture. However, the wasp's less general, more executive behaviors (digging, flying, walking, returning to the burrow) are not stereotypical at all but consist of finely tuned sensory-motor interactions with a lot of variability and complexity that require all intelligence AT can muster.

A good way to illustrate the smooth transition from instinct and learning to more evident forms of AT's modeling and planning capacities is provided by Dennett's metaphor of a tower to classify "the various design options for brains" (1996, p. 83). In this metaphor, organisms are classified by being placed on different floors of an evolutionary "Tower of Generate-and-Test." The floors signify different capacities for doing intelligent things in an environment.

On the ground floor of the tower, Dennett situates what he calls "*Darwinian creatures*" (ibid.). Darwinian creatures act adaptively in an environment because they are the result of a selection process. The selection process has eliminated all creatures that are not sufficiently adapted to their environment. New behaviors have to be tried out by evolutionary variation and selection. There is no (or hardly any) behavioral plasticity in the individual Darwinian creature. Darwinian creatures act strictly on instinct, the behavioral propensities that they are born with.

On the second floor, Dennett places "*Skinnerian creatures*" (ibid., p. 85). These form a subset of the Darwinian creatures. Skinnerian creatures have the inherited capacity to modify their behavior on the basis of the individual's encounters with the environment. Skinnerian creatures can try out various behavioral options and learn from the consequences of these behaviors (either positive, neutral, or negative) whether this behavior is to be repeated or avoided in the future.

The drawback of reinforcement learning is that new behavioral options have to be tried out first before they can be evaluated. As some of those options are lethal, and the whole process is rather time-consuming, there is room for improvement here. This improvement comes in the form of *"Popperian creatures"* (ibid., p. 88). Popperian creatures provide the prototypical case for AT's explanation of behavior. They incorporate a model of the external environment which they use to predict the consequences of optional behavior, and discard those behaviors from further consideration which (presumably) have unpleasant consequences.[9]

Of these three kinds of creatures, only the Popperian ones obviously reflect AT and its sense-model-plan-act cycles. In contrast, the behavior of Darwinian and Skinnerian creatures at any given moment is thought to be based on a preset structure—set in place by feedback derived from the creature's ancestors or its own individual reinforcement history. There doesn't seem to be any modeling and planning here. How then does this tower metaphor show that Darwinian and Skinnerian creatures also fit the conceptual framework of AT?

The key issue is that all three kinds of creatures are assumed to be already capable of basic behavior. The distinction between these kinds of creatures is based only on increasingly sophisticated ways to *change* this behavior. This categorization betrays the background assumption that making intelligent decisions about what to do is only required at an upper level of behavioral steering, while the subsequent behavioral execution of those decisions is supposed to be simple and kept out of focus. However, to generate basic behavior, complex problem solving is required at all levels of behavioral organization, not just on the upper level highlighted by the tower metaphor. To deal with the intricacies of behavior's sensory-motor interactions a real problem-solving mechanism is required.

The Tower of Generate-and-Test does not illustrate the evolutionary increase in problem-solving capacities for behavior, these capacities are present from the start. The Tower of Generate-and-Test rather illustrates the gradual increase in the *application* of problem-solving capacities to behavioral problems. Darwinian and Skinnerian creatures apply these capacities only to basic behavior while Popperian creatures apply this capacity to a higher level of behavioral organization as well. By identifying the width of application of behavioral problem solving as the distinguishing factor between these creatures, the seeming discrepancy between instinct and learning, and the mind-derived conceptual framework of AT, can be discarded.

AT is thus not limited to systems that exhibit the capacity to choose between different behaviors at a general level. The tower metaphor shows a gradual increase in behavioral capacities that are highly complex from the start. It also shows that it is possible to view this increase as the gradual extension of AT-styled processing to the guidance of increasingly global, or distal, forms of behavior. AT is a mechanism that applies to all levels of basic and nonbasic behavior.

5 AT's representational requirements

An essential ingredient of AT is a fully naturalistic concept of representation. How should this notion be drawn? The concept of representation is central to both cognitive science and the philosophy of mind and consequently has received a lot of attention. In this section, I will explicate the notion of representation on which AT is based. Again this will be a reconstructed position, reflecting AT's representational needs rather than a generally accepted view on representations. The aim is to elucidate the notion of representation one should hold if one is committed to defending AT. This discussion serves both as a fourth landmark to position AT within the general cognitive science landscape, and to mark the notion of representation against which interactionists react.

Above, representation in AT has been equated with modeling. A model consists of an internal structure which is isomorphic—possibly in an abstract way—with an external structure. A basic example is the sandpaper robot who carries a sandpaper around which is isomorphic to the table on which this robot moves. I take this description to be an unproblematic reflection of the general and rough view of the use of representation within cognitive science (see also Rosen, 1979, 1987; Gallistel, 1989, 1990b).

However, most philosophers within cognitive science who are engaged in formulating a theory to explain what makes representations representational are highly critical about the idea that representation consists of some sort of isomorphism. They tend to prefer a different account of the meaningfulness of representations. In this account, representational content derives from a dependency on external environmental states (Dretske, 1983; Fodor, 1987; Lloyd, 1989). This idea has been developed in a number of ways. I will refer to such 'informational' or 'causal' theories as perceptually oriented accounts of representation. To illustrate what such a representational theory looks like when it comes to basic behavior, I will give a short sketch of Dan Lloyd's version of the idea (Lloyd, 1989). Lloyd's approach is in many ways similar to the one followed here. He builds up his account of representation in the context of basic behavior as it is produced by "simple minds" that lie "just over the line of mindedness" (p. 10). It will be interesting to trace why he ends up with a perception-based interpretation of representation rather than a modeling-based one.

Lloyd derives his central theme from Dretske's theory of information (1983): "Events inside a representing system represent events in the outside world . . . because the internal events depend on the external" (Lloyd, 1989, p. 52). Although Lloyd distances his perception-based representations from Dretske's notion of information which involves a perfect correspondence between external and internal events, he does put a lot of stress on the accuracy of representations: "Representations, both inner and outer, have the pre-eminent capacity to capture and convey the way things are. A successful theory of representation, then, must explain how representations can accurately represent their objects" (ibid., pp. 12–13), and also: "The basic inspiration for this functional architecture is the need for reliability in signal detection" (ibid., p. 60). Lloyd develops this notion of representation further in the context of simple, artificial behaving systems, called Braitenbergian vehicles (Braitenberg, 1984).

The simplest example which Lloyd discusses is "Squint" (1989, pp. 52–54). Squint is a vehicle driven by a motor connected to a fat, cylinder-shaped wheel on the back. When the motor runs, it drives the vehicle forward in whatever direction it is facing. A photocell transduces light into an internal signal which turns the motor on. Squint thus moves when there is light and sits still in the dark. Squint provides the starting point for formulating a theory of reliable perception-based representation, and illustrates the need to make the system foolproof to ward off the possibility of false alarms and misses. These happen when the connecting circuit between transducer and motor is not reliable. For example, an energy fluctuation in the circuit may set off the motor when no light is present, or a genuine signal might not get through for some reason. The system can be made more reliable by adding connections, and also, as problems might arise in the transducers as well, by adding photocells. The motor can then be turned on by a majority vote of the multiple, parallel channels.

The use of multiple channels can be further elaborated by using directed transducers that react only to light in a restricted area directly in front of them. By placing two or more of these transducers at different angles at the front of the vehicle so that their receptive fields partially overlap, Squint becomes sensitive to light sources placed at a specific place in front of it. A single light source, situated at a place covered by more than one transducer, will activate all the transducers simultaneously. A light outside this special area will not. Mistakes can occur when multiple, properly placed light sources stimulate the several transducers at the same time, but this is a much more unlikely event than a single source at the right spot. By adding an extra wheel and motor, the vehicle can subsequently react selectively to these different situations. There are many ways for elaborating this kind of Braitenbergian vehicle. The connectionist road-follower ALVINN can be seen as a more advanced example. Lloyd treats more complex cases of representation, but this basic case suffices as a general sketch of the perception-based view that representation is a matter of internal events which depend on external events. Later additions do not change the essentials of the model.

The central difference between isomorphism-derived and perception-based representation then amounts to the following. In the case of isomorphism, representation consists of an internal model that can vary independent of the external situation. Of course, the usefulness of this model for guiding behavior depends on closely mimicking the external situation, but there is no direct dependency on the environment and it is possible that the model grossly misrepresents the external situation. For a perception-based account, representations derive their meaning from being 'welded' to an external state. The general problem here, and an important topic in representational theory, is to account for the possibility of error. Perception-based theories make representations represent whatever they are connected to. Still, one also wants to maintain that a representation can become connected to an external state which it does not represent. So far, none of the solutions that have been proposed for this error problem have been fully convincing.

Given AT's focus on behavior and a subpersonal level of organization, why would representation be a matter of isomorphism rather than be perception-based? There are at least three reasons. For one, many would hold that devices like Squint are not representing at all (Anderson, 1991; Fodor, 1986a; Beckermann, 1988). The whole point of invoking representations is the idea that behavior cannot be fully described in terms of reactions to configurations of external stimuli. One needs internal (representational) structure that is independent from the ongoing external environment. Representation that is defined as dependency on external states makes no sense in this perspective. This definition does not allow representations to do what they are supposed to do: Make organisms independent from the actual environment.

Second, there is also a lot more representational content necessary than can be plausibly provided for by sensory-dependence. In contrast to Squint-like robots, the basic behavior of multicellular biological organisms involves a complex musculo-skeletal system that requires a lot of spatio-temporal coordination before the organism does something interesting from an external point of view (such as moving forward). AT explains this spatio-temporal coordination by positing representations that instruct the motor apparatus in a detailed way. These representations will need to reflect the characteristics of the musculo-skeletal system in detail, and it is difficult to envision how all these representations acquire their meaning by means of a perception-based account.

Third, the stress of a perception-based view on reliability and accuracy seems to exaggerate their importance from an evolutionary and behavioral point of view. Evolution does not necessarily favor foolproof individuals, which reliably represent their environment under a wide variety of circumstances. It is necessary to have a reproductive advantage over competitors. If this can be accomplished with only moderately reliable 'representational' means, then that suffices. Speed of reproduction is very important in this context. More reliable representational means require more fancy and elaborate bodyforms that take more time and energy to mature and are less easily produced in large quantities. In this sense they are at a disadvantage.

Representational reliability thus depends on a trade-off with other evolutionary relevant factors and cannot be taken as the singly most important aspect of representation in biological organisms.

To conclude, the perception-based view of representation does not mix well with the needs of AT. But then, why the popularity of perception-based representational theories? The dividing line here seems to be whether one is interested in a personal (mental) or a subpersonal (behavioral) level of organization. While AT addresses a subpersonal level, the generally philosophical treatment of the notion of representation aims at the personal level. Representation is a core concept in the context of mind, intentionality and epistemology, all personal-level concerns. The goal of a representational theory here is to accommodate a number of generally agreed upon convictions regarding those personal-level topics. The guiding line for theory development consists of the philosophers' intuitive judgments concerning these topics. Thought-experiments, sometimes very exotic, are used to test whether a proposed theory remains within the constraints set by these shared intuitions. One important intuition that a theory of representation needs to accommodate in this approach is it being related to unique events in the external world. For example, how can representations be defined so that having the representation "I see Sophia Loren" represents seeing Sophia Loren rather than seeing an indefinite number of lookalikes of Sophia Loren? Making the internal representation dependent on the external event rules out the possibility of multiple meanings. Isomorphism is not an attractive option for making this kind of one-to-one connection between external and internal events. Isomorphism is radically nonunique and cannot distinguish between the real Sophia and a sufficiently similar lookalike. It is in dealing with these kinds of personal-level problems that perception-based theories have come to the fore.

At this point, it must be stressed that our present concern is with explaining the generation of behavior, a subpersonal-level endeavor. AT is formulated explicitly as a subpersonal explanation of behavior. The only considerations regarding representation that are to be taken into account here are those that directly impinge on the explanations it provides. Constraints that bear on personal-level, mental representations do not apply here, unless specific reasons can be given that make them also subpersonal level constraints. However, the concern about one-to one connections between external states and internal representational states does not fall in that category. The need for an internal model weighs much more heavy when it comes to AT's explanation of behavior.

It is highly gratifying in this context that Robert Cummins also defends the idea that representation derives from isomorphism (1996). Cummins bases his understanding of representation as isomorphism on a distinction between the content and the target of a representation.[10] The content determines what a representation is true of, while the target determines where a representation is applied to. Cummins argues that it is important to differentiate between these two different aspects of representation because one needs two degrees of freedom to deal with representational error, the key problem for perception-based representational theories. By making this distinction, the content of a representation can vary independently from the external target to which the representation is applied. Representational error then occurs when a representation is applied to a target it is not true of. Representation in Cummins's interpretation remains one step removed from external targets. Representations act as internal proxies for external circumstances in a way that allows for behavior that is independent from the directly sensed environment.

Cummins's opinion is particularly important because he is one of the few philosophers who explicitly tries to understand the role that representation plays in cognitive science, rather than to accommodate the intuitions of folk psychology (Stich, 1994). Cummins is committed to answering the same question as the one posed above: "What must we suppose about the nature of mental representation if orthodox computational theories (or connectionist theories, or whatever) of cognition are to turn out to be true and explanatory?" (Cummins, 1989, p. 13), He later comes to call this the "Explanatory Constraint" (1996, p. 2). In addition, and contrary to his choice of words, Cummins' aim is not to come up with an account of *mental* representations, intentionality or the mind. He discusses "cognitive systems rather than minds" (1989, p. 18), not all cognitive systems being minds, nor all aspects of mentality being cognitive. Cummins approaches the notion of representation thus in a way which is particularly suited to explicate the characteristics of AT's subpersonal representations and the present interpretation of representation is strengthened by his similar conclusions.

As AT attempts to explain the generation of behavior, its representations are best viewed in terms of an abstract isomorphism between internal and external happenings. At this subpersonal level, AT ought not to be constrained by personal-level concerns. Even so, Cummins does a great job in reconciling an isomorphism story with these concerns.

6 The Agent Theory in summary

AT explains the generation of behavior by postulating an internal representational structure which instructs the motor apparatus in such a way that specific goals will be achieved. This conceptual framework derives originally from the way in which human beings understand their own actions (belief-desire psychology or folk psychology). In AT it is turned into a lower-level, subpersonal mechanism that can function without the intentionality, consciousness, or other subjective features that characterize mind (Searle, 1992; Jackendoff, 1987). What does remain in AT are a 'translation' and 'retranslation' process. The external environment provides the behaving system with information which is 'translated' into a representational model of this environment. The model is used to plan a sequence of behaviors that will bring about a specific state of affairs in the environment which is beneficial for the behaving system. Subsequently, in a 'retranslation' process the planned behaviors are executed so that the planned state of affairs becomes an actual state of affairs.

The conceptual framework is summarized in figure 2.4. There is a general similarity to Brunswik's Lens Model as portrayed in figure 2.1 (section 2.2). The focus lies in both cases with the environmental and representational ingredients which provide the stable nonvarying entities. These stable points have to be connected by a variable set of (proximal/translation) events. AT states that the proximal variability is overcome by the instructions that are provided by the representing system. The distal regularities of behavior are thought to be the result of these specific instructions.

This conceptual framework is put to use at different scales of behavioral organization. The term 'distal' does not only apply to distant environmental goal-achievements such as finding food. An example such as the Ambler robot shows that finding a place to put a single foot and subsequently executing the leg's movement and footfall require the same form of explanation.

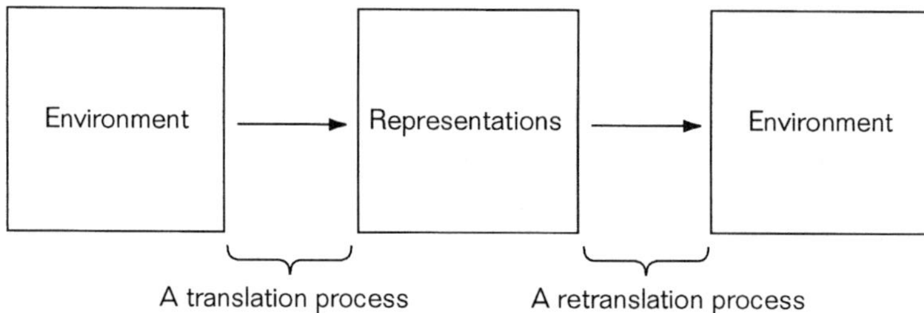

Figure 2.4
A schematic overview of the Agent Theory. AT highlights only the central state and the distal stimulus situation and distal achievements of Brunswik's lens model (figure 2.1).

The use of AT is not restricted to traditional cognitive contexts. The complexities involved in basic behavioral capacities, such as insect-walking, are still beyond the powers of cognitivist psychology.

In AT, representations consist of internal models that are used to predict the possible occurrence of future events, to plan actions in anticipation of these eventualities, and to provide instructions for the motor system. This behavior-oriented interpretation contrasts and is to be differentiated from the view where representations are defined as the results of a perceptual process (section 5).

In the following chapters, this particular modeling-based interpretation of representation will be the topic that is discussed and provide the target for criticism. I will interpret the discussion about representations between cognitivists and interactionists as a discussion about the merits and use of these representations.

At the same time, perception-based forms of representations—representations that derive their representationality only from a dependency relation on external events—will not be considered as representations at all. This means, for example, that many connectionist models such as ALVINN are considered to be nonrepresentational in this terminology. In these models, the notion of representation is not necessary to explain the system's behavior. This usage of the word 'representation' differs from the much looser general usage. However, as the modeling capacity is at the heart of the cognitivist, representation-based explanation of behavior, it seems appropriate to limit the term 'representation' to this particular form of representation.

The conceptualization of cognitivism as AT and pinning down the notion of representation allows a more concrete discussion between cognitivist and interactionist positions to take place. Cognitivists may still think that the notion of AT remains rather wide and general. That cannot be helped. The discussion is about the general conceptual framework with which we seek to understand behavioral phenomena. The pros and cons of individual models will not be discussed. This general conceptual framework is more abstract than the individual models in which it is implemented. It is a coarse framework which is used to interpret existing models and construct synthetic ones. There cannot be a totally clear one-to-one relation between AT and models. The case of feedforward connectionist networks, which are interpreted according to AT principles even when their actual organization hardly warrants this interpretation, is a case in point.

3

Why the Agent Theory Is a Bad Idea

1 An absolute and a comparative evaluation of AT

AT forms the establishment within cognition-oriented psychology. It probably is the most generally accepted and intuitively appealing explanation for behavior that is on the market. On the other hand, there are a number of reasons for being seriously dissatisfied with the offered commodity. As a consequence, bashing cognitivist psychology's basic premises has become a habit nowadays, and that includes what it has to say on behavior. This chapter will review a number of problems which accompany AT.

The goal of this chapter is to make it plausible that AT does not suffice to account for the generation of behavior. One way to do this is to look at its theoretical and practical accomplishments and make a decision on that count. This procedure amounts to an *absolute evaluation* of AT. Judgment is passed on the basis of a general evaluation of a conceptual framework. The problem with this procedure is the seeming impossibility to find and apply criteria that could ever force a conclusion to be generally accepted by the cognitivist community. Some philosophers and theorists may confidently proclaim cognitivism incoherent, circular, or a dead end (Bickhard and Terveen, 1995; Hendriks-Jansen, 1996; Shanon, 1993). Many others will disagree with the verdict or simply ignore it and insist that they should get on with the real, practical work. The discussion on Winograd and Flores's book and between Vera and Simon, and Clancey are cases in point.[1]

This latter group will be much more impressed by a *comparative evaluation*: set AT against a competitor and see which one does better. If models based on a different conceptual framework can be shown to outperform the results of those based on AT, it will be a much more generally accepted disclaimer of AT than all theoretical and principled objections put together. A conceptual framework that might become the source of such alternative models will be discussed in the following chapters. The problem with this alternative is its embryological, not fully crystallized state. In its present form, it cannot stand up to AT when it comes to providing a conceptual framework that provides intuitively plausible answers to all the questions that AT deals with in a taken-for-granted way. Consequently, some authors conclude that this alternative does not provide enough weight to act as a criticism of representation-based cognitivist psychology (Clark, 1997a; Clark and Toribio, 1994; Kirsh, 1991).

How does one proceed? I do agree that any definitive decision on the viability of AT depends on the availability of a different conceptual framework which does the same job better. But, I do not agree with the idea that being the best choice currently available vindicates AT. On the contrary, I think that the answers given by AT to behavioral problems are fundamentally flawed. The strategy that I wish to follow therefore is a mixture of the absolute and comparative approach. As a contribution to a comparative evaluation, a potential alternative—the idea of behavioral systems—will be sketched and further developed in chapters 4 and 5. However, this alternative conceptual framework is still immature and in need of a great deal of further improvement and elaboration. Only a lot of research could turn it into a full replacement of AT.

This chapter is therefore dedicated to creating goodwill for this research project, and will consist of an absolute evaluation of AT. I will argue that, irrespective of any alternative, AT does not do a good job at explaining behavior. And, even stronger, that it has not the potential to do much better in the future. I will try to change the default mind-set from (a) to (b):

(a) AT is good because there is no better conceptual framework to replace it.

(b) AT is bad, therefore a better conceptual framework should be developed to replace it.

It will be argued that AT is a local and not a global optimum in behavioral theory. Any deviation from AT may at first lead toward what seems to be less sophisticated models of behavior, but this is a path that must be taken if a more globally optimal explanation of behavior is to be reached.

Note that discarding AT is not a plea for the total abandonment of all of cognitivist psychology's models. It is the conceptual framework that is at stake. There is much leeway between actual models and the conceptual framework that they implement. For example, connectionist models are often interpreted in terms of AT, but different interpretations are possible. An alternative conceptual framework will give different directions for developing new models, but it will not describe in detail how such models look like. Vera and Simon argue that a lot of research in situated cognition can be interpreted in terms of conventional cognitivist psychology. That is correct. But it is not the issue. The issue is the general conceptual framework with which cognitive (behavioral) phenomena are interpreted. This framework provides the guidelines for constructing models and limits them to a specific *Bauplan*. A shift in the conceptual framework will be accompanied by a shift in the *kind* of models generated. Examples will be presented in this, and in the following chapters. The task of an alternative conceptual framework will be to set up a new conceptual *Bauplan* or framework for explaining the generation of behavior. This new conceptual framework should inspire the development of new kinds of models. At the same time all kinds of halfway models will be possible. There are not two, mutually excluding, sets of models. Compare it to two different business policies. Both will have their characteristic way of dealing with problems and can be clearly recognized for this reason, even though, in specific cases, both might do more or less the same thing.

The following will not provide an exhaustive review of all the difficulties that are raised for cognitivism. Many books are dedicated only to this purpose,[2] and I can't hope to replicate all the arguments and evidence in a small space. Instead of trying to enumerate everything held against cognitivism (including AT), I will go for a more systematic treatment of the problems that pertain to AT, based on the structure of AT's explanation of behavior.

An obvious way to downsize the amount of relevant criticism is the simple realization that the present topic is behavior. Much of the criticism applies to the cognitivist vision of mind. This will be ignored here. I will discuss only problems that apply to cognitivism's way of dealing with behavior. Only these are problems for AT.

The problems for AT will be divided into two groups. The first group consists of structural problems that derive from the particular way in which

AT is constructed. Proponents of cognitivism (AT) readily acknowledge these structural problems as real problems for the project of AT. The frame problem is the best known of these (Pylyshyn, 1987; Ford and Hayes, 1991; Haselager, 1997). Another problem is less obvious as long as one sticks to strictly cognitive tasks, but it is very troublesome for roboticists and workers on motor control. It concerns the translation of instructions into the movements that make up actual behavior. I will call this problem the instruction problem.

A second set of problems is meta-theoretical. These will be grouped around a phenomenon that I will call theoretical hitchhiking. These difficulties derive from the involvement of an observer (itself a cognitive system) in the process of explaining the operation of cognitive systems. Two separately stated problems can be brought together under the general heading of theoretical hitchhiking: the symbol grounding problem (Harnad, 1990) and the frame of reference problem (Clancey, 1989). The issues raised by theoretical hitchhiking make a lot of difference in the perception of the problems posed by the generation of behavior. They will both provide criticisms of AT and a set of constraints that any alternative conceptual framework will have to abide by.

2 Structural difficulties: what hampers AT?

In this section, I will discuss two structural problems for AT: the frame problem and the instruction problem. In addition, I will go into the issue of whether these problems—as problems for AT—might be overcome by combining AT with interactionist ideas.

2.1 The frame problem

Many people seem to know what the frame problem is. Only they don't agree with one another. Together, Haselager (1997) and Van Brakel (1992) list nineteen different problems that are all supposed to be connected to, or be a part of, the frame problem. Van Brakel even talks about a family of problems in this context. Despite this lack of agreement, there is enough coherence to locate the frame problem in the general area of "modeling change," an area which is highly relevant for behavior. Dennett (1987c) wrote the perfect introduction, a beautiful fairy tale about the tragic fate of three robots R1, R1D1, and R2D1.

These robots were designed to stay in one piece by actively counteracting the hazards of the world. As part of the testing program, the first robot, R1, was informed that its spare battery was situated in a room where a time bomb was to go off soon. R1 made a plan to rescue its precious battery by putting it on a wagon that was also present in the room and pulling the wagon outside. This would distance the battery from the room and its bomb and all would be well. Unfortunately, things turned out otherwise. R1 did pull the wagon out in time, but as the bomb was on the wagon too, R1 exploded together with its battery. R1 knew that the bomb was on the wagon. It just had not realized that moving the wagon would also move the bomb.

A new robot, the robot-deducer R1D1, was designed that should remedy the faults of R1. R1D1 did not only recognize the intended implications of its acts, but also its possible side effects by deducing these side effects from the descriptions it used to formulate its plan. R1D1 was put in the position where R1 had failed, and also came up with the plan to put the battery on the wagon and pull the wagon outside. At this point it considered which possible side effects this course of action might have. R1D1 had just decided that the colors of the room's wall would stay the same and that by its action the wheels would revolve more times than there were wheels on the wagon when time was up.

Finally the robot-relevant-deducer, R2D1, was made. R2D1 was to overcome the failings of R1D1 by making a difference between relevant and irrelevant implications of its actions. This was done by using a method of tagging implications as being either relevant or not. R2D1 did not survive the time bomb either. In the last moments before the bomb went off, the designers found the robot standing still in the room. "Do something!" they yelled at it, but R2D1 was too busy putting thousands of irrelevant implications on its ignore list.

All three robots were troubled by some aspect of the frame problem. The fate of R1 illustrates the need to regularly update the set of representations that describe the external situation. Things change out there, the representations that are used to instruct the behavior should keep up with these changes. This is particularly important when the robot acts. It should keep track of the consequences of the actions it performs, as R1 clearly did not. R1D1 adds the lesson that temporal and spatial constraints of an acting cognitive system preclude the possibility of considering *all* consequences of an act. Consequences have to be divided into relevant and irrelevant ones. Finally, R2D1 shows that the decision to ignore or pay attention should be made without actually reviewing all those consequences. Somehow, the decision for relevancy must be made beforehand, without knowing what the to-be-ignored consequences will be. All three problems are considered to be part of the frame problem, and all three have to do with the general puzzle of keeping the set of representations up to date when the state of the represented world is changing. This should give an intuitive understanding of the issue. In the following, I will give a bird's-eye view of the discussion that surrounds the frame problem.

The expression 'frame problem' was first used by McCarthy and Hayes (1969). McCarthy and Hayes tried to design a generally intelligent system. It should be capable of deciding what to do by inferring that a certain strategy will lead to a certain goal (Haselager, 1997). Their approach was based on the use of first order predicate logic. A central concept was the 'situation', defined by McCarthy as "the complete state of affairs at some instant in time" (Janlert, 1987, p. 5). A situation was described by a number of expressions in a first order logical language. From this set, the system could infer other expressions that also applied to the situation, but were not explicitly expressed before. McCarthy and Hayes conceived the world as a *sequence of situations*. These successive situations were to be connected by laws of motion. The frame problem arose when McCarthy and Hayes tried to represent those laws as deductive relations in first-order logic (ibid.).

> In the process of formulating laws of motion it turned out that the relevant laws were drowned in a flood of seemingly irrelevant but necessary *pseudolaws*. Deducing a new situation requires not only that changes effected by an action are inferable, but also that what *does not* change can be inferred. And, in fact, very little of what from a purely logical point of view could happen as a result of an action, does happen. (Janlert, 1987, p. 6)

Modeling change as a form of logical deduction required a very large number of so-called frame axioms that specified all the nonchanges that resulted from an action. The result was a system that got lost in performing endless deductions that are irrelevant to the task at hand. This was the original problem that McCarthy and Hayes baptized as 'the frame problem'.

Since this first encounter, the expression 'frame problem' has been used to refer to many different problems. These problems range from a relatively circumscribed technical difficulty—a result from using logic to model temporal relations—to a deep, principled problem that, unless it is solved, will prevent the development of generally intelligent AI systems—that is, systems capable of dealing with the sort of problems that humans habitually deal with.

McDermott (1987) can be placed in the first camp. He claims that the frame problem is challenging from a logical point of view, but it is not a significant issue for AI. AI is not committed to finding general and deductive solutions, as is logic. It can solve the frame problem efficiently by the sleeping dog strategy: "let everything lie, unless there's some positive reason not to. That is, unless there's some positive indication that a particular fact may be affected, the system will *totally* ignore it" (Haugeland, 1987, p. 84). As a consequence, according to McDermott, "it is still the case, as it has been since 1970, that *no working AI program has ever been bothered at all by the frame problem*" (McDermott, 1987, p. 116). He argues that, up to a certain level of complexity, the sleeping dog strategy works well enough to avoid talk about a deep, general frame problem. Above that level, it would be unreasonable to expect a computational system to accurately predict all consequences of an event (Haselager, 1997, p. 60). Humans, after all, do also not foresee all the consequences of the actions they undertake. So why expect more from AI systems?

The difficulty with McDermott's claim is the location of this 'certain level of complexity'. He gives the impression that AI systems, using the sleeping dog strategy, incorporate sufficient complexity to act reasonably well in normal (human) commonsense situations. "Yet, the problem is precisely that currently there are *no* such systems and that they are not likely to appear shortly" (Haselager, 1997, p. 61). Using the sleeping dog strategy is not sufficient to deal with the amount of complexity that humans habitually deal with. There is definitely a problem that remains, and this is precisely the frame problem, so it is claimed by those who favor a more general reading of this problem.

The insufficiency of the sleeping dog strategy is exemplified by the robot R2D1. How is it to know what not to consider, if it does not know what not to consider? After all, the relevant consequences do still have to come through, not everything can be ignored. At this point the general—in contrast to the more specific technical—version of the frame problem is often situated. Haselager (1997) distinguishes two versions of the general problem.

The general frame problem is described by Janlert as: "the problem of finding a representational form permitting a changing, complex world to be efficiently and adequately represented" (1987, pp. 7–8). Finding a suitable representational format is a major condition for the sleeping dog strategy to work. Only under certain descriptions does the world at large remain the same from moment to moment and only when this is the case can large portions of it be safely ignored. In this view, the big issue raised by the frame problem is to find this 'suitable' representational format. The other version equates the general frame problem to that of nondemonstrative inference; the problem of how to model higher cognitive processes by means of rule-determined processes (Haselager, 1997). In both guises the frame problem is turned into an extremely difficult issue. Passing over the actual discussion here, the immediately relevant question is whether this general frame problem can be solved at all. Well, can it?

Things do not look very hopeful. Fodor, probably the most staunch defender of classical cognitivist psychology, is very pessimistic. According to him some of the necessary key ideas are still missing, and cognitivist psychology has not made any *real* progress in solving (his version of) the frame problem. Equating it with the problem of scientific belief confirmation, he states:

> People since at least J. S. Mill have been asking themselves, "What is a good formalism for the fixation of hypotheses, fixation of belief by the scientific community, given a body of data?" . . . All of this is a total mess; nobody knows how to model any of this stuff except for the most local and uninteresting kinds of cases. (Fodor, 1986b, p. 158).

In his review of the frame problem, Haselager comes to a more positive conclusion. But this is primarily based on hope and a trust in future results: "A better understanding of non-demonstrative reasoning should ultimately make a solution to the frame problem possible, while staying within the framework of classical cognitive science" (Haselager, 1997, p. 145). He also discusses connectionism as a possible way to deal with the frame problem in its representational guise. His conclusion here sounds highly similar: Connectionist "distributed representations offer a *promising* candidate for those who favor the representational approach to the frame problem" (ibid., emphasis added). And those people like McDermott, who deny the existence of any deep principled problem for AI, still face the practical situation that actual progress in AI cannot disclaim the existence of such a principled problem.

All in all, the frame problem sets up an impressive challenge for AT. Basically, the sole reason to think that it can be solved at all is that this is what we do ourselves all the time. Hence, there must be a solution somewhere, even if no one has a clue how. For an explanation of the generation of behavior the frame problem forms an enormous challenge. It makes behavioral theory dependent on solving some very deep and not understood epistemological questions. If AT is true, a solid behavioral theory is not in the cards for a long time.

The latter conclusion is particularly hard to swallow from the perspective of behavioral theory. In contrast to research on cognition, behavioral research is not necessarily concerned with solving knowledge-related problems. Nevertheless, AT is bound to have the kind of trouble that the frame problem exemplifies: not necessarily because of the intrinsic difficulty of explaining behavior, but because of the intrinsic difficulties of a mechanism meant to explain it. Outward behavior is hypothesized to be the result from a set of internal instructions which specify its spatial and temporal organization. In other words, the structure which is present in the outward behavior is derived from the structure provided by the internal representations which embody the behavior's program. To accomplish this, the representations incorporate the external structure, a structure which is changing all the time. This way of dealing with behavioral phenomena is thus dependent on keeping up a continuous and detailed isomorphism between two independent structures. This explanatory construction is bound to create trouble. The need to maintain this elaborate isomorphism will always remain a brittle element in AT, making it susceptible to all kinds of disturbances.

2.2 The instruction problem

AT states that behavioral structure derives from representational structure. The latter provides the ingredients that are used to form programs that instruct the motor apparatus and through this produce outward behavior. Figure 3.1 illustrates the basic idea. This setup explains how behavior's adaptive and future-oriented, anticipatory characteristics are possible in a nonpurposive, causal world. The programs incorporate structure that is derived from past encounters of the organism itself (by learning) as well as

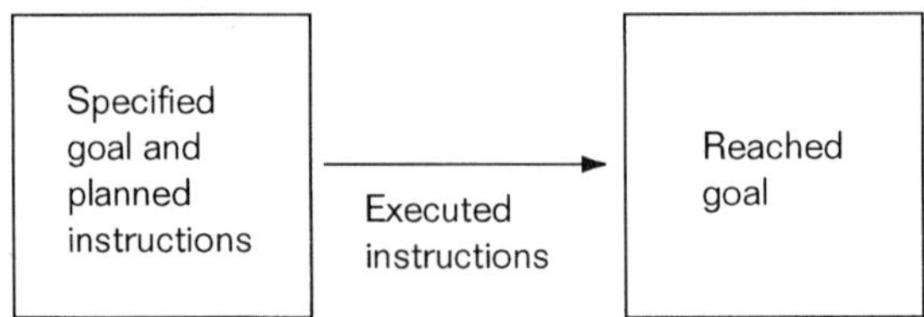

Figure 3.1
AT's representational specification model.

its ancestors (by selection) (Mayr, 1961; Dennett, 1996), and this structure is imposed on the motor system to produce behavior.

In simple cases, this setup definitely works. In more complex cases, however, this construction is bound to require too many instructions to be an efficient and even possible way of controlling behavior. It is like the soviet system of controlling the economy by central commands: increasingly costly and inefficient when the controlled system becomes big and complicated. There are too many things that need to be instructed in a precise way. A consequence is that AT seems to apply only to relatively simple sorts of behavior. I will call the difficulties that AT faces when it has to provide sufficient instructions to guide behavior in complex cases the *instruction problem*. The interesting question to ask is then, where lies the borderline between 'simple' and 'complex' cases of behavior?

I will argue that essentially all behavior exhibited by multicellular animals is complex. Behavior is never simple. Consequently, the complexity that made the detailed control of the soviet economy so difficult and ultimately unmanageable is present in human and invertebrate behavior alike. The reason that this problem does not show up all of the time is that, within cognitivism, behavior tends to be reduced to the notion of output. Much of behavior's complexity—which derives from performing physical movements in a changing world—is left out of consideration in this way.

The main focus of cognitivist psychology is on a general, 'cognitive' level of behavioral organization. It deals with problems that are thought to involve cognitive processes—for example, planning a route or a sequence of actions. Coming up with a plan at this level is considered to be the required output or behavior. Of course, cognitivism does not deny that behavior also consists of many intermediate outputs. As described in chapter 2, AT provides a theory of how a behaving system is capable of organizing its proximal behavior in such a way that it is capable of reaching distal goal-states. However, within AT the behavior-as-output is (almost always) formulated in distal terms. Proximal behavior does not play an important role in AT-based theories, it is a mere connection between a planned action and an achieved goal.

The neglect of the actual (movement involving) behavior becomes even more manifest in the tendency to leave unspecified whether an output consists of a *planned*, distal action or an actually *achieved*, distal goal state. In cognitivist psychology, having a plan and having it executed are often treated as if they amount to the same thing. The old story about the mice who thought that they had solved their cat-problem by coming up with the plan to bind a bell around its neck should be brought to mind here. Having a plan and having it executed are not the same. It will not do to merely assume that the planned behavior will be linked to the proper environmental state in a fairly direct way. To use the concept of output in a way that leaves this essential aspect indeterminate shows again how poorly the behavioral process is captured by the notion of output.

Dennett's story about the robots R1, R1D1, and R2D1 provides a good example of cognitivism's attitude toward behavior. The story focuses our attention on the reasoning difficulties that arise when robots have to solve some real-world task. At the same time, the story deemphasizes the instruction problem that these robots face. For example, R1's solution to the bomb problem took the form of 'pull the wagon out of the room'. This plan describes the robot's behavior in terms of an environmental result that is to be achieved. The sensory-motor coordinations that are necessary to connect a mere plan with an achieved goal state remains unspecified, and are (within the story) not considered as particularly problematical. The story simply assumes that the robot is capable of executing the plan.

As long as behavior is only considered at a distal level of description, the set of instructions that AT requires to connect plans and goal states looks manageable enough. But, this optimistic picture runs into difficulties when AT has to be implemented in a physical, behaving system. The complexities of the instruction problem arise as soon as one tries to build models that also encompass the behavior that has to connect a predefined plan to the actually achievement of the plan. In other words, when one tries to build a robot that executes these plans, thereby filling in the arrow that features in figure 3.1.

In contrast to an imaginary robot, a real robot must be capable of moving about and doing things. While an imaginary R1 can easily be assumed to be capable of performing many behavioral subtasks, a real R1 would actually have to perform those subtasks. Generating a plan for reaching a goal is only a first step. Executing the plan will be the next one. How does AT deal with this proximal executive behavior? The irony is that, according to AT, the execution has to be planned also. All the cognitive modeling and planning required to arrive at a relatively distal plan for action has to be repeated, but at a slightly less general and more proximal level.

Executing the general plan that a cognitive/behaving system comes up with is itself a problem that requires modeling and planning capacities to solve it. The problem is similar to that faced by a behaving system at a more general level: "what is to be done to achieve state X." Again, it has to decide what to do, given a large number of possible actions at a smaller scale. Again, it needs to forecast the results of several courses of action and to choose the one that will have the most beneficial consequences (given a specific goal). Again, the chosen action at a smaller scale has to be executed, after which the whole modeling and planning process repeats itself at an even smaller scale. This procedure is reiterated until it bottoms out in a set of instructions that the robot can turn into coordinated movements that will change the present environmental state into the environmental goal-state. Only then has something like behavior—and not simply some output—been modeled.

The awkward consequence for AT is that the kind of problems that it already has to deal with at a cognitive level of organization are repeated many times over at increasingly basic levels. The frame problem arises when the system has to keep up its representational structure at a fairly general level, corresponding to distal environmental regularities. To generate all the detailed instructions necessary to guide behavior at several scales of organization, an accurate and very fine-grained representational structure will have to be maintained that mimics proximal as well as distal environmental structure. This imposes huge demands on the amount of representational structure that is required for AT to work.

The situation becomes even worse when Brunswik's lens model is taken in consideration. The lens model specifies not only that there be 'a' link between a central state and some distal achievement. The lens model prescribes that there must be many such links connecting the two. When one path cannot be taken because of local (proximal) disturbances, another one will have to take its place. It is good to remember Ashby's law of requisite variety here: "only variety can destroy variety" (1956, p. 207). The behaving system needs complex behavioral capacities at a proximal scale—call it room for maneuvering—to counteract the many proximal disturbances that will always occur within a natural environment. Only in this way can stable distal regularities be ensured under these circumstances.

In biological practice this means that a behaving system consists of a many degrees of freedom musculo-skeletal system that enables the system to counteract many disturbances in an offhand habitual way. The need to perform distal tasks through a many degrees of freedom musculo-skeletal system enhances the extent of the instruction problem as it puts even greater demands on the amount of representational structure required.

The seriousness of the difficulties posed by proximal complexity can be witnessed in robotics where an AT based approach somehow has to overcome the instruction problem as good as it can. Here, the proximal complexity that is so characteristic of the behavior of biological organisms tends to be minimized as much as possible. One illustrative case of this principle is the use of wheeled robots (Keijzer, 1998b). Compared to walking, crawling, or any other form of animal locomotion, wheels simplify the task of generating forward motion enormously. Relatively 'interesting' (for anyone with a cognitive interest, that is) distal tasks become feasible without having to solve the intricacies of a walking system first. The drawback is that the robot remains limited to those surfaces that are flat and unobstructed enough to use its wheels. Of course, because of the difficulty of negotiating most natural surfaces by wheels (or even on foot), humans have turned vast areas of the Earth into a hard, flat surface making this much less the handicap it might have been. However, this merely illustrates the point that it is probably easier to adapt the environment to wheels than to adapt a robot to the variability of natural surfaces.

However, simplifying the proximal mediation of distal regularities is not a long-term solution for the instruction problem. All biological organisms display their distal behavioral regularities by means of proximal variability. Editing the problem of proximal variety out of the agenda of behavioral research amounts to editing out one of the most important features of behavior: *The key issue of adaptive behavior is not merely to achieve a distal goal, but to achieve this goal under always varying proximal circumstances.* Proximal variability is necessary to give rise to distal stability. To account for the behavior that biological organisms are capable of, proximal and distal behavioral tasks will both have to be dealt with by the same device.

The presence and necessity of proximal variability in behavior is one of the reasons for making a difference between behavior and movement (chapter 1, section 2.1). Usually goal-achievement is considered to be the criterion for demarcating behavior. However, without denying the importance of this functional criterion, the present point is that the criterion should rather be *consistent* goal-achievement under ever varying circumstances. The need for consistent goal-achievement turns behavior from a strictly functional phenomenon into a more structural one. Performing a set of stereotypical movements that lead to achieving the goal under restricted conditions is not characteristic of behavior. Behavior requires the presence of a many degrees of freedom sensory-musculo-skeletal system to counteract ever-varying circumstances. This thread will be picked up again in chapter 5.

To conclude, as a theory of behavior, AT cannot limit itself to a higher-level cognitive theory. The AT conceptual framework has to deal with lower-level proximal behavior as well. Once AT tries to deal with behavior in all its complexity, it becomes evident that it will have to do a lot more work than most cognitivist psychologists have reckoned with. Besides planning at a general level, AT has also to instruct the detailed execution of these plans, a task that is the more difficult because of the proximal complexity involved. Conceptualizing behavior as the consequence of a representational program that imposes its internal structure on a motor system and so on to the environment faces severe difficulties. Will AT be able to solve these difficulties? Some hold that there are no problems that the continuing increase in computing power cannot solve, and that we will have robots as intelligent and versatile as humans in a few decades (Moravec, 1999). On the other hand, exaggerated enthusiasm has ever been a mainstay of AI and robotics research. The news today remains that AT-based robotic architectures have not yet succeeded in modeling the basic behavior that we share with the invertebrates in a way that compares with the real thing. So far, there is more organization to behavior than representational instructions can provide.

2.3 Could AT be improved upon by combining it with an interactionist approach?

AT's source of structural difficulties should be clear by now. Interpreting behavioral structure as a derivative of an internal (representational) structure is a brittle construction. The representational structure has to be kept in synchrony with the environment somehow. It also has to be rich enough so that it can actually instruct behavior. Both are difficult to achieve. However, an understandable reaction at this point would be to question the lack of goodwill shown so far toward AT. AT may have these problems, but surely it can overcome them by making some suitable adaptations? In the picture sketched so far, AT is an inflexible and set conceptual framework. Couldn't a better case for AT be made if it were remodeled along lines that would ease the amount of required instructions?

The sketched difficulties for AT have not gone unnoticed. A number of developments are taking place in cognitivist psychology which are directed to solve or diminish the *kind* of problems mentioned above. These developments have above been referred to as a move toward an interactionist approach which stresses the embodiment and situatedness of intelligent systems. Clark (1997a, 1997b) argues that traditional, AT-styled explanations can be improved upon by being combined with an interactionist approach. Most relevant right now is the possibility of unburdening the representational structure that AT requires by relying on the structure that is already present in the bodily and environmental surroundings of the representing structure. If this can be made to work, it could make AT's representational requirements more manageable and thus AT itself more presentable.

To get the feel of the interactionist way of dealing with behavior, I will first discuss an example: the hopping robots build by Raibert and his coworkers (Hodgins and Raibert, 1991; Raibert, 1986, 1990; Raibert and Hodgins, 1993). They will provide a suitable case-study of a strongly embodied and situated approach in explaining the generation of behavior.

Seeing Raibert's hopping machines is an eerie spectacle that is difficult to dislodge from your mind. If you ever saw them on video, you are bound to remember them: machines that balance and move about by hopping on a single leg, a four-legged machine whose movements look like that of a genuine horse including gait transitions, a biped performing a somersault. Remarkable achievements indeed. How are they accomplished?

The one-legged robot—I will call it Hop for swift reference—consists of two primary parts: a body and a leg (see figure 3.2). Hop's body consists of an aluminum frame on which are mounted hip actuators, valves, gyroscopes, and computer interface electronics (Raibert and Hodgins, 1993, p. 332). The leg is a pneumatic cylinder with a padded foot. Its length is manipulated by changes in air pressure. A gimbal-type hip with two

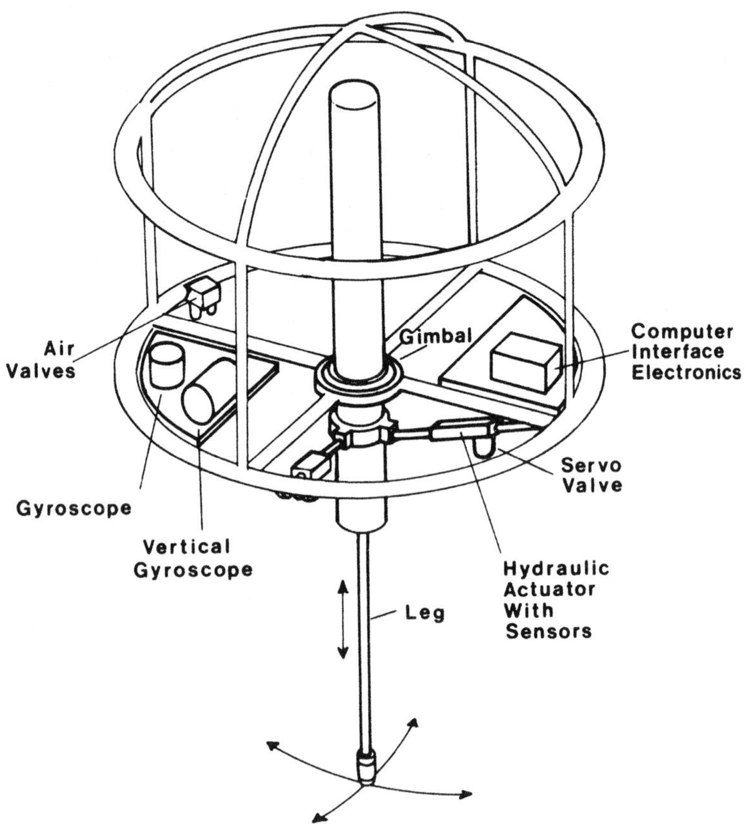

Figure 3.2
Raibert's one-legged hopping machine. (From Raibert and Hodgins, 1993.)

degrees of freedom connects the leg to the body. Two hydraulic actuators determine the hip angles. Sensors measure the length of the leg, the length and velocity of each hydraulic actuator, contact between the foot and the floor, pressures in the leg air cylinder, and the pitch, roll, and yaw angles of the body.

Hop's movements are based on the use of an elastic structure to improve energy efficient locomotion, a principle also used by animals. Hop's leg is springy because air in the leg actuator compresses when the robot lands on the leg and the leg shortens. To a large degree, the hopping motion is a passive elastic rebound that occurs when the springy leg reverses the downward motion of the body. The control algorithm responsible for hopping excites and modulates the bouncing motion, but does not specify the details of the trajectory. This is in contrast to the Ambler who plans each leg move exactly. Hop's control mechanism uses the dynamic interaction between the springy mechanical system and the control to generate the motion. Control of the leg spring rest length is used to inject or remove energy from the system in order to initiate, modulate, or stop the hopping oscillations. Hop stays upright by applying torques to the body during the support phase when vertical loading prevents the leg from slipping. Movement is induced by displacing the point of support from the projection of the center of mass (Hop tips itself over), and it is maintained, or changed, by manipulating the placement of the leg as well as the hip angles (ibid., pp. 334–335).

Hop and the other hopping robots built by Raibert and his co-workers illustrate some of the basic issues that are at the heart of a more embodied and situated approach. Instead of thinking about a nervous system or a control system as a center for commands to be executed by actuators, the body and the environment are taken as a system with its own dynamic characteristics. The preexisting dynamics of the body and the environment are only modulated by the controlling system, not really controlled. Raibert and Hodgins state: "We believe that the mechanical system has a mind of its own, governed by the physical structure and the laws of physics. Rather than issuing commands, the nervous system can only make 'suggestions' which are reconciled with the physics of the system and the task" (1993, p. 350). They also stress that it is necessary to deal with both the neural and bodily dynamics, while most research tends to address these topics separately: "It is ironic that while workers in neural motor control tend to minimize the importance of the mechanical characteristics of an animal's body, few workers in biomechanics seem very interested in the role of the nervous system" (ibid.). An embodied and situated approach to behavior strives to a more integrated treatment of both ingredients. Hop is an example where two coupled systems—a controlling structure and a physical system—together generate the total system's behavior.

In the following chapters, I will pay much more attention to the interactionist approach. The pressing question right now, however, is whether this kind of modeling offers a way for AT to overcome its problems. One of the background assumptions behind cognitivist psychology has always been that a higher-level cognitive explanation of behavior should delegate the problems of motor control to a noncognitive, so to say more 'mechanical', set of mechanisms. Having an AT-styled architecture do all of the work, down to initiating and controlling movements, never was an attractive prospect. Thus, it sounds both familiar and sensible to argue that AT's account of the generation of higher-level distal behavioral regularities are to be combined with a more embodied, dynamical approach that deals with the lower-level proximal issue of motor control (Clark, 1997a). A combination of the two sounds like a good way to have the best of both worlds.

Well, is there anything to be held against the view that AT can be improved upon by making it more embodied and situated, delegating the burden of instruction partly to the environment? Are there any reasons to suppose that there is any intrinsic *opposition* between AT and an interactionist approach? I think there are and I think also that these reasons are fairly straightforward. First, however, it is important to stress again what the present discussion is a discussion about.

The current discussion is about a *conceptual framework* (AT) that is being used to explain how behavior is generated by natural means. AT is a way of looking at behavior and of making sense of the process. The core of this conceptual framework consists of the idea that an internal (representational) structure provides instructions which are transformed in the outward behavioral structure: There is supposedly a linear connection between the instructions and the outward consequence. This general idea is widely accepted and has given rise to the supposition that the generation of behavior is not an unsolved riddle but a problem that is solved in principle. AT is thus a way of looking at—of making sense of—the generation of behavior. In this role, it provides a set of general guidelines for the building of many, concrete models of behavior. However, it does not consist of those models. In contrast to detailed engineered models, the performance of which can often be enhanced by ad hoc adjustments, the 'performance' of a conceptual framework is not improved upon by arbitrary extensions or combinations with conflicting ideas. Any addition has to fit in with the existing conceptualization. Thus, when the question is posed whether the conceptual framework of AT can be improved upon by making it more interactionist, it is not a matter of pragmatically combining different modeling techniques until a models works: At issue is the question whether the conceptual framework of AT allows the introduction of interactionist ideas.

Combining AT with an interactionist account will not do much good for AT. AT and interactionism compete rather than combine. They provide different conceptual solutions for similar problems. These solutions are difficult to reconcile with one another. To put it bluntly, AT's core idea is that behavior is the result of internal instructions, while the interactionist core idea is that behavior is *not* the result of internal instructions. It is difficult to see how these two will ever make a comfortable alliance.

In the field of movement science the clash between these two core ideas is known as the motor-action controversy (Meijer and Roth, 1988; Bongaardt, 1996). Motor-programs are thought to instruct the execution of movements in detail. Action systems (Reed, 1982; Kelso and Tuller, 1984) interpret movement as resulting from the closely coupled organism-environment interactions as exemplified by Hop. Within this controversy it is argued that both views provide valid and valuable contributions to a theory of movement, but also that they are incompatible models (Meijer, 1988).

Disregarding this incompatibility of both conceptual frameworks, of even greater importance is that the two do not complement one another. They compete. The general problem is to explain the generation of behavior: How do the regularities apparent in adaptive and anticipatory behavior—behavior's structure—come into being. If interactionism is to be of any assistance to AT, it will have to provide a solution to this problem. If the behavioral structure cannot be derived from an internal structure, it has to come from somewhere else. However, as soon as an interactionist story can be formulated that does the job, it will provide an alternative solution to the problem that AT set out to explain. For example, AT is used to explain the anticipatory and adaptive characteristics of basic behavior, among them the problem of motor control. Within AT, motor control is conceptualized in the same way as 'real' cognitive problems. In both cases, a set of representations has to be manipulated until they provide a set of instructions that specify what a behaving system should do to accomplish a goal. When an interactionist approach does away with the need to provide detailed instructions *and* accounts for the structure present in basic behavior, it will have replaced AT in that domain. And if it can replace AT here, why couldn't an interactionist approach do the same in more traditionally 'cognitive' domains? Once the first step is taken, there are no evident limitations in this respect. To repeat, such a conceptual framework will compete with AT, rather than help it to overcome its problems.

The only plausible way for AT to accommodate interactionism is by turning itself into a different conceptual framework. This move strikes me as a sensible thing to do, but the result will not be AT any more. We should keep our terminology crisp here and not call this a way to salvage the existing conceptual framework.

So far, the attention has been focused on AT's structural difficulties and the problem of overcoming them. AT has also problems of a different kind. These arise from the involvement of the observer when behavioral phenomena are conceptualized. In the following section, I will introduce the problem posed by theoretical hitchhiking. Theoretical hitchhiking instigates a serious misjudgment of the issues involved in adaptive behavior, a misjudgment on which much of AT's attractiveness depends.

3 Observer related difficulties: theoretical hitchhiking[3]

Hitchhiking is an easy way of gaining mobility. It enables you to go to any place you might want to go in a way that is fast and low-cost, and without the need to worry about the means that get you to your destination. You only have to stand at the side of the road and wait for somebody going in your direction to take you along. This brings into focus the only real drawback of hitchhiking: You are always dependent on somebody else to get to where you want to go.

Theoretical hitchhiking in (cognitivist) psychology amounts to an easy way of introducing explanatory concepts in a manner that is fast and low-cost, and without the need to worry about the means that enable you to use these concepts. As in the real-life case there is a drawback, however. The explanatory properties of hitchhiking concepts do not derive from the entities or processes referred to by these concepts; rather, these properties derive from the cognitive processes of the person using these concepts. Hitchhiking concepts do not 'move' on their own; they are dependent on the psychologist to take them around. At the same time, hitchhiking concepts *are* taken around (by the psychologists) so that a surface equivalence with genuinely 'self-propelled' concepts is maintained. Because of this outward equivalence, it is difficult to distinguish hitchhiking concepts from self-propelled ones. As hitchhiking is also much cheaper than providing one's own transport, hitchhiking concepts may seem very attractive from an explanatory point of view. It makes the complex look simple.

The overall effect of theoretical hitchhiking is the unwitting and widespread introduction of explanations in cognitivist psychology that look like subpersonal explanations, while they actually depend on higher-level cognitive properties. To use Dennett's phrase, loans of intelligence are taken, but without anyone being aware that it occurs. I will argue that two of the central notions on which AT is based—representations and distal environmental descriptions—depend on hitchhiking and are left unaccounted for at a subpersonal level.

3.1 Theoretical hitchhiking: preliminaries

Theoretical hitchhiking arises in the context of naturalism. As discussed in chapter 1, naturalism amounts to the idea that there is a hierarchy of organizational levels in nature, each level with its own properties and dedicated natural science, and each lower level forming the basis for each higher, supervening level. Physics sets the stage for less general pursuits like chemistry, which does the same for biochemistry and so on. Higher levels have higher-level properties, which involves, among other things, an increase in explanatory possibilities. Consider the enzymatic function of large protein molecules composed of amino acids (Grobstein, 1973). These molecules fold in a specific way, which gives them a spatial form that enables them to function as catalysts for specific chemical reactions. The catalyst and the reactants fit together like a lock and key. In this case one starts with a string of amino acids and ends up with enzymatic functioning. Darwin's theory of evolution provides another example. It postulates the lower-level properties of random variation and subsequent selection, and so explains the higher-level property of the species adapting to their environment at larger spatio-temporal scales. The property of adaptation can, in turn, be used to explain even higher levels of organization (Rosenberg, 1978).

So, only physical properties may be used as a basis for understanding chemical properties, while physical *and* chemical properties can be used in understanding physiology, and so on. Each level introduces additional constraints by which higher levels must abide, leading to an increase in explanatory potential at each successive level. At the same time, this higher-level explanatory potential cannot be used at any of the lower levels. Higher-level descriptions do not apply to lower-level properties. The former are to be derived from the latter. Neglecting this limitation results in a quasi-explanation where the explanandum is (mistakenly) used as a part of its own explanans.

Psychology places itself within this natural science hierarchy. The challenge faced by psychology is to account for personal-level properties by means of a theory that only involves subpersonal properties. It has to explain how a 'cognitive transition' comes about. Above this transition, personal-level theories that rely on properties like 'intelligence' or 'rationality' may be applied to a score of areas, ranging from economics to self-narratives. On the other hand, an account of the *generation* of these properties has to steer free from this abundance of cognition-dependent, explanatory possibilities. As said above, the use of personal-level properties for this purpose would result in a quasi-explanation where the explanandum acts as its own explanans.

The use of intelligent processes to account for intelligent phenomena was baptized by Dennett (1978) as taking a 'loan of intelligence'. According to Dennett, intelligence loans are not necessarily bad. They alleviate the need to solve all problems relating to intelligence at once, leaving some issues to a later date. The intelligent properties, taken on loan, can be seen as the agenda on which psychology still needs to work. However, to be willing to pay back such loans of intelligence, it should be evident when a loan has been taken. I will argue that there is a complex demarcation problem here.

It is very difficult to distinguish properties that are 'fully paid' for from those that depend on loans of intelligence. To understand why, let's bring in the observer.

Not only does naturalism place cognition and behavior within a hierarchically organized, natural order. It places the *study* of cognition and behavior within the same natural order (Campbell, 1973; Kornblith, 1985; Quine, 1969). For a naturalist, the world is described from within, not from an external 'God's eye' point of view (see figure 3.3). Theories, explanations, and descriptions do not stand apart as a nonnatural, abstract, Platonic realm of ideas. They are themselves aspects of the hierarchically organized natural world, as described by the different natural sciences. How science can occur as a natural phenomenon goes beyond present concerns. What is clear, however, barring some *very* serious, pan-psychic rewriting of physics, is that any such account will involve the activities of persons doing science. It is inconceivable how one might have scientific explanations in a universe without intelligent (cognitive) beings. As Maturana and Varela said: "Everything said is said by someone" (1988, p. 27).

Whenever there is a theory, explanation, or description proposed, refuted, or discussed, there is necessarily somebody involved (a cognitive system) who proposes, refutes, or discusses. The cognitive system fulfilling this particular role will be referred to as the *observer*. The observer is the person, or cognitive system, handling a description at any particular moment, giving it existence. It is crucial to realize that the observer is not some abstract theoretical notion—a notion about which the question may be raised whether or not it is a necessary one. Talking about the observer is

Figure 3.3
A schematic overview of the position taken in by the observer among the multiple hierarchical levels of the natural world: an observer describes the world from within.

meant to make *you* self-conscious of your own constant activity as a cognitive system. As *you* are now reading this chapter, you act as the observer who is right now actively interpreting and judging this particular text. The thought of whether we could do without the observer as a relevant theoretical factor when dealing with behavioral theory is only entertained because we, as observers, consider it. The observer is the ever-present, inescapable entertainer of theories, descriptions, and explanations.

The important implication for present purposes is that cognition and behavior are studied from the observer's intrinsically personal-level perspective. The observer is (you are) a fully operational, acting cognitive system who readily applies the rich explanatory cognitive vocabulary of mental processes, rationality, intentionality, and so forth, in all sorts of situations. The natural sciences have waged a long battle to expel personal-level explanations from areas where they do not apply. Lightning was once seen as bolts thrown by a god, plant-growth as a result of the powers of a goddess. Arriving at our present understanding of these natural phenomena has not been easy. The task faced by psychologists looks particularly daunting however. To account for the 'cognitive transition', a subpersonal explanation has to be formulated. But, this to-be-developed account is situated just below the level where all those personal-level properties actually do apply. The divide between the two levels is here very thin indeed.

At this point, the observer, functioning above the cognitive divide, needs a lot of self-restraint to set aside those explanatory properties which do not apply to the subpersonal situation, even when they seem from the observer's cognitive perch extremely well suited for an account of behavioral phenomena. To guide such self-restraint, a clear demarcation between personal and subpersonal properties is required.

The problem is that the demarcation between personal and subpersonal properties is rather fuzzy. We do not know beforehand which subpersonal properties will be relevant for generating higher, personal-level properties. The discovery of suitable lower-level properties is an important aspect of explaining the occurrence of higher-level ones. Psychology needs a set of properties which apply at the subpersonal level *and* which can be strung together so that behavioral phenomena come about. It is uncommon that such useful properties are already formulated within a field that limits its focus to these lower-level processes. For instance, as long as we are interested in the chemical structure of molecules, the spatial folding of these molecules is not necessarily a matter of concern. But to understand how enzymatic functioning takes place, folding turns out to be a key issue. The relevant properties are not known in advance, they need to be discovered.

Neither do we always know beforehand whether a proposed lower-level property can actually be provided for. The very problem of giving an account of the emergence of some higher-level property is to hypothesize, model, and test potential lower-level processes until a plausible story can be formulated that does the job. The properties that feature in such a story tend to be hypothetical at first. Often it is only much later that they can be unequivocally connected to some independently established, lower-level counterpart. In the case of Darwin's theory of evolution, it took about ninety years before the lower-level counterpart of Darwin's 'variation' finally bottomed out as the double helix of Crick and Watson.

To summarize the situation faced by psychology: (a) For the observer's consistently cognitive perspective it is very convenient to use personal-level explanatory properties. (b) To account for the generation of behavior and cognition, a set of subpersonal properties is necessary that are situated just 'below' the very convenient (for us) personal-level ones. (c) There are no firm and definite criteria that delimit personal and subpersonal properties. This is, finally, the context in which theoretical hitchhiking takes place.

3.2 Theoretical hitchhiking: taking intelligence loans without knowing it

Theoretical hitchhiking occurs when the cognition-dependency of a hypothesized subpersonal property is consistently obscured by the observer's own personal-level perspective. A hitchhiking property is not really present at the subpersonal level. It only looks that way to us, the observer. The difference goes unnoticed because there is no way to avoid the observer's personal-level perspective. An observer decides on the acceptance of a proposed subpersonal property as a part of an explanation of behavior, while all observers are prone to make the same systematic mistakes. We are all *Homo sapiens*, with a shared evolutionary background, a similar physiology, and, when it comes to psychologists, a similar upbringing and years of training. We are not neutral spectators. To study cognition and behavior, all researchers have to look through the same distorting glasses. It is difficult to disentangle the distortions produced by the glasses from the properties of the phenomena themselves.

A consequence of theoretical hitchhiking is the creation of explanations that are really only quasi-explanations. The means used to explain higher-level properties are themselves dependent on these higher-level properties. The result looks solid and convincing to the observer, but it does not incorporate the organization that is necessary to generate the higher-level property in the world. Theoretical hitchhiking affects a serious misjudgment regarding the ability of the subpersonal situation to uphold explanatory properties. In this way, it obscures the difficulties involved in accounting for higher-level phenomena.

When such hitchhiking properties are incorporated in an explanation of the 'cognitive transition', this explanation will depend on loans of intelligence. However, because the loan-dependency of the hitchhiking property is kept up in a consistent way, it is very difficult to distinguish it from genuine subpersonal properties. The cognitive processes at work within the observer will automatically fill in the gaps, so that these gaps never show. On the outside it will therefore give a very solid, naturalistic impression, even when on the inside large chunks are missing. As long as the observer is present to invest hitchhiking properties with the power they need to do their explanatory work, everything looks fine. And as there is always an observer present when someone investigates the explanation, everything looks fine all the time.

Given the phenomenon of theoretical hitchhiking, three questions come to the fore. The first question consists of two subquestions, (a) does theoretical hitchhiking actually occur within cognitivist psychology at a large scale, and, (b) if so, how does it affect AT? Second, how is the presence of theoretical hitchhiking ever to be discovered, if there is no way to avoid the observer's perspective? Third, how can hitchhiking ever be avoided? First, let's address the second and third question.

If no one can distinguish hitchhiking properties from those that are actually provided for by the subpersonal level, why make the distinction at all? It would be no more than an academic nicety. The distinction does show up very clearly, however, in an indirect way. A 'real' subpersonal property will be actually present at the subpersonal level. Its characteristics can subsequently be replicated in an artificial context and used to build an artificial, behaving system, a model. A hitchhiking property, on the other hand, provides only the illusion of being present at the subpersonal level. Models based on hitchhiking properties will reflect this incorrect analysis of the subpersonal situation that they are supposed to approximate. Crucial characteristics will be left out and the resulting model will remain flawed and not live up to expectations.

This pragmatic criterion for establishing the actual occurrence of theoretical hitchhiking does also provide the criterion for deciding when hitchhiking does not occur. If a theoretical account does consistently lead to models of behaving systems that actually work, then it seems safe to conclude that the account is a sound one.

The occurrence (or absence) of theoretical hitchhiking thus becomes visible in a roundabout way: in the modeling results it generates. Even here, judgment is difficult to pass. The causes for disappointing models are not always obvious, nor whether a result is actually disappointing rather than sobering reality breaking in on overly high expectations. The history of artificial intelligence is a good example of the inconclusiveness of interpreting disappointing modeling results. Theoretical hitchhiking may show up when theories are put to the test in models; but it will be difficult to establish the definite, unquestioned occurrence (or absence) of theoretical hitchhiking. Also, the question could be raised, why should one bother with the notion of theoretical hitchhiking at all? So far, it looks like a roundabout way to name good (probably no hitchhiking) and bad modeling (possibly hitchhiking).

The real relevance of the notion of theoretical hitchhiking lies not with any definite shoot out between models to decide whether hitchhiking does or does not occur. Rather, the relevance of the notion of hitchhiking derives from the critical attitude that it instigates concerning standard, commonsense interpretations of the processes that are involved in connection to the operation of behaving systems. We should not trust our commonsense interpretations in this context. Compare it to astronomy where the actual movements of the heavenly bodies were only discovered when the systematic effects caused by the movement of the earth itself (and thus of everyone studying the skies) were recognized and accounted for. Our own high-level perspective on behavioral phenomena should not be accepted at face value. Theoretical hitchhiking is definitely an issue and avoiding it a matter of concern—as well as an option.

The notion of hitchhiking provides a diagnostic as to why difficulties with modeling arise. Theoretical hitchhiking can also be used to guide a process of conceptual pruning in which an account of behavior is scrutinized in search of any probable reliance on hitchhiking. Once identified, steps can be undertaken to replace a presumed hitchhiking property by one that looks more solid. If the replacement leads to better modeling results, this will be evidence that an instance of hitchhiking has been pruned. In the following sections, I will attempt such a conceptual pruning of AT.

How does theoretical hitchhiking bear on AT? Within cognitivism there is a strong dedication to modeling, and in that sense the occurrence of hitchhiking should be minimal. The conceptual framework of AT may be derived from a higher-level context, but it is rephrased and elaborated on in significant ways. Most important, it is changed in such a way that it does lead to the building of operative models of a large number of cognitive tasks. AT does not call in any obvious, unexplained higher-level notions, such as rationality or intentionality. On the contrary, cognitivism prides itself in its strict requirements concerning the need to provide some model if an explanation is to be deemed any good. Is AT thus free from hitchhiking?

I think not. I think that theoretical hitchhiking is a widespread phenomenon within cognitivist psychology. The general shortcomings of cognition-based models of behavior fit in very well with this position. Of course, the verdict that such models consistently underachieve will be contested. Some might think it an excessive demand to require them to mimic insect-like behavior at insect-like speeds (e.g., avoid being stepped on by a human). No one has a clear standard of what models of behaving systems ought to be capable of to be considered good or bad. Still, there are strong theoretical considerations that point in the direction of hitchhiking.

Theoretical hitchhiking can be subtler than is hinted at so far. The problems created by theoretical hitchhiking for cognitivism are not connected to the introduction of *obvious* personal-level properties into a subpersonal context. This introduction occurs, of course. AT is defined by this introduction. But AT introduces these properties with an awareness that its cognitivist account has to be recast in such a way that it is fully consistent with the subpersonal situation. As described in chapter 2, a lot of care is taken to alleviate any improper use of obvious personal-level properties.

The real venom of hitchhiking strikes at much less circumspect places. These places lie at the heart of AT, and form very strong reasons for disqualifying AT as a conceptual framework that helps us understand how behavior is generated. Two central properties on which AT is based derive their self-evident simplicity from theoretical hitchhiking: representations and distal environmental descriptions. These can be associated with, respectively, the symbol grounding problem (Harnad, 1990) and the frame of reference problem (Clancey, 1989).

3.3 The symbol grounding problem: how to avoid hitchhiking representations

The first major concept of AT that ought to be scrutinized with an eye to theoretical hitchhiking is the notion of representation. The notion of representation lies at the heart of AT and forms the basis for its explanation of behavior. Given the phenomenon of theoretical hitchhiking, the question that needs answering becomes: Can representations be constructed as a subpersonal property, or is there only a seemingly subpersonal integrity, which in reality depends on our own cognitive powers?

Theoretical hitchhiking focuses our attention on the issue of how subpersonal representations become representational—that is meaningful, semantic—entities. Leaving aside philosophical attempts at a theory of representation, the standard practice in cognitivist psychology is to *postulate* that certain entities in a model—such as syntactic symbols or network nodes—simply are representations. These entities are given labels that are meaningful to *us*, as observers. They can be designated to mean anything that takes our fancy. The problem, of course, is how such designated representations can have any semanticity at all, independent from us investing meaning into them. If the semanticity comes from us, then the use of representations would be a case of theoretical hitchhiking.

Despite cognitivism's commitment to building computational or connectionist models to back up its account of some cognitive task or behavior, the problem of the hitchhiking dependency of representations is acute. The difficulty with these models as signifiers of an observer-independent use of representations is that they depend heavily on the observer's interpretation of the model. The observer's interpretation is essential to determine what the model is supposed to approximate. The observer decides on the semantic interpretation of the syntactic symbols or the nodes of a neural net. It does not help when the representations are connected to an external domain, as long as this domain consists of a set of abstractions, provided by the observer. The input vector of the same neural net can as easily be taken to encode mines, phonemes, or members of the Duck family, all at the whim of the observer (Verschure, 1992). There is nothing intrinsic to such models that makes the representations hook onto the world by means that are independent from the observer's interpretation. This form of representation needs an observer for continuous maintenance. In other words, it depends on hitchhiking.

As discussed earlier, the need to provide an observer-independent account of meaning has been a long-standing issue for cognitivist psychology's philosophers. More recently it has become recognized as an issue by the more practically minded. Of those, Harnad provides a nice label for this problem. He calls it the symbol grounding problem and describes it as follows: "How can the semantic interpretation of a formal system be made *intrinsic* to the system, rather than just parasitic on the meanings in our heads?" (Harnad, 1990, p. 335) The problem consists of creating a way to connect the 'representations' to—to ground them in—the worldly properties that they are to represent. This grounding will involve the linking of the representations to the environment by sensory connections and behavioral capacities. It requires an embodied and situated system to effect this grounding. Genuine subpersonal representation cannot be had as an abstract domain, set apart from any implementing, physical system. Representations set apart from any particular physical context can only be had in the context of the observer, and this makes them personal-level representations.

As soon as the need to avoid hitchhiking representations is taken seriously, it becomes obvious that representations are not a readily available commodity. The use of representations as a subpersonal entity can only be upheld if there is a plausible way to have representations that do not depend on an interpretation by an observer. The long-standing philosophical worry about representational meaning becomes an urgent problem for cognitivism.

In the previous chapter, I described how a subpersonal form of representation, as required by AT, might be constructed: AT's subpersonal representations can take the form of a modeling capacity, tied to a behavioral context (section 5). This was partly done in anticipation of the hitchhiking issue to make the case for AT as strong as possible. In this section, I will argue that these countermeasures against the risk of hitchhiking representations are not sufficient.

AT's representation derives from an isomorphism between an internal structure used to predict external happenings and to instruct the motor system, and parts of the external, environmental structure. It can be argued that the isomorphism does not derive from any interpretation by an observer. According to AT, the outward behavioral capacities bear witness of the existence of this isomorphism. Testing the existence of this isomorphism in any particular case will of course always involve the activity of observers. But this is a necessary part of all science. What matters is whether it is plausible that these internal representational models function independent of an observer who infuses meaning into them. In other words, can this conceptualization of representation be considered as a (subpersonal) naturalistic property?

The obvious, intuitive answer will be that these model-based representations are definite, subpersonal properties. There are clear cases to proof it a fact. Longuet-Higgins's sandpaper robot is maybe the simplest example, the Ambler a more complex one. In both cases there is an isomorphism between an internal structure and the external world that will not go away when we all leave the room and stop thinking about these machines. The existence of this isomorphism is guaranteed because of the role it plays in the robots' behavior. Does this close the case?

There are complications. It is one thing to present a way in which subpersonal representation can be had. It is another to live by the rules imposed by that particular way of having representations. If the threat of theoretical hitchhiking is taken seriously and the use of representations restricted to model-based ones as described above, it would be the end of cognitivist psychology as we know it. The implication is that any representation-based cognitive theory can only be used within the context of an embodied and situated behaving system for whom the representations figure as a guiding model. Cognitivism can do two things here. It can (re)style itself as an enterprise dealing with higher, personal-level phenomena. In the personal-level context, the existence of agents, exhibiting relatively complex behavior, can simply be assumed, and the use of representations as a generally available commodity can be continued. A higher-level psychology deals with the questions that are traditionally the terrain of folk psychology or Dennett's intentional stance: Why did agent X do so and so rather than such and such. It concerns the choice between different, *existing*, behavioral capacities. This project is both naturalistically respectable and important, but it does not address the problem how those behavioral capacities are generated in the first place.

On the other hand, a part of psychology could focus on the problem of behavioral capacities, and restrict its theorizing and model building to a behavioral context. For those psychologists who want to pursue the question of behavioral capacities the relevant issue is: Can AT stave off the risk of hitchhiking representations by limiting their use to model-based representations in the context of behaving systems? I think it cannot. Model-based representation provides a cure that kills the patient: AT. The sandpaper robot, the Ambler, and similar machines provide existence proofs for AT and its use of subpersonal representations in a behaving system. They show that AT can explain the generation of behavior in simple cases. But, these models do not show that this construction can be scaled up to much more complex cases, without *presupposing* complex behavioral capacities. And that last move cannot be made because it would defeat the whole idea of AT.

AT consists of the general idea that behavioral structure (to a large degree) derives from representational structure. To avoid hitchhiking representations, the latter has to be made dependent on behavioral structure. The presence of behavioral capacities is a precondition for ascribing (subpersonal) representations. To summarize, AT states that behavior derives from representations, while the representational theory on which it depends states that representations require behavior for being considered representations in the first place. Representation and behavior thus mutually presuppose one another. This mutual presupposition disqualifies AT's basic idea that behavioral structure can be derived from representational structure.

One could shy away from the strong conclusion that AT ought to be rejected on the grounds of the mutual presupposition of representation and behavior by arguing that the two can be had in one go, like the stones of an arch, mutually supporting one another even when they would fall down on their own. However this story veers away from AT in essential ways. The simple beauty of AT's conceptual framework is its straightforward claim that the origin of behavioral order lies in a stored program or set of representations (of course always modifiable and extendable). When representation and behavior become *mutually* supportive, this strikes at the core of AT, and thereby changes it.

What to think of those cases in which AT does work, such as the Ambler? A good way to visualize both the achievements and the shortcomings of these models is by viewing them in terms of Brunswik's lens model of behavior (figure 2.1). The lens model shows how a perceptual and a behavioral proximal lens produce a unitary distal focus, both internally and externally. The focal points are the most salient to us as observers, and AT takes these as the basis for its account of behavior. Behavior then becomes the process of turning an internal distal goal-representation into an achieved external distal goal-state. AT-based models, such as the Ambler, reflect this distal focus. They are models that translate a distal goal-representation into a distal goal-state, preferentially as efficiently as possible. Brunswik's lens also conveys the intuition that the focal points are not to be taken as a part of the premises, but rather as a consequence of an organism's activity at a proximal range. A proximal 'focusing process' generates the distal focal points. The proximal activity has to be in place and have a certain complexity before distally focused behavior can be expected to occur. How does this bear on the AT approach?

When we, as observers, provide the representational and the environmental focus it becomes possible to make a model that connects the two under certain circumstances by following the AT-guidelines as described above. However, the focal points are in this case not derived from any proximal behavioral complexity of the model itself. They derive from the observer's focusing powers. The setup of this construction is exactly the mirror image of the one suggested by Brunswik's lens. The latter starts out with proximal, behavioral capacities that allow the behaving system to attain its own distal behavioral regularities or distal focus. In the AT case, the observer's distal focus is the starting-point while an arbitrary device is built to perform the translation between the preset focal points. As the device is not developed as a focusing mechanism, the proximal variability is kept as low as possible to minimize the amount of instruction needed. Brunswik's lens is kept as flat (vertically) as possible. Proximal mediation is cast in the role of efficient translation rather than the generator of behavioral potential. As a result, such a behaving system will always be comparatively vulnerable to environmental disruptions. A behaving system with limited proximal variability cannot reach the same goal in many different ways.

The Ambler and similar models still depend on theoretical hitchhiking. Such models start out with a highly specific capacity for representation, a capacity which is used to achieve a behavioral goal via a prespecified and limited set of events. This organization is physically possible, but it is not very stable. It requires the work of observers to set it up and any unforeseen disruption of the thin line connecting the two will put an end to this form of behavior. It is like a sandcastle that also exists independent from its builders, but which needs these builders to maintain it, and which withers away as soon as they call it a day. The only way in which sandcastles and AT-based behaving systems are kept in existence is by the care of a behaving system that takes the effort to keep it in shape. An AT-based behaving system does not do its own distal focusing.

The need to avoid using representations that derive from hitchhiking makes life extremely difficult for AT. As a consequence, it becomes increasingly plausible that AT's account of a subpersonal mechanism is not a sound one. This conclusion will be further reinforced in the next section. The need to avoid hitchhiking puts heavy demands on the environmental descriptions as well.

3.4 The frame of reference problem: a hitchhiking environment

When we look at a behaving system, we see it moving about and behaving in the same environment that we inhabit ourselves. It reacts to lights, sounds, objects, other behaving systems, and so on. All are stimuli that are recognizable by us (if necessary by using equipment to amplify or add to our failing perceptual system). Together they make up what we deem to be an independently existing environment, which is lying ready 'out there' for the behaving system to be perceived and be acted on. A well-demarcated and specified environment is an essential prerequisite for AT: It specifies what is there for a behaving system to perceive, it constrains the content of the system's plans, and it provides the stage on which the system can act out its plans. What happens to this important notion of a firm and objectively present environment when it is prodded with our theoretical hitchhiking stick?

A concern with hitchhiking makes one ask the question whether the environment as we know and describe it for ourselves (the environment as it consists of cows, grass, carnations, gas stations, and such) can be incorporated in a subpersonal account of the generation of behavior. This concern does not extend to the environment within personal-level descriptions. I agree with Fodor when he says that "*we* do see shirts, and it's loopy to deny that we do, and there's an end of it" (1986a, p. 17; emphasis added). The concern is whether a (human) nervous system can be said to be geared to an environment consisting of recognizable objects and events. Or is the environment as we know it only there because our brains and bodies do a lot of work in rearranging an unspecified environment into our commonsense world?

Clancey (1989, 1993) provides a convenient terminology to discus this point.[4] He dissociates the set of (environmental) descriptions that are used by the observer from the descriptions that can be derived from the behaving system's own dynamical interactions with the environment. He uses the notion of a "frame of reference" to refer to the several different descriptions. Each frame of reference corresponds with a different "ontology," a different specification of the entities in the environment, either for the observer, looking at the behaving system from the outside—a third-person view—or for the behaving system itself—a first-person view.[5] The frame of reference problem consists of the difficulty to establish which frame of reference is to be used when designing an artificial intelligent (behaving) system.

To avoid an environmental frame of reference that depends on theoretical hitchhiking, AT has to use the subpersonal behaving system's frame of reference. It is important to stress that subpersonal does, among other things, imply that the behaving system is not to be interpreted as an agent (which is the behaving system at a personal level), but as a neural, embodied system. Physically this amounts to a large collection of cells (when the system is a biological one) or a collection of electronic and other components (when it is a robot). The problem can be formulated as follows: Can AT use the observer's frame of reference as the frame of reference of a collection of cells or mechanical parts, without *us* providing and maintaining this frame of reference?

Brunswik's Lens model provides a quick way to argue that AT cannot presuppose the distal environmental descriptions on which its conceptual framework depends. The (extended) lens model consists of two lenses and three focal points (figure 2.1). The focal points are the distal stimulus situation, a central state, and distal achievements. In the previous section, it was argued that the central state—the representational mechanism as we would now call it—is a consequence of the behaving system's activity (its so-called focusing capacities) rather than a prerequisite. If the representations are treated as a prerequisite within AT, they will depend on the focusing capacities of the observer, and thus on hitchhiking. The same reasoning leads to the conclusion that the other two focal points, the distal stimulus situation and the distal achievements, are also a result of these focusing capacities, either our own (as observers) or those of the organism that is being studied. When this reasoning holds, it can be concluded that the distal environmental descriptions which are used to specify what a behaving system perceives or does, cannot be used as a part of AT's explanans because they belong to AT's explanandum. The reasoning is rather quick here. In the rest of this section, I will present further evidence for this conclusion.

A number of considerations support the conclusion that the (distal) environment cannot be described without taking into account for whom, or for what it is to be a description. I will first discuss von Uexküll's idea of an *Umwelt* to make more specific the claim that the frame of reference should derive from the organism under description and not from the observer. Second, I will discuss some examples to show how the human environment, the one inhabited by the observer, depends on a specific neural system and embodiment. All this lends credit to the idea that 'what is out there' depends as much on the system that uses the descriptions as on 'what is out there beyond the descriptions' in an unlabeled and uninterpreted world.

How does the environment look like for crabs, dragonflies, or other multicellular (and unicellular) organisms? Jacob von Uexküll was a biologist, heavily influenced by Kant, who posed and tried to answer such questions (Von Uexküll, 1964). Von Uexküll is nowadays almost exclusively remembered as the originator of the word *Umwelt*. However, his ideas are very relevant for the present discussion and warrant more attention. Von Uexküll was born in 1864 in the Baltic, then a part of Germany, as the youngest son of a German aristocratic family (ibid.). His biological research was on comparative physiology and behavior. He had an important influence on Konrad Lorenz, one of the founding fathers of ethology. As said, Von Uexküll's most lasting fame lies with his "*Umweltlehre*" (Von Uexküll, 1921, 1980).[6] The *Umweltlehre* was proposed as a theory for the integration of physiology and behavior, although it was also much more generally applied as a sort of biological philosophy of life. Von Uexküll used his words in a highly idiosyncratic way, which is difficult to catch in English and which explains the many German words in the following discussion.

Von Uexküll studied the physiology and behavior of many different, mostly marine, invertebrates. His interest lay both with the available behavioral capacities of organisms, dependent on their physiology, and the environmental stimuli that triggered and influenced the behavior. As a result of this comparative approach he came thoroughly aware that the physiology of different organisms coincided with different behavioral capacities and different sensory sensitivities. This led him to propose that the environment, as far as it was relevant for the organism, should be conceptualized in a way that fits the organismal organization. This organism-bounded environment was called its *Umwelt*. The *Umwelt* of an organism is characterized by a double relation to the organism. It provides the stimuli that the organism's sensors are sensitive to and it provides the grip-surface (*Angriffsflächen*) for the organism's motoric capacities (Von Uexküll, 1921, p. 45).

Together, the organism and its *Umwelt* constitute a closed, reciprocally adapted system. Von Uexküll tended to talk about each *Umwelt* as consisting of crab-things, dragonfly-things, and so on. The stimuli and motoric system are internally connected by neural connections. On the outside the connection runs via the *Gegengefüge*, the opposing (environmental) structure that transfers the effects induced by the motor apparatus back to the organism's sensors. Together it constitutes a circular organization, which Von Uexküll called the *Funktionskreis* (Dewey's (1896) reflex-arc could be used as a translation, or, more modern, sensory-motor- and perception-action-loops). The *Umwelt* consists of the environment as it is wedged in between motor and sensory parts of the organism. The *Funktionskreise* in which an organism partakes suspend it in its *Umwelt*.

Von Uexküll's *Umwelt* provides a comprehensive way to think about the frame of reference for a particular behaving system. The notion of *Umwelt* gives a more clear meaning to the idea that the organism's frame of reference differs from that of the observer. Von Uexküll also had interesting ideas concerning the means by which (across species) the different *Umwelten* became more and more extended. The *Umwelt* of paramecium consists only of fluidity with and without (chemical or tactile) stimulation (ibid., p. 39). But those of larger and more complex organisms involve more and more *Funktionskreise*.

Starting out with multicellular organisms containing a nervous system, Von Uexküll notes that for the most simple organisms the motor capacities are often highly sophisticated, even when the sensory capacities are relatively simple (ibid., pp. 165–166). The prominence of the motor-related parts of the nervous system disappears by more complex organisms. When different species of differing complexity are compared, there are no principled differences between their motor systems, except for a general subordination of its multiple nerve nets to a central neural system. On the other hand, the sensor-related parts proliferate exceedingly in more complex organisms. This is not only due to the addition of extra sensory capacities, but mainly by adding more (neural) 'depth' to a set of sensors. These sense-related parts make up an increasingly large percentage of the nervous system. This increase is associated with a decreased dependency on the particulars of proximal sensor stimulations and an increased capacity to act on more (abstract) distal environmental structures. Von Uexküll explained this by arguing that the increasingly expanded nervous systems of more complex organisms allow organisms to act no longer on direct sensor stimulation, but on patterns generated by the nervous system's own structure (ibid., pp. 168–169). The organism incorporates a *Gegenwelt* of its environment (*Umwelt*).

Heider (1959) and Brunswik (1952; Campbell, 1966), already discussed above, later extended the idea that complex organisms gain independence from their immediate (proximal) environment by an extended nervous system. A suitable neural organization can provide substitutes that make up for the absence of direct distal stimulation and allow the organism to behave nevertheless in a way that is tuned to adaptively important (distal) environmental characteristics. This capacity gave rise to Brunswik's lens that models how proximal variability gives rise to distal unity. Later, Fodor (1986a) took the same proximal indeterminacy of distally oriented behavior as the phenomenon that AT is supposed to explain. Fodor brings us back to the now familiar conceptual framework of AT. However, the biological route that led us here comes with a different perspective. In contrast to AT which takes the environment as the primary structure, to which an organism can be sensitive in a greater or lesser degree, the environment is now an extension of the organism's capacities to sense and act, capacities that derive from the specific neural and bodily characteristics of the organism. The organism and its *Umwelt* are reciprocally adapted and together they make up a single, circular organization (a set of *Funktionskreise*).

The conclusion to be drawn here is that the environment, as a relevant feature for behavior, cannot be taken as a prerequisite. It is dependent on the behaving system. AT cannot assume an independently given environment which is there to be perceived by the organism. If AT assumes such an independent environment it relies implicitly on the observer's own *Umwelt* or frame of reference. This observer dependence of seemingly objective environmental features shows up quite clearly with color (Varela, Thompson, and Rosch, 1991).

To us, as observers, color looks like a clear physical property of the environment, ready to be perceived by any behaving system with the proper perceptual apparatus. However, color may not look like something that we impose on the environment and therefore it may look like an unproblematical primitive in cognitive and behavioral theorizing, current insights in the operation of the perception of color spell otherwise. The straightforward physical story is that color signifies a set of wave-lengths of electromagnetic radiation, ranging between approximately 700 nanometer for the border between infrared and red and approximately 400 nanometer for the border between violet and ultraviolet. However, the correspondence between the colors as we perceive them and these objective wave-lengths is not one to one. Perceived color is a result of three color channels in the visual system. The characteristics of this system give color their particular characteristics such as the complementarity of red and green, yellow and blue, and black and white. The characteristics of the system also make that a combination of light of different wave-lengths can be indistinguishable from light of a single wave-length (e.g., the combination of monochromatic red and monochromatic green light is seen as a yellow which is indistinguishable from monochromatic yellow light). The colors we perceive are the construct of a specific perceptual (color) system, and only in a complex, roundabout way related to objective changes in electro-magnetic radiation (Hardin, 1988; Varela, Thompson, and Rosch, 1991). Color is not something existing independently in the outside world which subsequently imposes itself on a nervous system. It is a construct that derives from the organization of the nervous system and which offers the behaving system a handy tool to deal with the environment in an adaptive way.

Another way to make the same point is by looking at the many new ways to turn abstract scientific data into forms that can be visually inspected (Hall, 1992). Computer-driven animation is used to turn satellite data about the scattering of ultraviolet radiation in the earth's atmosphere into a visible hole in the ozone layer, or to turn X-ray diffraction patterns of crystallized biochemical substances into three-dimensional models of these macromolecules. These animations can be very vivid, in particular by the ample use of color to highlight different molecules, gradients, or whatever needs to stand out. These modeling techniques make the otherwise theoretical and abstract suddenly look very concrete and 'real' to us. At the beginning of the twentieth century, the atom was a theoretical entity, whose material existence was a matter of intense debate by philosophers of science. Since then, and in particular since the invention of the scanning tunneling microscope (SCA), the atom has become a thing that can be 'seen' and even moved about. The consequence of these modeling techniques is that previously abstract and theoretical entities can acquire a status as entities that are intuitively as 'real' as any of the human sized objects to which our biologically given senses are tuned. The difference consists of a contraption that turns unintelligible signals into something which is intelligible to the system.

Considering these cases, it follows that: (a) What we take to be 'out there' in the environment is sensitive to the contraptions that are available—and used—to change 'raw data' into a format that allows us to notice it and deal with it efficiently. (b) It requires a hell of a lot of work to create contraptions that are capable of performing the functions mentioned. (c) Once such a contraption operates, it delivers very succinct and clear patterns that are useful to guide our actions in the modeled domain. These patterns are not the same as the raw data fed into the apparatus.

The analogy between the operation of a more complicated nervous system and these animation techniques is that both make visible the previously invisible—thereby bringing it into existence as far as the observer is concerned. From a bottom-up, naturalistic perspective, environmental labeling is a complicated task that the nervous system achieves one way or another (Edelman, 1992). The difference between computer-driven animation and the perceptions generated by our nervous systems is that in the former case it is still evident what kind of raw data were used to create the animations, while in the latter case we have only direct access to the result of our neural animations. In the latter case it is much more difficult to look 'through' the fancy, interpreted environment and get a glimpse of the patterns that give rise to our perceptions.

To conclude, when an account is to be given of the generation of behavioral capacities, such as AT professes to do, then it cannot rely on the environment under our own (neurally enhanced) descriptions, but it has to start with the environment as it is for what is to become a behaving system. Simply integrating 'self-evident' environmental descriptions in such an account of behavior glosses over one of the most serious problems for psychology.

3.5 Theoretical hitchhiking as a conceptual prodding stick

The need to avoid theoretical hitchhiking puts a heavy burden on the feasibility of the Agent Theory. Intuitively, AT looks like a plausible and consistent way to explain the generation of behavior. The notion of theoretical hitchhiking breaks into this seeming self-evidence because it forces one to be more critical toward the notions that feature in AT's conceptual framework. Once the fundaments of AT are put to the light, they turn out to be rather shaky and not a sure footing at all. The notion of representation is only a cheap, readily available commodity once intelligent, behaving systems exist. Using it at a subpersonal level can only be done under very restrictive conditions, restrictions that make AT much less plausible. AT's interpreted environment is also problematic when hitchhiking is to be avoided. It cannot fulfill its role as a primitive factor in AT's explanations.

None of these problems for AT are exactly new. Both have been pointed out before repeatedly. Cognitivist psychology's philosophers have been worrying about the representation-related problems for many years. But that is also what it remained, a philosopher's worry. The difficulties with the environmental frame of reference have also been pointed out repeatedly

(Clancey, 1989, 1993; Maturana and Varela, 1980, 1988; Putnam, 1987, 1988; Varela, Thompson, and Rosch, 1991; Winograd and Flores, 1986). These criticisms probably have been too divergent from almost everyone's background assumptions concerning intelligence and realism to be taken overly serious, or to be properly understood. Still there has for a long time been (and often still is) a general reluctance to apply these criticisms and take them to heart.

The nice thing about the notion of theoretical hitchhiking is that it works as a conceptual prodding stick that prompts the proponents of AT to stand up and say how AT might avoid the difficulties referred to. Once one starts scrutinizing AT with an eye to theoretical hitchhiking, the burden of proof changes. No longer can it be assumed that AT stands until proven otherwise. Proponents of AT now have the task to make it plausible that AT abides by the general (naturalistic) constraints that they profess to uphold. These proponents will have to specify how the properties on which AT depends are accounted for at a subpersonal level. Problems which are otherwise easily hushed up now have to be dealt with. Once one starts trying to deal with these issues, AT becomes a much less attractive theoretical framework.

The need to avoid theoretical hitchhiking makes life difficult for cognitivists. It might be wondered whether it makes cognitivist psychology impossible. Hitchhiking can occur everywhere. Maybe the cases discussed above are only the tip of an iceberg. Maybe we should become even more restrictive in accepting explanatory concepts. How can we be sure that hitchhiking is ever avoided? The possibilities for experimentally testing the observer independence of cognitive or behavioral models are all delicate and often inconclusive because of the thick layer of observer interpretation involved in any such testing. There is no general guideline that unequivocally restrains the use of personal-level explanatory properties at a subpersonal level. Psychology cannot get rid of its observer and it will never have any observer-independent access to the subpersonal level. Is the need to avoid theoretical hitchhiking too strong a constraint on psychology?

The ultimate and very pragmatic criterion to decide whether an account depends on hitchhiking is the ability or the inability to create working models of behaving systems on the basis of that particular account. When this succeeds, the account can be considered sound. If the efforts remain unsuccessful, there is a reason for suspicion. At such a moment, there should be a theoretical investigation of the account, to determine whether these difficulties could result from unsound premises that rely on a hitchhiking process. If the diagnosis of hitchhiking is rendered plausible on conceptual grounds, steps should be taken to replace the unsound parts of the account, or to come with a different account. After that the account should again be used for model-building, and so on.

Theoretical hitchhiking is not something about which we can make sure that it never occurs. If that was demanded, it would indeed be the end of psychology. The notion of hitchhiking provides a conceptual tool to be used when a proposed account for behavior is found wanting. It provides a useful heuristic aid to investigate the possible origins of such problems.

4 AT: the collapse of Brunswik's lenses

This chapter promised to give an 'absolute' evaluation of AT, irrespective of any competing conceptual frameworks that would do a better job at the same problem. It is time to make up the balance and pass verdict.

AT provides a conceptual framework which professes to explain how behavior is generated (in a general sense) by subpersonal means. AT derives from our own personal (higher) level of description and consists of applying the personal-level framework in a lower-level (subpersonal) context. Given the growth of cognitivist psychology, this is a successful strategy, up to a point. However, when looked at up close, AT looks untenable. Its higher-level origins come to the fore again and again and make it both a brittle and a questionable solution.

AT focuses on the general (distal) order present in behavior (e.g., reliable stimulus relations or achieved goals). It tries to connect readily identifiable (distal) stimuli and behavioral results by a mechanism that models the environment at this general scale. However, between these ordered points there is a lot of variability at a proximal scale. An organism may consistently go out for food every evening, and find it, but the smaller scaled behavioral events that lead the organism to exhibit this regularity are never (exactly) the same. This proximal variability is a nuisance for AT, which must go to great lengths to overcome it. A lot of knowledge is necessary and the motor apparatus has to be instructed in elaborated ways. As a result, AT-based models have so far not succeeded in dealing with environments which impose even a moderate variability in between the general focal points.

When AT is pictured in terms of Brunswik's lens model (see figure 2.1) its problem consists in overcoming the variability of the 'lenses'. The only way in which AT-based models have succeeded so far in generating interesting distal oriented behavior is by collapsing (or minimizing) the proximal variability. The lenses are kept as flat as possible. However, in the real world there is always a lot of proximal interference, and to counteract this interference variability is necessary. As long as AT cannot deal with this issue, its models will remain brittle and their behavior easily disrupted.

The need to avoid a conceptual framework that is based on theoretical hitchhiking makes further difficulties for AT. The general (distal) order, which it assumes from the start, is not given, it is the phenomenon which needs to be explained. From the perspective of the observer, the elements that figure in this distal order might look like subpersonal features. However, when the observer does not step in to impose this order, it can only be applied once a behaving system operates. That is, it can only be applied after the problem of the generation of behavior is solved. AT thus uses what it needs to explain as a part of its proposed solution.

To conclude, AT does not stand up to scrutiny. However, this conclusion is based on an 'absolute' evaluation, and for many it will not be convincing enough. There are always possibilities to extend, improve, or tamper with the conceptual framework until it does a somewhat better job. The conclusion will never be considered final, given such possibilities to amend the framework. A final denunciation of AT will only come from a comparison with an alternative conceptual framework that performs better. Without such an alternative, AT will remain the best choice available, and its failings a reason for demanding improvements rather than its abandonment.

The following chapters will be dedicated to describing and developing a potential alternative conceptual framework. Again, Brunswik's lens model offers a good way to introduce it and contrast it with AT. AT is based on the focal points in the lens model. The lenses—the proximal variability occurring between the focal points—are *obstructions* that must be overcome. The alternative conceptual framework on the other hand takes the lenses—the proximal variability—as its starting point and takes them as the *origins* of the distal regularities.

4

Behavioral Systems Theory: Organism-Environment Interaction as a Potential Alternative

1 Behavioral systems: the very idea

The idea of behavioral systems is not finished or clear-cut. The idea of behavioral systems derives from a set of tentative intuitions, hunches, practices, and convictions. These intuitions, hunches, practices and convictions all stress the importance of the direct, physical interactions between an organism (or a robot) and its environment. They form the heart of the interactionist approach in cognitive science. In this chapter, I will discuss several attempts to transform this loose agglomerate of ideas into a cohering conceptual framework, a conceptual framework which can be set against that of AT.

The core of the idea of behavioral systems is that behavior is a result of the fine-grained interactions between an embodied behaving system and the specific structure which is present in the environment in which the behaving system acts. Together, the behaving system (the organism) and the environment on which it acts constitute a single *behavioral system*. Other names are "organism-environment system" or "organism environment interaction system" (Smithers, 1994). In all cases it is stressed that a behaving organism (or a robot) and the environment together make up a single, cohering system. In the following, I will call the conceptual framework that is based on the idea of behavioral systems the Behavioral Systems Theory, or BST. It should be understood that BST is at present more a desideratum than a well-established framework. The work discussed provides some provisional ways to give body to BST.

BST ought to provide a general conceptual framework that explains the generation of behavior in a way that differs from AT. However, even more so than in the case of AT, BST is a reconstructed position. Many authors profess ideas which lie in the general direction of BST, but there is no consensus as to what the idea of behavioral systems exactly amounts to. BST will be my own reconstructed and systematized version of the organism-environment interaction approach to explaining the generation of behavior. BST is a fairly grand term for this loose set of ideas, referring more to what might become than what is. It should also be stressed that this reconstruction is done with the purpose of formulating a conceptual framework that stands in opposition to AT. Many of the ideas that are connected to a behavioral systems approach are also accepted by defenders of an AT-styled approach to behavior. The rejection of AT, as implied by BST, does not transfer to everyone who is sympathetic to a behavioral systems styled approach. Many, and probably even most, researchers hold a mixture of the two positions.

Presenting interactionism in the form of BST—and thus in strict opposition to AT and, more generally, cognitivism—is not a matter of unnecessary and willful antagonizing. The present discussion is about *conceptual frameworks*, about different ways to conceptualize, to interpret, behavioral phenomena. The opposition between AT and BST is not always, and not necessarily reflected in an opposition of detailed models of behaving systems. The opposition comes to the fore in the interpretation of such detailed models according to a particular conceptual framework. For this project, it is important to specify the different conceptual frameworks as clearly as possible. Combining an interactionist approach with AT-styled representations does a disservice here. Rather then leading to a clear statement of the behavioral systems idea, it seems to obscure in advance how a behavioral system approach could be used as an explanation of behavior on its own.

BST consists of two central commitments, one positive, one negative.

a. The behavior of organisms (as well as of BST-based models) results from multiple, dynamical, reciprocal interactions between a neural system (or another control structure when it comes to the models), a sensory-musculo-skeletal system (or just embodiment in the robotic case) and an interaction space (the environment incorporated in the behavioral regularities).

b. The postulation and use of subpersonal representations (interpreted as an internal structure, isomorphic to the behaviorally relevant environment) to instruct behavior is rejected.

In addition to the unquestioned importance of the neural system, the first commitment stresses the equal importance of embodiment and situatedness. Both concepts have been mentioned above. They form the core of BST and reflect a departure from AT's focus on an abstracted and disconnected cognitive (neural) controlling structure. Embodiment conveys the importance of the specific set of sensors and actuators to which a neural control system is connected, as well as the dynamical regularities that derive from the embodiment. The body is a cohering system, which imposes its own dynamical regularities on the behavior. For example, Raibert's hopping robot (referred to as Hop in chapter 3) shows how the springiness of a leg acts as an important dynamical principle in making a robot that balances. The dynamics of the movements are not prescribed by internal instructions, they derive from the physical characteristics of the embodiment. The same goes for situatedness. The embodied agent is situated in an environment. The structure present in the environment is used by the behaving system to generate behavioral regularities. For example, Hop is situated on a hard, flat surface in a gravitational field. When Hop jumps, the gravity will pull the robot down again, compressing the air in Hop's leg, which is subsequently used in a second jump. The behavior exhibited by Hop is highly dependent on the characteristics of the environment. The control structure for such embodied and situated behavior does not instruct the movements; rather, it influences the dynamical relations that are already present in the embodiment and the environment. The general idea is pictured in figure 4.1, which shows the three systems that reciprocally influence one another. Together the neural (control) structure and the sensory-musculo-skeletal system make up the behaving system. In turn, the behaving system in conjunction with its situatedness (the interaction space)[1] constitute the total behavioral system.

Note that the interaction space is considered to be a part of the total behavioral system. Von Uexküll's *Umwelt* provides a way to think about this point. An organism comes equipped with a specific sensory-musculo-skeletal system that limit the environment it deals with. The sensory-musculo-skeletal system constrains the environment that becomes integrated in the behavioral relations initiated by the organism. The environmental processes that come to take part in the regular organization of a behaving system can be thought of as belonging to an extended metabolism, just as in

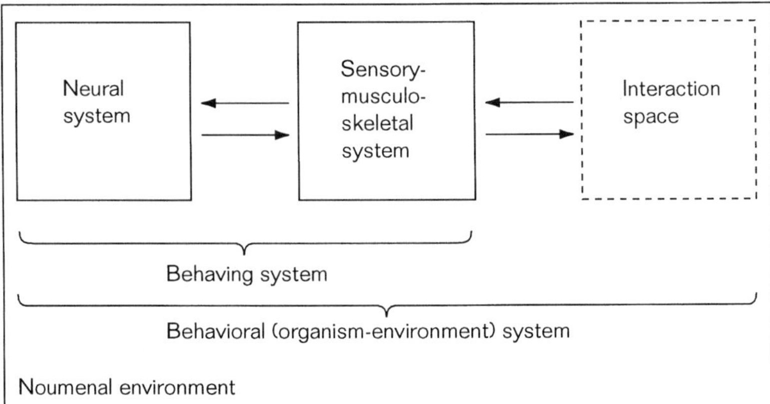

Figure 4.1
The idea of a behavioral (organism-environment) system.

the regulatory network that makes up the cellular and bodily metabolism. This extended metabolism can be said to define that part of the *noumenal* environment that forms the interaction space of the behaving system. It forms the environment as it is projected by the behaving system, not as it is interpreted by the observer.

The word 'coupling' will often be used to denote the reciprocal influencing between a behaving system and its environment. In the following sections, more specific interpretations of this general idea of coupling will be discussed. Maturana and Varela introduce the notion of structural coupling (section 2), while Van Gelder derives the idea of dynamical coupling from dynamical systems theory (section 4). Both interpretations fall within the more general notion of coupling as it is used here. However, neither is sufficiently broad to act as an actual replacement for coupling in the general sense.

The negative central commitment of BST—the rejection of a set of internal instructions—is already implied by the stress on the embodiment and situatedness as components which bring their own structure to bear on behavior. When this is accepted it follows self-evidently that behavior is not a derivative of internal instructions (provided by a modeling and planning mechanism). The important implication is that behavior has to be explained by different theoretical means then what is provided by AT. How a behavioral theory might eventually come to explain the adaptive and anticipatory behavior of animals and humans without representations might look like an awesome problem. However, it should be noted that explanations that do rely on representation do themselves not score very well in dealing with basic behavioral capacities.

In the following sections, I will discuss three ways in which BST has been developed so far. The first is a presentation of the ideas of Maturana and Varela as they bear on the idea of behavioral systems. Maturana and Varela's theory of life and cognition has been very influential within the interactionist approach to cognition and behavior (Beer, 1990, 1995a; Smithers, 1994; Winograd and Flores, 1986). Maturana and Varela are important for achieving a conceptual switch that lies at the basis of the behavioral systems idea and which involves an explanation of generating behavior without any agent-like entity or mechanism. Second, the field of Autonomous Agents Research (AAR) will be discussed. AAR is a practical enterprise that seeks to develop the notion of behavioral systems by building artificial agents that act in a natural environment. Third, the theory of dynamical systems will be discussed as another way to fill in the notion of behavioral systems. The theory of dynamical systems consists of a set of mathematical concepts and theories which can be used to model systems, consisting of many interacting parts. This set of ideas is sometimes presented as a way to make the idea of behavioral systems more concrete and sophisticated.

In all cases it will be argued that the theory or approach is a promising and stimulating way to *begin* to make sense of an explanation of behavior in terms of behavioral systems. However, there are important shortcomings with these attempts as they now stand. In their present form, they do not turn BST into a conceptual framework that can stand up to AT.

2 Maturana and Varela: behavior as a part of living organizations

Maturana and Varela have a long-standing reputation as the originators of some rather eccentric ideas on biology, cognition and language (Maturana and Varela, 1980, 1988; Maturana, 1978; Varela, Thompson, and Rosch, 1991). To illustrate what I mean by 'eccentric', here is a citation. Its meaning will become more clear later on.

Living systems in general, and their nervous systems in particular, are not made to handle a medium, although it has been through the handling of their medium that they have become what they are, such that we can say what we can say about them (Maturana and Varela, 1980, p. 56).

Despite the initial strangeness of their ideas, as well as the (sometimes) cryptic way in which they express them, the work of Maturana and Varela has been very influential in the interactionist movement. Their books "Autopoiesis and Cognition" (Maturana and Varela, 1980) and "The Tree of Knowledge" (ibid., 1988) are standard citations by proponents of an interactionist approach,[2] and their ideas have had a strong influence on the development of the idea of behavioral systems. Their work has in particular been an important inspiration for work on artificial autonomous agents (Beer, 1995a, Smithers, 1994) as will be discussed in later sections.

In 1959, Maturana co-authored the now classical article "What the frog's eye tells the frog's brain" (Lettvin et al., 1959). The article proved that the retina of the frog's eye did not send a more or less complete copy of the pattern of incoming light rays to the frog's brain. Instead, what was sent consisted of the presence (or not) of a small number of basic and highly specific features, corresponding with relevant environmental factors like, for example, small moving dots (flies) and large shaded edges (predators). His reputation settled, his work shifted to more generally theoretical issues related to biology. Among them were two central questions: "What is the organization of the living?" and "What takes place in the phenomenon of perception?" (Maturana and Varela, 1980). Finally, he decided that both questions addressed the same phenomenon: "cognition and the operation of the living system—its nervous system included when present—were the same thing" (ibid., pp. xvi–xvii). Working together with his former student Varela, this insight led eventually to the two books mentioned above.

Probably the most interesting contribution of Maturana and Varela to the idea of behavioral systems is their consistency in formulating a conceptual framework which is not a mechanized, subpersonal version of the personal-level descriptions of a behaving, thinking system. More specifically, they approached the issues of behavior and cognition as aspects of a living organization: A theory of behavior and cognition has to fit the fact that these phenomena are to be produced by a local operating nervous system, situated in a body, interacting with an environment. They carefully avoid the problems associated with theoretical hitchhiking. Following this premise they ended up with a view on behavior and cognition which may look strange at first. Still, given the sound premise on which it is based it should receive our due attention.

The following will be a skewed introduction of Maturana and Varela's ideas, primarily dedicated to their contributions to BST.[3] I will focus on what they call the *operational closure* of the nervous system, as well as the *structural coupling* in which it takes part. The notion of operational closure is a consistent source of difficulties and confusions. It is sometimes interpreted as anti-realism, and thought of as the problematic part of Maturana and Varela's position (Clark, 1997a; Mingers, 1990). However, operational closure is also at the heart of a conceptual switch that separates the conceptual framework of AT from that of BST: It leads to an account of behavior which does away with the view that the operation of a nervous system is somehow 'agent-like' and replaces it by a more consistently subpersonal approach. Getting clear on this issue is important to understand how exactly BST is different from AT.

2.1 A long-standing puzzle: naturalism's tendencies towards idealism

According to Maturana and Varela, behavior and cognition—both the phenomena itself as well as our (the observer's) knowledge of it—are to be explained by naturalistic means. These premises lead them to ideas that do not correspond with the common sense notion of an independently existing world, which is subsequently perceived by humans and other animals. This implication of a strict naturalism is not only noticed by Maturana and Varela. It is a logical—and troubling—consequence of the naturalistic position.

The ideal of a fully naturalistic science of the mind is not new. While eighteenth century philosophers already toyed with the idea, in the nineteenth century there was a genuine scientific attempt to incorporate mental phenomena into the physical, world as described by the natural sciences (Young, 1970). Explanations involving mental phenomena should no longer refer to nonnatural entities. Such explanations should (ultimately) be based on the activity of the nervous system.

Surprisingly enough, it turned out that the 'tough', materialistic and naturalistic point of view which envisioned mind as a product of a physical brain tended to shift into its opposite, a subjective idealism. While at first the physical world was thought to give rise to mental phenomena, the view suddenly changed into one where the positions were reversed: mind was seen to give rise to the physical world! This paradoxal relation was quickly pointed out. Gottlob Frege, for instance, wrote in 1879: "This flowing into idealism is the most remarkable in physiological psychology, because it is in such sharp contrast to its realistic starting point" (Sluga, 1980, p. 31). The existence of this relation has always haunted naturalism and has often been used to attack the internal consistency of the naturalistic position.

The basis for this relation between naturalism and idealism was laid by Johannes Müller, one of the great German physiologists of the first half of the nineteenth century. He formulated a "Law of specific nerve energies" (Müller, 1848; Reed, 1987). Müller noted that the sensory quality of a stimulation is a function of the stimulated nerve, irrespective of the actual, external source of the stimulation. Hitting the ear produces the sensation of sound, while pressing the eye makes us see light without either sound or light being present. Müller concluded thereupon that "external agencies can give rise to no kind of sensation which cannot be produced by internal causes, exciting changes in the conditions of our nerves" (Müller, 1848, p. 115). But if we do not know the external objects themselves, but only what is produced by the nervous system, then it opens up the possibility for all kinds of skepticism regarding the reality of the external world. Everything sensed consists ultimately of brain states, without a guarantee that these will correspond with the real, external situation. Acceptance of the naturalistic point of view implies that mind should abide by the constraints set by the underlying physiological substrate, just as someone traveling by train cannot make a trip which is rendered impossible by the train's timetable. As a consequence, what we (can) see and think depends on the brain, rather than on the world.

The resulting puzzle is nicely worded by Bertrand Russell: "If physics is true then we are aware not of the world, but of our brains; yet, if this be so, it is well-nigh impossible that we could have come to have knowledge of the physical world" (Reed, 1987, p. 216). The idealistic implications of a strict naturalism are so patently absurd—in particular for most naturalists themselves—that almost no one sees it as a serious issue for a fully naturalistic psychology. One simply maintains the position that cognitive processes have to be realizable by physiological means, *and* the idea that cognitive processes incorporate knowledge which goes beyond the brain and touches on a 'real', independently existing, external world. The centrality and importance of both assumptions seems to suffice to convince most people that there can be no serious discrepancies between the two. Still, the question remains: how both are to be combined?

How to deal with this situation? Maturana and Varela make an important theoretical move here, which gives a different twist to the problem. Instead of providing an answer as to how a nervous system could overcome its intrinsic limitations, they state that a nervous system does not (need to) overcome these limitations. A nervous system does not 'know' what happens external to it, but at the same time it operates in such a way that adaptive behavior, as witnessed by an external observer, is produced. The result is a theory which "is like walking on the razor's edge" between realism and relativism (1988, p. 133). On the one hand there is the impossibility of accounting for cognitive phenomena when the objective world of independently existing objects is simply assumed, and on the other hand there is the arbitrariness of relativism in which the objective world of independently existing objects is said not to exist (ibid.). Both are to be avoided.

2.2 Life and behavior as autopoiesis: operational closure and structural coupling

Maturana and Varela state that behavior and cognition are aspects of a living organization. Thus, to understand behavior and cognition it is necessary to start out with the nature of living systems. The first of Maturana's two initial questions addresses this topic: "What is the organization of the living?" The ideas of Maturana and Varela on behavior and cognition are extensions of their theory of the living organization.

What do all living systems have in common? The answer that Maturana and Varela give is 'self-production', a process for which they invented the term *autopoiesis*. Autopoiesis takes place when there is a circularly organized network of interactions which maintains itself over extended periods, and which has a well-defined border or membrane— limiting the organization in space—which is also maintained by the circular organization (Varela, Maturana, and Uribe, 1974). The most basic form of autopoiesis is at the cellular level, and autopoiesis is also most easily explained in that context. At a cellular level, the autopoietic organization consists of a network of chemical reactions, which together produce the same network of chemical reactions at a later time, and so on. The principle is that of autocatalytic sets (Kauffman, 1995). An autocatalytic set consists of a network of chemical reactants that mutually catalyze their own production from an abundance of simple, raw chemical ingredients. Initially, there are few of these reactants, but because of their reciprocal catalyzation which works as a positive feedback loop, the substances within the autocatalytic set are continuously produced until they exist in (comparatively) large quantities. An autocatalytic set can maintain itself over time, as long as there are sufficient basic ingredients and sufficient energy to maintain the reactions.

An autopoietic organization is more complex than a simple autocatalytic set. First because an autopoietic organization also involves the production of a boundary which contains the circularly organized network of reactions and prevents dispersal of its components. Second, it involves much more self-regulation than an autocatalytic set. The latter is a large, positive feedback loop which will expand as long as its requirements of basic components and energy are fulfilled. The autopoietic organization is self-regulating, involving checks and balances. It modulates its own self-production.

Maturana and Varela stress that the notion of autopoiesis refers to self-production and that this does not necessarily involve self-reproduction (Varela, Maturana, and Uribe, 1974). Their theory applies to the living organization itself. They state that the universal capacity of biological organisms to reproduce themselves is essential to understand how life developed on Earth. However, autopoiesis refers to the kind of organization that has evolved and that is reproduced from one generation to the next: The organization which is manifest in every individual living system. The autopoietic organization is neutral with respect to evolutionary processes, although its current manifestations are all the result of evolutionary processes.

An autopoietic organization allows the continuing existence of intrinsically unstable processes—chemical reactions which would run down as soon as their ingredients are exhausted, or their boundary conditions (e.g., temperature or acidity) changed. Because an autopoietic system maintains its own organization it acquires a certain autonomy from its environment. Instead of being dependent on an external source of, for example, catalytic ingredients, it manufactures its own. Similarly, it can develop energy storage capacities which makes it less dependent on a continuous source of energy provided by the environment. As a result, an autopoietic organization can maintain its integrity under a variety of environmental states and is autonomous in that sense.

Here, the two concepts can be introduced that play a crucial role in Maturana and Varela's account of behavior (and cognition) as this bears on BST: operational closure and structural coupling. *Operational closure* refers to the bounded, environment independent nature of an autopoietic system. An autopoietic organization has its own structure which is independent from the structure present in the environment. The structure of a living organization is produced and maintained by the autopoietic system itself. A living organization on a beach does not derive its structure from the sand or the water that are present; it creates its own organization. The environmental structure cannot be injected into the circularly organized network of interactions that make up the autopoietic system. The metabolism of a cell is a self-contained set of interacting processes. An environmental process outside the cell does not impose its own order on the cellular metabolism. On the other hand, external happenings do affect the closed, circular organization of the autopoietic system. This brings us to the complement of operational closure, *structural coupling.*

"We speak of structural coupling whenever there is a history of recurrent interactions leading to the structural congruence between two (or more) systems" (Maturana and Varela, 1988, p. 75). A living system is closed insofar that its organization is self-produced and not derived from external circumstances. At the same time, these external circumstances are essential for the continuation of the autopoietic system. Some environmental disturbances can destroy the autopoietic organization. The system can only produce its own components and maintain its integrity as long as the external conditions fall within certain limits (e.g., temperature, the presence of an energy source, or chemical conditions). When these limits are exceeded, the system will collapse and disintegrate. On the other hand, there are also external circumstances which will only perturb the autopoietic organization. A perturbation will not lead to the disintegration of the system, but it will trigger a series of changes (where the capacity to change derives from the living organization) which will allow the living organization to maintain its integrity by counteracting the perturbation. A cell can change the permeability of its membrane to counteract fluctuations in the chemical makeup of its surroundings. When this works repeatedly, it constitutes a history of recurrent interactions between the system and the environment, in which both are "structurally congruent" and where the autopoietic organization will maintain its integrity over extended time-periods.

Thus autopoiesis involves two separate, but intimately intertwined processes: an operationally closed living organization with its own structure, and a structural coupling of the living organization with an external environment which can perturb the living organization in repeatable ways so that the living organization makes appropriate changes in its current processes that will help it maintain itself given the new external circumstances.

Maturana and Varela see behavior and cognition as extensions of this basic autopoietic organization. Behavior and cognition extend the structural couplings of the living organization beyond the molecular, physicochemical processes occurring at a cellular scale. The extension relies on the same autopoietic principles. Leaving the behavior of cellular organisms alone, the behavior of multicellular organisms is tied up with the activity of a nervous system. Maturana and Varela view the operation of a nervous system as a local process, in this sense not different from that of any other bodily organ. It consists of the interactions of a collection of neural cells, whose activity is bounded by the states of the sensors and the motor-neurons. This neural activity does not incorporate external happenings or instructions for external effects. The activity of the nervous system is limited to manipulating the states of the sensor surfaces by varying the states of its motor-neurons. Changing the way in which the muscular system is activated leads to systematic readjustments of the measure and kind of stimulation received by the sensor surfaces. Movements of the head cause systematic shifts in the patterns of stimulation falling on the retina, and the proprioceptors monitoring this part of the muscular system. The relations between effectors and sensors so form a loop, by which activity generated within the nervous system feeds back again on the operationally closed nervous system.

One consequence of this interpretation of the nervous system's operation is, for example, Maturana and Varela's protest against information processing as a basis for psychology. The generally held idea in cognitivist psychology is that a cognitive system takes in and processes information coming from the environment by means of a perceptual process and subsequently uses the information to guide its behavior. Maturana and Varela deny that the operation of the nervous system is to be described in terms of information processing. The environment can never *specify* changes within the cognitive system. The environment does not deliver information which is picked up by and then internally replicated by the nervous system. The environment can only trigger processes that the nervous system is capable of, just as Müller's Law states. The idea can be clarified by a comparison with the accelerator of a car. The foot's pressure on the accelerator does not set the car in motion. Rather, a car is built in such a way that it is capable of self-movement. What happens is that this structure is connected to the accelerator so that the movement of the car is made dependent on the presence or absence of an external perturbation. The foot's pressure is not turned into the movement of the car, but the foot's pressure brings the car in a state in which it moves. In the same way Maturana and Varela hold that a nervous system does not take in external stimulations which are subsequently processed. The structure present within the nervous system is independent from the structure present in the environment, the former merely changes its internal states under the influence of external perturbations. It is misleading to use the notion of information without involving the system for which such system-bounded-triggers are supposed to form 'information'.

The operational closure of the nervous system is only half the tale that Maturana and Varela have to tell. The relevance of this closed, circular organization for the maintenance of a living system by autopoiesis hinges all the time on the external happenings which are its results. A part of the circular organization runs, as if it were by accident, through the environment of the organism. The nervous system operates independently from the environment, but at the same time it hangs in a web of relations with the environment which enable the operationally closed organization to have specific environmental effects. As a result, changes and variations of the internal process consistently bring about external effects which are beneficial for the chances of survival for the organism. For example, the activity of the nervous system modulates the sensory-motor system in a way that brings edible substances into the mouth. Maturana and Varela's insistence on the operational closure of the nervous system is therefore not a plea for studying the brain and forgetting about the environment. Their point is that the brain operates independently of the environment, even when it takes part in a constant interaction with the environment. To use the quote that I started with:

> Living systems in general, and their nervous systems in particular, are not made to handle a medium, although it has been through the handling of their medium that they have become what they are, such that we can say what we can say about them (Maturana and Varela, 1980, p. 56).

To summarize, Maturana and Varela interpret the operation of the nervous system as a circular, strictly local process, which takes place independently of the external environment. In no way is it presupposed that the nervous system represents the things happening outside of it. At the same time this operationally closed system is in continuous interaction with the external environment. When the closed organization is perturbed by an environmental feature to which it is "structurally congruent," the closed organization changes its internal processes in such a way that the environmental disturbance is dealt with in an appropriate way. This splitting up *and* intertwining of the internal operation of the nervous system and the external organism-environment interactions is a central point of Maturana and Varela's ideas on behavior and cognition. However, to be able to describe the behaving system in this way it is essential to explicate another important factor: *who* is describing the system?

2.3 The submarine in the noumenon

Maturana and Varela connect the operational closure and structural coupling of behaving, living systems to two complementary perspectives on cognitive systems, an internal and an external one. The internal perspective is a description from the inside, constrained within the borders set out by the effectors and sensors of the cognitive system. An internal perspective does not extend beyond the brain or, more generally, the nervous system. In this case, the environment is only present as the perturbations it imposes on the living system, something which depends on the available neural structures. In contrast, an external perspective is provided by an external observer who views the system from the outside. An external observer is not bounded by the first system's physiological borders (of course, when it comes to its own operation, the observer-system is in turn limited by its own physiological borders). From an external position it is possible to view both the behaving system and the environment in which it acts. And only in this case is it legitimate to view the cognitive system as an entity which acts adaptively in an independent, external environment. To illustrate how a 'blind' brain can produce adaptive behavior, Maturana and Varela use the following analogy:

> Imagine a person who has always lived in a submarine. He has never left it and has been trained how to handle it. Now, we are standing on the shore and see the submarine gracefully surfacing. We then get on the radio and tell the navigator inside: "Congratulations! You avoided the reefs and surfaced beautifully. You really now how to handle a submarine." The navigator in the submarine, however, is perplexed: "What's this about reefs and surfacing? All I did was push some levers and turn knobs and make certain relationships between indicators as I operated the levers and knobs. It was done in prescribed sequence which I'm used to. I didn't do any special maneuver, and on top of that, you talk to me about a submarine. You must be kidding!" (1988, pp. 136–137)

A nervous system is situated in a position similar to that of the submarine's navigator. The nervous system doesn't have any access to—it doesn't know about—anything that happens outside of it. It is organized so that it modulates a number of parameters, made available by the make up of the system (an indicator for it has to be present), which are relevant for maneuvering the boat in that environment. The activity of the nervous system (the navigator) based on this internal organization and local sensor disturbances is sufficient to guide the boat through a complex environment. This latter description in terms of adaptively relevant behavior is however not available to the behaving system itself, but only to an external observer who has an overview of the system and the environment in which it acts.

I like the submarine story as a way of visualizing an otherwise very abstract set of ideas. It illustrates how the internal (operationally closure) and the external (structural coupling) perspectives are different, as well as how they come together in the living organization. The story also offers a handle to discuss a number of complexities that are connected to Maturana and Varela's conception of living and behaving systems.

For one, the submarine story illustrates the idea that behavior results from a local operating system, just like any other natural system. Behavior results when a behaving system—a system which can only access a number of parameters to which it happens to be sensitive because of its particular construction—interacts with an undefined external situation (for this behaving system). The nervous system is not invested with personal-level powers such as knowledge, information, or intentionality in order to understand its operation in the context of behavior.

Second, the story conveys the idea that the submarine establishes its own interaction space or *Umwelt*. The sensor readings to which it is sensitive allow a structural coupling with only certain aspects of the external environment. The world as it features in behavioral theory is made relative to the behaving system. The world of the external observer and the one of the behaving system do not (self-evidently) coincide.

The submarine story is also instructive for its flaws. When a nervous system is in the position of the submarine's navigator, then the same would apply to the nervous system of the observer who is watching the actions of the first submarine from the outside. Given Maturana and Varela's model, the external observer will herself only be capable of inspecting her own indicators, when monitoring the activity of another submarine. When the two submarines are more or less similar, the two navigators will access similar indicators. The observer will see a remarkable example of lever pushing and knob turning on its indicators and will send a remark to that effect. In turn, the compliment will be received by the first navigator in the form of some other indicator-states. The confusion, described in the story, will never take place, which, of course, nicely concurs with our daily experience.

At this point, the question can be asked how the submarine story does relate to our everyday subjective experience. The vocabulary of an internal and an external *perspective* suggests a personal-level theory involving a person whose perspective it is. This may be, and Maturana and Varela definitely attend to the topic of human experience (see also Varela, Thompson, and Rosch, 1991). However, the present aim is subpersonal and behavioral, and the ideas of Maturana and Varela are used as a contribution to the idea of behavioral systems. In this context, there is no room for experiential, personal-level subjective positions. The two perspectives are better interpreted as two idealized positions suitable for describing behaving living systems (see also note 5, chapter 3).

Under this interpretation, the internal perspective is that of the (subpersonal) nervous system, not that of the personal-level, cognizing individual. It is an abstract theoretical description of the activity of the nervous system. The external perspective is also highly abstract. It describes the interaction of a cognitive system with 'the real world', the reefs and the submarine in Maturana and Varela's story. These reefs form the world as it exists independently of the behaving system and in which the behaving system has to act. Given Maturana and Varela's model, an independently existing environment is an impossible element within a description. We are all submarine navigators. None of us can look further than his or her own indicator states, the environment as specified by our own nervous system. The 'real' environment, as figuring within the external perspective, consists of a Kantian *noumenon*, a thing as it is in itself, independent of our knowledge of it and therefore by definition beyond our knowing it. The external position then is a perspective which no observer can truly hold. It shows the 'strictly impossible' task faced by psychology of developing a theory which specifies how a nervous system situated in a body is capable of initiating and maintaining an evolutionary adaptive (autopoietic) interaction with a *noumenon*. The external perspective is an idealization, important to understand the operation of cognitive systems, but in practice it forms a limiting case which we can never actually reach. The internal and external perspectives are, as is so often the case in science, idealized theoretical points of view. They must not be equated to subjective positions held by human beings. The submarine story is a didactic analogy which brings into focus an otherwise difficult to understand aspect of the interactions between cognitive systems and their environments. It is comparable with Einstein's vision of himself riding on a light-ray: impossible but insightful.

The submarine story also provides a convenient way to illustrate Maturana and Varela's razor's edge position with respect to realism and relativism. Within the story, the sea, the reefs, surfacing, and so forth consist of *noumena*, entities that are beyond the indicators available to the navigator. In this respect Maturana and Varela advocate relativism. An autopoietic organization can never know the external world as it (really) is, independent of its interactions with this external world: All we have is specific neural structures that allow us to see things in certain ways and not others. Their position is a realist one, insofar that the performance of differently structured 'submarines' (or organisms) is highly variable and dependent on an external 'something'. The navigator may not know what is really happening outside the submarine, but the sequences used by the navigator to push levers and turn knobs, as well as the available indicators, all are highly relevant for traversing the *noumenon* successfully. If the navigator had been sloppy the reefs would not have been avoided and instead of surfacing beautifully the submarine would have sunk. The internal structure may not 'reflect' reality, it is far from arbitrary either. The structure of the nervous system does not derive from the *noumenon*, but its existence depends on its capacity to deal with it. Consequently, except for malfunctions, most nervous systems that will be encountered in life have a strong structural congruency to a particular environment.

Does the capacity to deal with the *noumenon* not imply a straightforward realist position? Evolutionary epistemologists, for example, steer toward the conclusion that (some form of) truth and realism can be based on adaptationism (Campbell, 1973; Lorenz, 1973; Plotkin, 1994). For good reasons, Maturana and Varela oppose this interpretation and profess their own razor's edge position between relativism and realism. First, adaptation is no proof that there is an internal description of the external situation. The legs of a horse do not describe a relatively flat surface in a gravitational field. The legs of a horse only make it possible to traverse such surfaces efficiently. Second, the important implication of their ideas is that the external environment (as a *noumenon*) is always fluent and transient. It can never be tied down in any permanent way, independent of a particular living organization. An analogy that I find useful in this context is to compare the *noumenon* with the mathematical notion of an infinitely large number. Infinity is always out of reach. Any finite number, however big it is, is not infinitely large. Within the realm of finite numbers, we can compare different numbers, compute their difference, and so on in a nonarbitrary way. It makes sense to say that 10 is bigger than 5, or that 95 is closer to 100 than 94. However, the question of which number is closer to infinity is of a very different stature. No finite number can be considered to be closer to infinity than any other. Compared to an infinite difference, any finite difference, no matter how large, is negligible in comparison. To translate this analogy into the *noumenon* context, the message is that the choice of neural structure is extremely important as our continuing existence depends on it (realism), but at the same time no structure can be said to come any closer to the *noumenon* (relativism).

So far, the principled inaccessibility of the *noumenon* has been stressed. This is an important issue, because it points at the fluidity, and transient nature of any environmental description. However, in practice we can, and must, use particular descriptions as (good-enough) approximations of the *noumenon*. For example, when the behavior of a *Sphex* wasp is described, we, as observers, can take our own description of the environment as an approximation of the *noumenon* to which the wasp's behavior is oriented. Subsequently, it can be investigated how this wasp succeeds in generating its own *Umwelt* within this *noumenal world*. Such an approximation is usually sufficient to track the structural couplings between the behaving system and its *Umwelt*. However, any description will never be more than an approximation of the real thing.

This matter of principle has important practical consequences when constructing artificial behaving systems (see section 3). While a robot has to behave in a *noumenon*, it is often much simpler to develop first a simulated robot that behaves in a simulated environment. A simulated environment is a fully described environment, while the used descriptions derive from the observer. A simulated environment (and embodiment) will always miss aspects of the real environment and embodiment. When a robot is developed and tested first in a simulation and found adequate there, it happens often that the resulting design does not perform adequately when it is turned into hardware. The real world tends to have many unforeseen characteristics that can be overlooked and left out of the simulation (ranging from sensor variability, unforeseen surface-reflectances, and so on). Only with hindsight is it shown that such features are essential for the behavior. The message should be clear: The environment as we describe it for ourselves is not the environment in which a behaving system has to act.

2.4 Maturana and Varela's contribution to BST

Why should the view put forward by Maturana and Varela be accepted? One good reason is their thorough naturalism. Their view follows from the premise that behavior and cognition are aspects of a living system. Their first priority lies with giving a fully naturalistic model of life, behavior, and cognition. They do not take our subjective, personal-level view at face value as a veridical *description* of the processes involved in behavior and cognition. In this they depart from AT-based cognitive theorizing with its roots in the Anglo-Saxon philosophy of mind. Maturana and Varela incorporate the idealism-related (or relativistic) tendencies of naturalism rather than try to develop a theory that opposes this tendency.

The contrast shows up clearly when the submarine story is compared to a classical thought experiment in cognitivist psychology: the Chinese room of John Searle (1980). The Chinese room consists of a closed room in which an English-speaking person sits who computes by hand. The whole Chinese room so forms a computer in which a human being does the computations. The Chinese room runs a program which enables it to answer in Chinese questions posed to it in Chinese, while the person inside the room does not speak Chinese at all. He just instantiates the program. The result is from the outside a Chinese-speaking room which from the point of view of the person inside does not know what it is doing.

The Chinese room and the submarine story are much alike. However, the interpretations given to these stories couldn't be more different. Searle uses his story as a criticism of computational models. The Chinese room shows, according to Searle, that there is no internal 'understanding' of the externally viewed behaving of the room, and therefore computational models ought to be dismissed as models of cognition. In response, those who disagree with Searle's conclusion try to show that computational models and even the Chinese room can actually be said to have the 'understanding' that is denied by Searle (Hofstadter and Dennett, 1981). However, Maturana and Varela use their similar thought experiment to show that there is no need to postulate such internal 'understanding' when you want to explain how a system is capable of adaptive behavior.

These differences in interpretation hang together with Searle's and with Maturana and Varela's different starting positions. Searle takes the commonsense idea that we have knowledge of an independently existing world as a basic fact which has to be taken at face value and accounted for by cognitivist psychology. A theory which doesn't fulfill this demand is to be criticized for it. Maturana and Varela, on the other hand, start from the position that we are living organisms who can know the world only as far as the make up of our nervous systems allows it. What this 'knowing' amounts to remains an open question which still needs to be answered. In this perspective, commonsense ideas concerning knowledge and realism do not have to be taken at face value: There is no reason to presuppose that current common sense forms a solid basis for describing the relation between cognitive systems and their environment. The result is a liberation of cognitivist preconceptions of adaptive behavior as a result of an intelligent (or intelligently programmed) agent that executes its plans (or programs) in a preset world.

The change in outlook on the generation of behavior, as provided by Maturana and Varela, is an important step in formulating Behavioral Systems Theory as a conceptual framework that may eventually replace AT. This change of perspective has been a source of inspiration for the building of relatively simple robots that can behave adaptively in the real world. Despite the fact that such robots are not living systems, designing and building them involves a starting position very similar to that of living systems that are to behave: How can a collection of parts, including sensors, effectors, and a control structure be put together so that, in a particular environment, adaptive behavioral regularities result? Maturana and Varela are important as they claim that there is no need to use an AT-styled architecture and that it is important to work with real environments rather than with a description of it (as is done in simulation work in contrast to real robotics).

On the other hand, the work done with robotics is important for the ideas of Maturana and Varela as well. Robots provide a way to put their ideas to the test and to see whether these ideas do actually result in a better account of the generation of behavior than AT provides. This practical work is also essential to develop the idea of behavioral systems in a more concrete way, and as such it is a further step in giving BST a definite form.

3 Autonomous Agents Research[4]

Artificial Life is the general and now quickly developing enterprise of producing all sorts of life-like phenomena by artificial means (Langton, 1989). Autonomous Agents Research is one of its branches. It is the project of developing agents or 'animats' which are capable of adaptive behavior in a real-world environment. This is usually done by handcrafting such animats (Brooks, 1989, 1991b), but attempts are under way to evolve them by means of artificial evolution (Harvey, Husbands, and Cliff, 1993). AAR seeks primarily, but not exclusively (Brooks and Stein, 1993), to build 'simple' animal-like agents such as insectoids or wheeled vehicles capable of doing tasks like moving about in an office environment. Within AAR it is the organism-environment interaction which is deemed most important, not the complexity of the agent involved in such an interaction. Preferably, modeling takes place with real, non-simulated agents and environments. In real-world circumstances there are always unsuspected disturbances and noise with which the agent must cope if it is to behave successfully and which will never be fully captured in a simulation. Nevertheless, for matters of feasibility a lot of research is actually done either as, or in close coordination with, simulation studies (Meyer and Wilson, 1991; Mondada and Verschure, 1993). However, the real challenge within this field remains real-world artifacts.

3.1 AAR's interpretation of behavioral systems

On a small scale, the building of simple behavioral agents has been going on for almost a century. Loeb (1918) reported a light finding automaton of the Braitenberg variety (Braitenberg, 1984); Tolman and Hull, leading behaviorists in the thirties, both used 'artificial organisms' to elaborate and test their ideas (Tolman, 1939; Cordeschi, 1991); and in the fifties, under the influence of cybernetics, Grey Walter (1953) built his famous Turtle creatures. While building autonomous agents was never more than a fringe affair for psychology, in the sixties and seventies people were even less interested in building simple 'creatures' as a way to understand behavior. In that period, interest shifted in a massive way toward the modeling of the internal cognitive system, as prescribed by AT, which computer modeling was then just turning into a respectable and viable research area (Arbib, 1975). In the new *cognitive* science, behavior was seen as the execution of preformed 'plans for action', and the problem of adaptive behavior was turned into that of getting the cognitive control structure right. This picture changed in the eighties when people working in robotics became more and more dissatisfied with the 'cognition first policy' (Brooks, 1991c). Their part was to fill in the last stage of the AT strategy; to put all separate sense, model, plan, and act bits together to form a real agent. Thus, they were also the first to really encounter the limitations and problems of AT as a framework for understanding behavior. The robots made according to this principle simply did not perform well in real-world environments. The real world is always cluttered with objects and full of unpredictable events, which makes it difficult or even impossible to succeed using detailed, preconceived plans. Such robots spent too much time thinking, leaving no time to act.

Confronted with this situation, Rodney Brooks achieved a major breakthrough by simply omitting the cognitive architecture prescribed by AT. He started to build simple robots which did not 'know' what they were doing and which did not plan any actions. They were designed so that they would first exhibit basic but real behavioral capacities. Subsequently, more complex behavioral capacities were added on top of the existing ones. In this way a robot became capable of increasingly complex behavior (Brooks, 1989, 1991a, 1991b).[5] The result consisted of insect-like robots which had very robust behavioral capacities and which were much more successful in real environments than anything built up to that time. In this way Brooks's autonomous robots and those subsequently developed by the AAR movement which sprang up in his foot steps form a basic challenge to the established AT solution to the problem of behavior.

In the wake of this material success, several ideas important within behavior-based AAR became popular and somewhat convincing as an alternative for AT. Of extreme importance was the acknowledgment of the fundamental relevance of embodiment and situatedness (Brooks, 1991a). The idea of a cognitive system computing an abstract input-output function was discarded. Intelligence came to be viewed as intrinsically related to the capacity for adaptive behavior, a capacity which depended on the specifics of the body and the environment of the agent (Barwise, 1987; Beer, 1990). A body and an environment were said to be their own model. Their characteristics did not have to be replicated within the agent's cognitive structure. For example, forward motion does not involve first planning a possible trajectory and subsequently executing the plan. Instead, an embodied structure generates movements which in a particular environment result in forward motion. The trajectory does not exist beforehand as a plan; it emerges for the first time when forward motion occurs. The controlling structure does not represent the structure of the embodiment and the situation but relies on their continuous presence to accomplish adaptive behavior. The internal cognitive system necessary for this task is much less general and complicated than an AT-styled general problem solver. In other words, a relatively simple controlling architecture helps create relatively complex behavior. The stress on embodiment and situatedness makes AAR an enterprise dedicated to the behavioral systems idea. The agent and the environment together make up a more general system in which adaptive behavior takes place. Compared to the classical conception, here the input and output have themselves become part of the system of interest.

Brooks also drew attention to a point that has already been discussed above: The basic behavioral capacities that humans share with the other vertebrate and invertebrate animals is much harder to achieve than most researchers on cognition and behavior tend to think. To solve the problems that arise in this area, basic behavior needs much more attention. Truly intelligent robots should be capable of dealing with the same environment that humans and other animals inhabit. They should be capable of moving about, pass over obstacles, avoid running into things, and make sure that it is safe to cross a street. Behaviors that we perform without paying attention to them provide extremely difficult tasks for a roboticist. And, as it turned out, the same goes for almost all of invertebrate (insect-like) behavior. Thus, irrespective whether there are good models for dealing with 'really' cognitive domains, these basic behavioral capacities have to be tackled by roboticists. This awareness imparted great relevance to the study of simple biological agents, as a route to understanding and modeling more complex organism-environment interactions.

In summary, AAR arrives at the following interpretation of the behavioral systems idea: Behavior consists of the outcome of an integrated system consisting of a computational (or a neural) control structure in close interaction with a specific embodiment and situatedness. The specifics of observed behavior arise from the makeup of the embodied agent, the environment in which it acts and the ways in which they physically interact. It makes no sense to talk about the cognitive control structure without considering the embodiment and environment to which it is tied. AAR studies and models the resulting organism-environment interactions by building animats which exhibit adaptive behavior in real environments (a *noumenon*). Intelligent behavior is accounted for without resorting to higher-level, agent-related concepts.

3.2 Behavioral systems as incremental robot-building: the subsumption architecture

AAR is a very practical affair. Its strength derives primarily from the physical robots that are built and which provide hard to ignore evidence of the soundness of its principles. Given this base in practicality, the best way to sketch AAR's way of handling the idea of behavioral systems is by considering its method of creating robots. Most notable here is an incremental approach to robot building, leading to what Brooks calls a *subsumption architecture* for robots (Brooks, 1986, 1989, 1991a).

This approach starts by creating a robot with at least some behavioral capacity, however simple. This capacity provides a bottom layer of both behavior as well as a control structure. The subsumption part consists of using this basic capacity as a building block to construct more complex ones. These, in turn, can become elements subsumed in even more complex behavioral capacities. For instance, a six-legged robot and control structure is built which, from an initial 'body-grounded' position, stands up and remains standing when perturbed. When this works, a second control structure can be added on top of the original one, which remains intact, to make the robot move forward. When the robot falls down, the first level sets it on its feet again and the robot can again try to move forward. Once the new two-level structure has been tested and debugged, the robot is capable of both standing up and moving forward. The same procedure can be repeated to add increasingly complex behavioral capacities. Every behavioral capacity involves sensing, control, and behavior. Brooks contrasts the resulting subsumption architecture of robots built in this way to the AT-styled sense-model-plan-act architecture (figure 4.2).

Let's look at one of Brooks's six-legged robots in some detail (Brooks, 1989). As said, the robot has six legs, is about 35 centimeters long, has a leg span of 25 centimeter, and weighs approximately 1 kilogram. The legs are rigid. Each one is attached to a shoulder joint, has two rotational degrees of freedom, and is driven by two orthogonally mounted, position controllable servo motors. These motors are called the α motor (α for advance) and the β motor (β for balance). The α motor swings the leg back and forth. The β motor lifts the leg up and down. The sensors consist of a crude force measurement on each axis of the legs (derived by tapping the internal servo circuitry of the motors when the leg is not in motion along that axis). Further there are two front whiskers, two inclinometers for pitch and roll, and six passive infrared sensors that cover a 45 degrees forward looking span.

The control system consists of a network of augmented finite state machines (AFSMs). These augmented finite state machines consist of registers, an internal timer (clock), a combinatorial network, and a regular

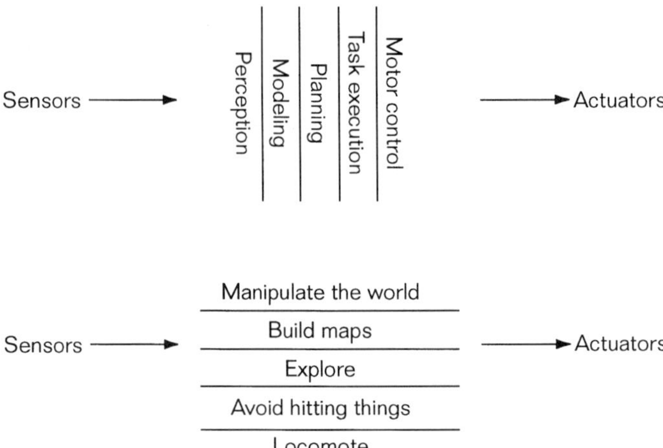

Figure 4.2
Brooks' subsumption architecture (bottom) contrasted with AT's sense-model-plan-act architecture (top). (Redrawn from Brooks, 1991c. Reprinted with permission from R. A. Brooks. Copyright 1991, American Association for the Advancement of Science.)

finite state machine (a computer with a limited number of internal states). Registers can be written by attaching input wires to them, over which messages coming from other machines or sensors are sent, erasing the former content of the register. The arrival of a message, or the expiration of a timer, can trigger a change of state in the finite state machine. The output of the AFSM goes to other AFSMs, or are direct commands to actuators.

An initial network of these augmented finite state machines provides the robot with a certain behavioral repertoire. A new network can be added to the old one as a second layer on top of the existing one. The new layer leaves the old layer intact; it only provides additions to the existing network. In this way, after testing and fine-tuning the combined network, there is a robot with its previously existing behavioral capacity intact, while a new behavioral capacity is added.

The additions can influence the existing network in several ways. For one, new inputs can be connected to the registers of existing AFSMs. Second, new AFSMs can inhibit the output or suppress the input of existing AFSMs by being connected as side-taps to existing wires (see figure 4.3). Inhibiting requires a continuous flow of messages along the new, tapping

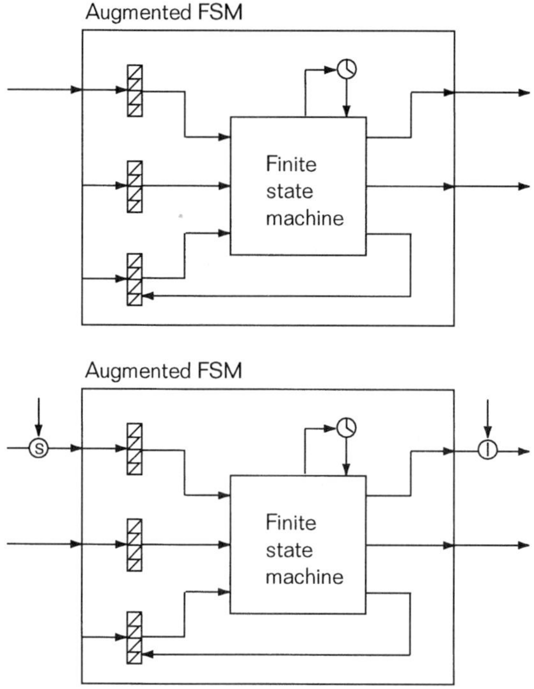

Figure 4.3
An augmented finite state machine with registers, a timer, and a combinatorial network (top). A new layer is added by making new connections to the existing AFSM's (bottom). (Redrawn from Brooks, 1989.)

wire. When an input signal is suppressed, the signal of the new, tapping wire is also allowed through to the AFSM and masquerades as coming from the original source. When the procedure of adding a new layer to the previous ones is repeated a number of times, it results in a layered control architecture where each layer (in connection with all underlying layers) initiates a behavior pattern for the robot, and where each layer is implemented as a network of message-passing augmented finite state machines.

The initially most basic behavioral level of the robot is to stand up. It is achieved with only two AFSMs per leg. These two use a register to hold a set position for the α and β motors and ensure that the motors are sent those positions. The initial values for the registers are such that on power up the robot assumes a standing position. The AFSMs also provide an output that signals the most recently commanded position of the leg to other AFSMs in the network.

To this basic network a new control layer is added to make the robot walk. The additional layer takes the form of extra AFSMs and connections. For example, a leg-down AFSM is added for each leg which notices when the leg is not in the down position and writes to the register of the AFSM controlling the β motor in order to set the leg down. More AFSMs are added that make all legs that touch ground move slightly backward (propelling the robot forward), while any leg that is lifted swings forward. An up-leg trigger is also added which can give a command to lift a leg by suppressing the leg-down AFSM. Finally, walking sequences are initiated by adding an AFSM which sends an appropriate pattern to the six up-leg trigger AFSMs. This can be a pattern in which three legs form a tripod to support the robot (the first and last leg on one side and the middle leg on the other), while the other three legs swing forward to be placed and provide the next stride's supporting tripod, and so on. It can also be a standard back-to-front ripple gait by sending a trigger message to a different leg at some regular interval.

The described control system lets the robot walk, but it is insensitive to the terrain and has a tendency to roll and pitch excessively as it walks over rough terrain. A next layer compensates for this problem, while another modulates the height to which the legs are lifted when they move forward. Then, whiskers are added to detect obstacles beforehand so that leg-lifting modulation doesn't have to wait until actual collisions occur. Then a prowl-layer is added which makes the walking activity dependent on the activity of the infrared sensors picking up the presence of a person (the robot operates in an office environment) by its body warmth. A steered prowling layer influences the backward swing of the legs on the side where the infrared sensors are triggered, making the robot turn in that direction. The robot can follow a slow-walking person in this way.

The subsumption architecture which results from this incremental approach to robot building is not a form of AT. It is not organized around an internal model of the external environment that guides the motor apparatus in an appropriate way. A subsumption architecture is a collection of mutually coordinated mechanisms that happen to be organized in such a way that at a global-level behavioral regularities result. It is the particular makeup of the control system, together with the particular characteristics of the embodiment, and the particular characteristics of the environment that together produce behavior. The behavior emerges from the local interactions of all these components. This way of robot building is a very concrete way to fill in the idea of behavioral systems.

There does not seem to be any obvious upper limit to this incremental approach. AAR's founding father Brooks claims that it is possible to increase behavioral capacities up to a human level without the sense-model-plan-act cycles of AT. To prove his case he started some years ago the Cog project, a bold scheme to build a humanoid robot, Cog (Brooks and Stein, 1993; Dennett, 1994). If this ongoing project succeeds, it would mean that 'psychology' could explain the generation of behavior without AT by dedicating itself to robotics, and to build those robots without using AT's representational ideas. There are however reasons for concern about the 'if' part of this favorable view on AAR's prospects.

3.3 Drawbacks of AAR's way of filling in BST

AAR fleshes out the concept of behavioral systems in a concrete way. By doing so, it offers an explanation for adaptive behavior which remains independent of AT, a necessary step if it is to provide an alternative for AT-based explanations of behavior. However, there are serious drawbacks to AAR's way of dealing with the concept of behavioral systems. Most important, it constitutes an *a-theoretical* approach which remains tightly centered around the practical task of building autonomous agents. A-theoretical should not be misunderstood or be read in a derogatory way. AAR's working practice uses of course many theoretical ideas. Without them the techniques that allow a roboticist to build robots wouldn't be there. In addition, integrating the many theories and techniques into an operational artifact requires lots of ingenuity and deserves our due respect. In contrast, 'a-theoretical' refers to the hands on approach involved in engineering. Sticking close to practical issues allows AAR to steer free from AT's conceptual framework but it does not, all by itself, provide a different conceptual framework for understanding behavioral phenomena.

Within AAR, the knowledge-based AT approach to robotics is rejected and replaced by the *practice* of building or evolving robots capable of real-world behavior. This shift toward a practical bottom up approach for building robots is, of course, accompanied by a set of ideas which stress the importance of system-environment interactions. Nevertheless, the behavioral systems idea provided by AAR is primarily a practical and not a theoretical affair. These ideas are useful guidelines for building better robots, not a theoretical background for understanding the generation of behavior.

For example, the subsumption idea does not explain how the more complex goal-oriented and intelligent characteristics of adaptive behavior come about without invoking AT. It merely states that complex behavior can be arrived at by an incremental approach in robot building. Adaptive behavior is seen as a technical engineering problem, not as a theoretical one for which the proper conceptual tools still have to be developed. AAR does not take the generation of behavior to be a general problem that can be made sense of in a general way. Rather, it is held that there are individual cases of adaptive behavior (ants, humans, ducks, glowworms), and these individual cases seem to require individual solutions (Harvey, personal communication). Some systems, properly put together, just have behavioral properties. In line with this view, the behavioral systems concept provided by AAR is primarily a set of separate cases of animat-environment systems, together with a design strategy for building such animats.

The claim that subsumption provides a way to develop increasingly complex behavioral agents without relying on AT is convincing because it is backed by material evidence (animats). This a-theoretical, engineering-oriented approach allows AAR to remain aloof from the conceptual framework provided by AT. At the same time, this approach prevents it from opposing AT at a more theoretical or conceptual level. Thinking about behavioral systems as a collection of individual cases is not sufficient in this respect. A model by itself is not more than a single example. On its own it does not provide an alternative way of thinking about behavioral phenomena. As a consequence, AT is not replaced, but only temporally pushed back. Without an explicit and convincing alternative conceptual framework one cannot really succeed in moving beyond AT's way of thinking about behavior. Whenever, a problem or setback arises, AT, with all its commonsense plausibility, will bias AAR to play by its rules again.

A sign that AAR is under this pressure to revert back to AT consists of the tendency to combine a subsumption approach with elements stemming from AT (Bonasso, Kortenkamp, and Murphy, 1998; Gat, 1998). The objective of this chapter is to develop the idea of behavioral systems. For this purpose, I have focused on the radical side of AAR which explicitly rejects, or is critical about, the use of representations. This radical side is largely inspired by the work of Brooks (but see also Beer, 1990; Webb, 1994; Harvey, 1992; Rutkowska, 1994). However, many researchers within AAR harbor a far more lenient attitude toward the AT-framework.

So far, the accomplishments of a strict animat approach are limited to basic behavior that is purely reactive. Reactive behavior is fully under the guidance of the immediate environment of a behaving system. A next goal is to develop animats exhibiting anticipatory behavior, which is not fully guided by the immediate environment. Clark calls the problems posed by anticipatory behavior "representation hungry problems" (Clark, 1997a; Clark and Toribio, 1994). These problems are precisely the ones where AT stands most strong, and here the idea of behavioral systems faces its primary challenge.

The willingness to combine AT and interactionist elements results from the current shortcomings of the newer approach. The subsumption idea provides insufficient theoretical guidance as to exactly how more elaborate, anticipatory goal-orientations are to be achieved. As a result, many workers in AAR fall back on AT. Situatedness and embodiment are still held to be central to a good understanding of adaptive behavior. At the same time, these researchers seek to extend the capacities of their animats by combining a subsumption approach with classical modeling and planning components (Bonasso, Kortenkamp, and Murphy, 1998; Gat, 1998). They use a hybrid approach that combines AT and AAR.

A hybrid approach has the advantage of overcoming some of the immediate limitations of nonrepresentational modeling. However, a hybrid approach is not attractive given the very general and far-reaching difficulties associated with AT. From the present perspective, the point of interest is not the *possibility* of combining AT and AAR. Rather, it is the tendency to do so. This tendency suggests that the regular AT-based explanation for the generation of behavior remains attractive for those in the field.

The explicit reliance on a representational framework by many researchers within AAR—committed to the importance of situatedness and embodiment—warrants the conclusion that an a-theoretical, engineering interpretation of behavioral systems runs short as an independent and alternative conceptual framework for thinking about adaptive behavior. AAR provides valuable insights into the concrete operation of behavioral systems, but it does not provide the necessary theoretical backbone. AAR's current independence from AT is maintained by a stream of practical results. However, when this stream dries up, or has difficulties in dealing with specific behavioral capacities, the old conceptual framework of AT reasserts itself. In particular the representation hungry, distally oriented characteristics of anticipatory behavior remain a problem for a purely engineering oriented approach and seem to warrant a return to AT.

4 Coupled dynamical systems

Dynamical Systems Theory is another, currently important, context in which the behavioral systems idea is being developed (Skarda and Freeman, 1987; Van Gelder, 1991, 1995, 1998; Van Gelder and Port, 1995; Beer, 1995a; Thelen and Smith, 1994). Dynamical Systems Theory, or DST, has its background in physics. Ever since Newton, precise dynamical laws have been the established way to describe the temporal changes occurring in physical systems. Until the twentieth century the exact predictability of physical systems by means of such dynamical laws was always stressed. Around the turn of the century the mathematician Poincaré discovered that there were severe limitations to the exact predictions of quantitative dynamical models (Ekeland, 1988). As a remedy he lay the foundations for a more qualitative, analytical approach to describing dynamical relations. Since then, in particular helped by the invention of the computer, this qualitative method of analysis has developed into a mathematical and conceptual framework which is capable of describing the behavior of complex systems in a mathematically precise way. The framework is nowadays known as DST (Abraham and Shaw, 1992) and has become a general and important mathematical instrument within the natural sciences. It forms the mathematical background of newly developing fields such as chaos theory (Gleick, 1987), self-organization (Prigogine and Stengers, 1984; Haken, 1987; Kauffman, 1993), and complexity (Waldrop, 1992). DST is used to describe many different phenomena (air turbulence, neural networks, prey-predator relations, and so on) which are nevertheless alike in that they all consist of a large number of interactions between constitutive parts. Our present interest in DST arises from its potential to provide a theoretically sophisticated conceptualization of the behavioral systems idea (Van Gelder, 1995, 1998; Beer, 1995a). DST is put forward as a conceptual framework which will allow us to understand the generation of adaptive behavior in a way which does not depend on AT.

4.1 Behavioral systems interpreted as two coupled dynamical systems

For a long time, DST did not have much impact on cognitivist psychology. Only when connectionism reintroduced the use of neural nets in cognitive theorizing did this situation begin to change (Smolensky, 1988; Van Gelder, 1991). In contrast to Von Neumann machines, neural networks are easily interpreted as complex dynamical systems (Van Gelder, 1995; Van Gelder and Port, 1995), and this opened a gateway for introducing DST thinking into mainstream, cognitivist psychology. Smolensky's "subsymbolic hypothesis" is one of the early examples of applying the language of dynamical systems to the cognitive domain: "The intuitive processor is a subconceptual connectionist dynamical system that does not admit a complete, formal, and precise conceptual-level description" (Smolensky, 1988, p. 7). Since then, DST thinking has begun to have a continuously growing impact on cognitivist psychology and related fields (Van der Maas and Molenaar, 1992; Van Geert, 1991; Thelen and Smith, 1994; Miller and Freyd, 1993; Vallacher and Nowak, 1994). Much of this work, like that of Smolensky, remains within the AT paradigm. But there are also more radical proponents of the DST view who have come to the fore. In particular Van Gelder has made an influential case for an explicitly noncomputational and nonrepresentational dynamical systems account of cognition (Van Gelder, 1995; Van Gelder and Port, 1995; see also Beer, 1995a; Thelen and Smith, 1994; Smithers, 1994). Van Gelder proposed that the computational, representational conceptualization of cognition should be replaced wholesale by a dynamical account which describes the relation between agent and environment in terms of two coupled dynamical systems.[6]

In this radical view, DST is presented as an alternative for AT along lines which follow the general behavioral systems idea: Organism and environment are interpreted as the two, dynamically coupled, parts of a single organism-environment system (Beer, 1995a). This makes it interesting for our present purposes. The DST fleshing out of the idea of behavioral systems is independent of the efforts within AAR to do the same. In contrast to research on autonomous agents, DST is not limited to a specific ontological domain of which it is a theory. DST provides a general formalism which is useful for describing any system consisting of many interacting parts. The relation between agents and their environment is just one more application of the general framework. As a consequence AAR and DST do not necessarily imply different interpretations of the behavioral systems idea. The two can be easily combined, in which case DST provides a stronger formal backup of AAR engineering and model building (e.g., Beer, 1995a; Smithers, 1994).

The DST interpretation of the behavioral systems idea relies on a large set of mathematical tools which enable the modeling and abstract conceptualization of many different complex phenomena. These tools consist of concepts like state space, trajectory, fixed point, attractor, and coupling. Their meaning is tied to the general theoretical framework of DST and they are very much a package deal. Short introductions of some of the main ideas can be found in Beer (1995a) and Thelen and Smith (1994). Here I will focus on the concept of *dynamical coupling*, the key concept in the context of behavioral systems. Dynamical systems theory can be used to describe the changes of a system over time, its dynamics. This is done using a set of differential or difference equations which specify the future state variables of the system, given initial conditions. One of the major innovations of DST is its use of a spatial metaphor to get a global understanding of a system's dynamics. All state variables are interpreted as defining distinct dimensions in a 'state space'; the possible values of a variable become the extension along the dimension defined by that variable. In this way, every possible state of the system, described by a specific configuration of the state variables, becomes a point in state space, while the dynamics of the system can be interpreted as a trajectory in this state space (Abraham and Shaw, 1987). The idea of a state space allows the dynamics of the system to be traced as geometrical objects and to visualize abstract dynamical properties. The flow through state space can be described in terms of, among others, repellors and attractors. Repellors are unstable states of the system. When initial conditions put the system at such a position, it tends to move away from that position into the direction of an attractor state.

The system's dynamics, its change over time, can then be visualized as a flow from a 'high' peak (a repellor) toward a 'low' valley (an attractor). The layout of these landscape features is determined by the values of a set of parameters, the constants figuring in the equations which describe the dynamics of the system. As long as the parameters remain the same so does the form of the landscape. Hills and valleys remain in the same place. However, the landscape can be changed, sometimes quite dramatically, by changing the ordinarily constant parameters within the equations. Hills may rise or fall and the dynamics of the system will change accordingly. Here the concept of dynamical coupling acquires its meaning. Suppose you have two separate dynamical systems, each described by its own set of equations. In this case, the state variables of the first system are the parameters of the second system and, vice versa, the variables of the second system are the parameters of the first one. The result is two systems in which the dynamics of each one has a strong influence on the dynamics of the other. When the first system moves through its state space, it changes the layout of the state space of the second system. However, the changed dynamics of the second system will in turn change the state space topology of the first system, and so on. Each system therefore effectively influences the topology of the other's state space. The result will be an extremely complex interaction between the two systems, leading to more intricate and complex behavior than either of the two dynamical systems would have been capable of alone. This is the concept of dynamical coupling as used by Van Gelder (1995) and Beer (1995a) and elaborated on by Smithers (1994).

Dynamical coupling is a mathematically sophisticated way to understand the complex mutual influence between two different systems. For this reason, dynamical coupling is presented as a much more detailed and specific way of characterizing the relation between agent and environment than a description in terms of representation could ever be (Beer, 1995a; Van Gelder, 1995; Wheeler, 1994). The organism does not represent its environment in a static and relatively well-defined way. Instead there is a continuous mutual influence which is too complex to allow description in the impoverished language of representations (Van Gelder, 1995, p. 353). The example Van Gelder uses to back up his case and illustrate the concept of dynamical coupling is the centrifugal governor. The governor is a simple feedback mechanism formerly used to control the speed of a steam engine's flywheel.

> It consisted of a vertical spindle geared into the main flywheel so that it rotated at a speed directly dependent upon that of the flywheel itself. Attached to the spindle by hinges were two arms, and on the end of each arm was a metal ball. As the spindle turned, centrifugal force drove the balls outwards and hence upwards. By a clever arrangement, this arm motion was linked directly to the throttle valve. The result was that as the speed of the main wheel increased, the arms raised, closing the valve and restricting the flow of steam; as the speed decreased, the arms fell, opening the valve and allowing more steam to flow. The result was that the engine adapted a constant speed in the presence of large fluctuations in pressure and load. (Van Gelder, 1995, p. 349)

The centrifugal governor is an example of the dynamical coupling between a system and an environment (ibid., p. 357). One of the state variables for the engine, its speed, acts as a parameter for the governor, while one of the governor's state variables, its arm angle, functions as a parameter for the engine. Van Gelder contrasts the image of the centrifugal governor with that of a computational governor. The latter does the same job as the centrifugal governor, but it is built according to an AT-inspired solution of the problem. The continuous, reciprocal, dynamical interplay is cut into several independent parts according the principles of AT's "sense-model-plan-act" cycles. First the speed of the flywheel and the steam pressure are measured, subsequently adjustments to the throttle are made, measurements are made again, and so on. In contrast, the centrifugal governor provides an evocative image as to how the fine-grained interaction between an organism and its environment consists of a continuous interaction which is most easily described in the language of dynamics, without the need to introduce a computational-representational mechanism.

4.2 An example: Beer's insect's leg

Van Gelder's example of the dynamical systems approach remains fairly abstract and general. Beer provides an example where a dynamical approach is used in a behavioral context (Beer, 1995a, 1995b). His example centers around what he calls the "Synthesis Problem" and the "Analysis Problem" (Beer, 1995a, p. 186). The Synthesis Problem is formulated as follows:

> Given an environment dynamics *E*, find an agent dynamics *A* and sensory and motor maps **S** and **M** such that a given constraint *C* on the coupled agent-environment dynamics is satisfied. (ibid.)

The constraint *C* refers to particular adaptive demands that a behaving system has to fulfill, such as, for example, forward locomotion.

Beer's example of a solution to the Synthesis Problem consists of a simulated insect with six rigid legs. The legs can move up or down, swing forward when up, and swing backward when down. All three movements have their own effector. Forward movement only takes place when three legs are down and form a tripod that supports the body (see section 3.2). Each leg possesses an angle sensor that measures its angle relative to the long axis of the body. The control system consists of a continuous-time recurrent network (see figure 4.4). Each leg is controlled by a fully interconnected network consisting of three motor neurons (whose outputs drive the three effectors) and two interneurons. All five neurons receive a weighted input from the leg's angle sensor. Six copies of this network are combined in an architecture roughly resembling the neural circuitry underlying insect locomotion. A genetic algorithm was used to find network parameters such that the dynamics of the network instigates forward motion in the body.

The search algorithm found three different classes of locomotion controllers. (1) When the readings of the angle sensors were available to the network then *reflexive pattern generators* evolved, which depend on the sensory feedback for its operation. They are not robust to sensor loss. (2) If the sensors were disabled during the parameter search then *central pattern*

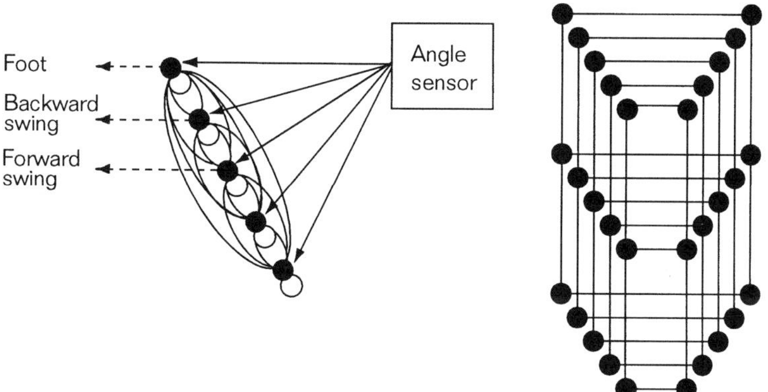

Figure 4.4
Network architecture of the locomotion controller of Beer's insect. A leg controller (left). Coupling between adjacent leg controllers (right). (Redrawn from Beer, 1995a.)

generators evolved. These generate the rhythmic control signals necessary for walking without any sensory input. However, the patterning is stereotyped and can make no use of sensory feedback to fine-tune its operation. (3) If the presence of the sensors was unreliable during the parameter search, then *mixed pattern generators* evolved that work best when the sensors are intact, but which also manages without sensory input.

Beer's solution to the Synthesis Problem is a simulated version of the animat building as described in section 4. The real input of a dynamical systems approach comes to the fore when he deals with the Analysis Problem:

> Given an environment dynamics *E*, an agent dynamics *A*, and sensory and motor maps **S** and **M**, explain how the observed behavior $\mathbf{M}(x_A)$ of the agent is generated. (Beer, 1995a, p. 193)

The example that Beer uses to illustrate how a dynamical systems can be used to analyze the interaction of a behaving system and its environment consists of the synthetic insect just described. However, as Beer says: "a dynamical analysis of these 30 neuron networks would be far too complicated for our illustrative purposes here" (ibid.). Therefore he reverts to an analysis of a (simulated) single-legged insect with only a single five-neuron network to control it, while the environment consists of the leg angle as indicated by the angle sensor. The characteristics of this simpler system are highly similar to those of the larger one, while the five-neuron network is much more amenable to a dynamical analysis.

When the single-legged insect's behavior is analyzed, the most simple case is the model developed with the angle sensor disconnected. In this case the network acts as a central pattern generator, keeping up a rhythm without any sensory input. The neural system keeps repeating itself. In terms of a state space, the system exhibits a *limit cycle*. A limit cycle is an attractor that does not consist of a fixed point (which means that there is no change), but of a cyclic trajectory through the state space that—once the limit cycle is reached from an initial state—is endlessly repeated, at least as long as the parameters are unchanged. As the central pattern generator is an autonomous dynamical system, without external influences, it keeps repeating itself. Figure 4.5 provides a motor space projection of this limit cycle. The output of the foot, backward swing (BS), and forward swing (FS) motor neurons are plotted. The foot is considered to be down when the output of the foot motor neuron is above 0.5 and up otherwise. A stance phase (foot

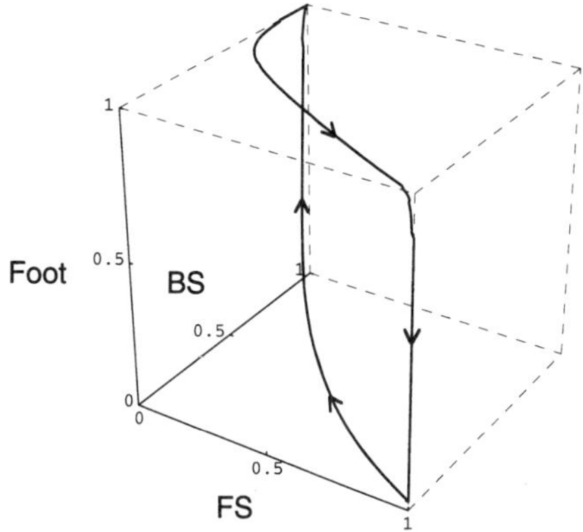

Figure 4.5
A motor-space projection of the limit cycle generated by a typical central pattern generator. (From Beer, 1995a.)

and BS neurons active, FS neuron inactive) is situated at the back-upper-left corner of the projected state space, while a swing phase (foot and FS neurons active, BS neuron inactive) is situated at the front-lower-right corner.

Coupling between two dynamical systems, as described above, occurs in a reflexive pattern generator. Due to the presence of a sensory feedback signal, a reflexive pattern generator is a nonautonomous dynamical system. The motor space projection of the reflexive controller also exhibits a suitable limit cycle (see figure 4.6, top). However, the rhythmic behavior takes only place as long as the reflexive controller is coupled to the body which provides the sensory feedback of the angle sensor. How does the interaction between the two produce the observed limit cycle?

Beer states that we can "think of a reflexive controller as an autonomous dynamical system whose flow is parameterized by the sensory input that it receives from the leg's angle sensor. At any given point in time, the network's state is flowing toward the attractor in whose basin it finds itself. However, because the angle of the leg is constantly changing, the structure of the network's flow is changing also" (ibid., p. 195).

The network never completely traverses these instantaneous trajectories that correspond with the transitory parameterizations, because these parameterizations—and thus the lay out of the state space's landscape features—changes continuously as the leg moves. These instantaneous trajectories are

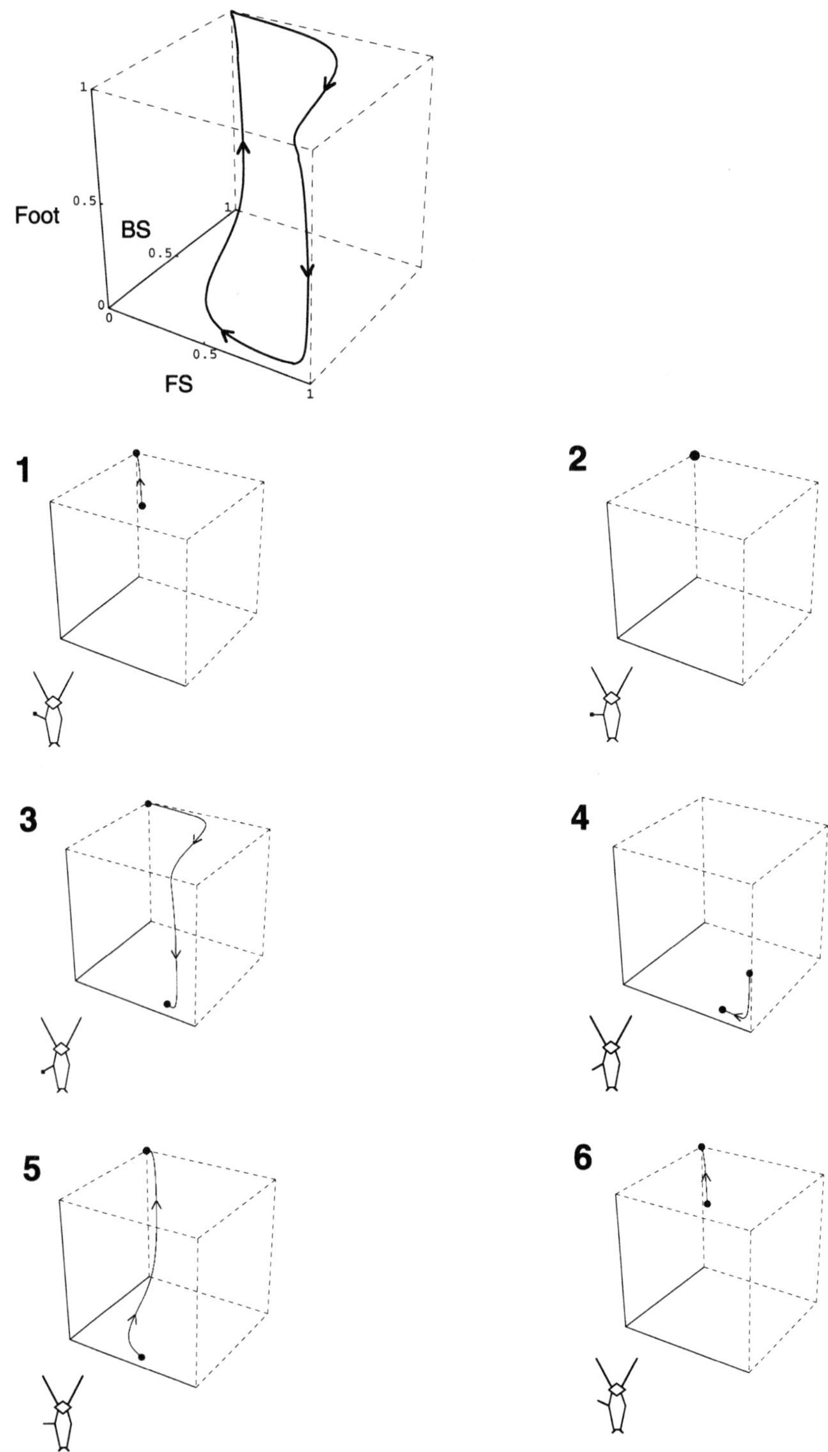

Figure 4.6
Operation of a typical reflexive pattern generator. (From Beer, 1995a.)

depicted by plots 1–6 in figure 4.6. By piecing together these different pictures at many different moments in time, the picture of the reflexive controller's limit cycle (center) can be build up.

The reason why the reflexive controller breaks down when its sensor is removed can now be explained. It is an effect of locking the controller dynamical system into one particular parameterization of its state space. Within this particular parameterization, the controller is governed by a point attractor instead of a limit cycle. Beer modeled the missing signal by setting the angle sensor's signal to zero, the same value that signals otherwise that the leg is perpendicular to the long axis of the body. The controller is subsequently governed by the dynamics of plots 2 and 5, leading it to a stable point.

Beer's example provides a general outline how a dynamical systems approach can be used to model the behavioral interaction between an organism and its environment. The question now is: Does dynamical coupling and, more generally, Dynamical Systems Theory turn the idea of behavioral systems into a convincing Behavioral Systems Theory?

4.3 Drawbacks of filling in BST as dynamical coupling

The interpretation of behavioral systems in terms of a dynamic coupling has several positive features: In contrast to AAR's interpretation it is a *theoretical* framework. Its solid mathematical, physical background makes it a respectable bottom up approach. It does not seem to involve a high-level interpretation in terms of an agent perceiving its environment and planning suitable forms of action. Also, as the characteristics of specific couplings between organism and environment are a direct reflection of its specific embodiment and situatedness, it fits in nicely with the now well-established importance of these factors for behavioral regularities. Another positive point is the formal characterization of organism-environment coupling. This allows DST to move away from the commonsense characterizations and interpretations of adaptive behavior and provide a more abstract and systematic description of this phenomenon. The latter has obvious advantages when, for instance, the behavioral capacities of artificial agents have to be assessed in a way that does not depend on theoretical hitchhiking.

The general implications of dynamical systems theory for psychology cannot yet be fully gauged. The introduction and use of these ideas has only just begun and will influence the study of intelligence in many and very diverse ways. This chapter is, however, concerned with one specific question: Does DST make a good BST that can act as a viable alternative for AT's sense-model-plan-act explanation of behavior? Despite the strong points, a straightforward DST interpretation of the behavioral systems idea has serious shortcomings: It does not deal with the specific conceptual demands an alternative for AT has to cope with. Instead it seems to hope that just bringing in an elaborate mathematical apparatus will be enough to describe and explain organism-environment interactions in a satisfactory way. Without any additions, DST provides an explanation that consists of a total description. Such an explanation suffers from a lower-level hyperconcreteness that must be replaced by suitable, higher-level (superneural-subpersonal) conceptualizations that provide a more tractable account of organism-environment dynamics.

Without suitable, simplifying conceptualizations a dynamical systems approach to the generation of behavior will stumble over the complexity involved. Any complex system—such as a behaving system—requires many parameters and variables. It is difficult to envision how these can all be accounted for without explicit conceptualizations that allow us to order this complexity. The fact that Beer restricted his analysis of an already relatively simple simulation experiment to a single insect-leg is illustrative of the difficulties involved in adequately modeling any complex dynamical system. Somehow, somewhere the problem will have to be simplified. To do so more explicit theory of behavioral systems is necessary.

The problem that needs answering can be stated as follows: How do the lower-level physiological, biomechanical, and other physical processes generate the higher-level, psychological regularities of adaptive behavior? DST's answer consists of a conceptual image of two coupled (embodied and situated) dynamical systems whose interaction has to produce the future oriented purposiveness of adaptive behavior. However, dynamical coupling gives no hint as to how the specific purposive characteristics of behavior come about. The DST account treats behavior just as it would any complex process involving interactions between many elements. It does not specify how the properties of behavioral systems differ from those of other dynamical systems which do not exhibit agent-like characteristics at a higher level.

DST is mainly a mathematical framework, to be applied when a few abstract dynamical relations reliably describe the system's overall behavior. On its own it does not say anything about the processes which generate the dynamics. For example, the speed with which a chemical reaction takes place can be described by an equation. When the reaction is speeded up by injecting a new enzyme, the change in dynamics can simply be accounted for by changing some of the parameters in the equation. But this only works because we have a theory of chemical reactions and enzymes which specifies the parameters to be included in the mathematical model. The same goes for the interactions between an organism and its environment which amount to behavioral regularities. The mathematical framework of DST can be used to describe the regular coupling between organism and environment. However, first the relevant parameters which govern those regularities will have to be discovered (Kelso, 1995). DST needs to be supplemented by a theory of the implementing substrate which specifies the relevant parameters and variables for the generation of adaptive behavior. DST can be used to formalize a model based on the idea of behavioral systems. It does not suffice as a model by itself.

The conceptual shortcomings of a nonrepresentational DST approach have not gone unnoticed. The primary motivation to uphold this view nevertheless seems to be a negative one: The strong intuition that there is something amiss with traditional computational-representational explanations of behavior and cognition, and an alternative is urgently needed. However, a nonrepresentational DST position without an additional explanatory account of the anticipatory, future-orientedness of adaptive behavior is not attractive (Keijzer and De Graaf, 1994). Van Gelder himself seems to admit this point when, after his long argument against the representational-computational view of cognition, he concedes that he does not oppose the use of representations per se and states that DST "offers opportunities for dramatically reconceiving the nature of representation in cognitive systems" (Van Gelder, 1995, p. 376). The need to include representational elements within a dynamical systems approach is also articulated forcefully and at greater length by Miller and Freyd (1993). They hold that DST is very good in bringing the important issues of time and dynamics to the center of psychological attention. But they criticize the idea that DST does away with the need for using representations in psychological theorizing. Instead they advocate 'dynamic representations' which combine "a broad dynamical cognition view" and "a broad representationalist view" (p. 15), thereby doing away with any dichotomy between the two. Clark also argues that acceptance of dynamical relations does not detract from the need for explanation by means of representation (Clark and Toribio, 1994; Clark, 1994).

The persistent plea for a combination of a dynamical approach and an AT-based representational framework is significant. First, it shows that acceptance of a dynamical approach does not necessarily imply a criticism of the Agent Theory. The two can be easily combined. Second, just like in the AAR case, it illustrates that the representational account still works as a seemingly self-evident, default explanation for behavioral phenomena. DST alone does not give a satisfying conceptualization of how an organism-environment system produces adaptive behavior.

5 Behavioral Systems Theory: what do we have and what is still missing?

At the outset of this chapter I said that the idea of behavioral systems is still very tentative and preliminary. To what extent does the work discussed turn BST into a more definite conceptual framework, capable of dealing with the generation of behavior?

Maturana and Varela provide a way of looking at behavioral phenomena that does away with the idea that the internal, neural, system necessarily reflects the external environment. Operational closure, together with structural coupling, provides a skeleton conceptual framework that is thoroughly subpersonal and that can be further filled in or amended as need dictates.

On the other hand, neither Autonomous Agents Research nor coupled dynamical systems have so far succeeded in turning this outline into a coherent conceptual framework that provides a genuine alternative for AT. Still, AAR and DST may not be anything near the final story, but they do cover a lot of ground in moving toward a presentable BST conceptual framework. The existence proof provided by AAR shows that it is not necessary to rely on an agent-like mechanism to explain the generation of behavior. In addition, modern ideas on dynamical systems, and, in its wake, self-organization and complex systems (Haken, 1987; Kauffman, 1993; Kelso, 1995; Goodwin, 1994) provide new theoretical tools to handle the complexity involved in behavioral systems.

Together, this opens up a whole new area for developing theories along the general lines of BST. Without the mental straightjacket provided by AT there is a lot of conceptual freedom that can be used to find solutions for the problems that BST faces. So far this freedom has been insufficiently used. When it comes to explicit theory building at a more general, explicitly conceptual level, the territory opened up by AAR and DST remains largely unexplored and virginal.

The theoretical or conceptual shortcomings of BST can be divided into two categories. The first category consists of mere puzzles for a BST conceptual framework. These are problems that arise naturally within an interactionist approach and that evidently need a lot of work to solve them in a satisfactory way. To name just two examples, BST will probably need to make more extensive use of proximal behavioral variability to generate distal, behavioral regularities. The model systems discussed have all—compared to biological systems—very limited sensory and motor capacities. If Ashby's Law of Requisite Variety that "only variety can kill variety" (chapter 3) is to be made good use of, then the complexity of the organism-environment interaction used in modeling still needs to be greatly enhanced. It then follows, and this provides a second puzzle, that BST requires new ways to handle this complexity. New conceptual tools are necessary that make these interactions theoretically manageable, possibly by better descriptions of behavior (Jacobs et al., 1988), or by a search for general dynamical regularities (Kelso, 1995). Puzzles like these, however fundamental they may actually be, have in common that they look like problems that can be dealt with by an interactionist approach. In this they differ from the second category of current BST's shortcomings.

The second category of current BST's shortcomings are those kind of problems for which we have the tendency to think that they are *in principle* beyond a purely interactionist approach (even when some of the problems of the first category are at least as fundamental). AT was formulated in the first place to account for distally oriented, anticipatory behavior, behavior that is oriented toward environmental factors that are not reflected in the current sensor-stimulation. This behavior consists of representation hungry problems. For many it is inconceivable that a nonrepresentational BST could ever provide an account of (representation hungry) anticipatory behavior. To deal with such behavior, a large group of workers in AAR or with DST fall back on AT. Evidently, the idea of behavioral systems as it now stands does not provide a satisfactory story for anticipatory behavior in the eyes of these people.

While the difficulties of the first category are at least as important for BST, those of the second category are of a more immediate concern for this book. Here lies the motivation to postulate a representational structure as an essential aspect of an account of the generation of behavior. The very conceivability of a genuine alternative to AT is put into doubt. If BST is to be this alternative it must have a convincing story on anticipatory behavior. In the next chapter, I will get into this problem. Besides tidying up the behavioral systems idea somewhat further by relating it to scale relations, I will argue that BST can provide an account of anticipatory behavior by borrowing a set of ideas developed within the field of embryology.

5

Behavioral Systems Theory and Anticipatory Behavior[1]

1 Can BST do without representations which specify what to do?

BST, as it is presented above, is not a definitive, finished conceptual framework, providing answers to everything we want to ask about the generation of behavior. Nevertheless, I gave it a favorable review in the last chapter. Part of the motivation to look at BST in a benevolent way derives, of course, from the conviction that an alternative to AT must be found. In the eagerness to find this alternative, there is the risk that potential shortcomings of BST are too easily glossed over. Any positive well-willing judgment of BST should be tempered by a clear appreciation of the difficulties that it faces.

Chapter 4 ended with two general, theoretical problems for BST (besides numerous practical ones) that spell trouble for accepting BST as a conceptual framework for interpreting behavioral phenomena. The first problem is the general state of the BST conceptual framework. It is not yet very elaborate and remains a rather tentative set of ideas. The second problem is more specific. It concerns the question how BST could ever solve the representation-hungry problems of anticipatory behavior, without relying on representations (as defined in chapter 2). In this chapter, I will present an elaborated version of BST's conceptual framework, which should be able to account for anticipatory behavior. Any answer to the problem of anticipatory behavior will automatically involve a step toward a better conceptualization of the BST framework in general. Therefore, by concentrating on the issue of anticipatory behavior I hope to kill two birds with one stone.

What was again the problem raised by anticipatory behavior? In chapter 1, it was described as a specific kind of goal-achieving behavior.[2] Goal-achieving behavior generally can be guided toward the goal by the changes in its current sensor states as the behavior unfolds. Anticipatory behavior is the kind of behavior where the changes in current sensor states are insufficient to enable successful goal-achievement, and additional internal states are needed to accomplish goal-achievement. These internal states are standardly interpreted as representations. Hence, anticipatory behavior provides a problem for BST, which denies the usefulness of these representations, and it provides a strong point for AT which is built upon the notion of representation.

BST banks on the finding that the body and the environment provide much more structure than was previously thought, and consequently that most—if not all—(human) behavior is not anticipatory at all, but a result from immediate organism-environment couplings. The term used to denote this opposite of anticipatory behavior is *reactive behavior*. The problem of where to draw the border between reactive and anticipatory behavior will be discussed later on (section 4.3). BST's all-out denial of the occurrence or at least the importance of anticipatory behavior has not been generally accepted, and consequently the problem remains.

How can this close link between anticipatory behavior and AT's representational explanations be broken? In this chapter, I will sketch the outlines for an extension of the interactionist account of BST. The key idea underlying this extension is that behavior is a multiply scaled phenomenon. Behavior involves patterns at many different scales of organization, ranging from changes within a neuron's ion channels, to spatially and temporally extended actions like 'walking to Rome'. Similarly, the coupling between organism and environment occurs at many different spatio-temporal scales. I will argue that conceptualizing the idea of behavioral systems as the coupling between multiple scales of dynamical organization offers a better way to understand organism-environment interactions. This conceptualization provides a basis for extending the idea of behavioral systems in such a way that it is (in principle) capable of giving an account of the long-term, distally oriented patterns of anticipatory behavior.

If the scale-related approach can be made to work, it will offer a theoretical basis for understanding anticipatory behavior without relying on representational specifications. There will be no representations involved of the kind that feature in AT. On the other hand, there will be important internal states and processes that could be interpreted as some form of representation.

The chapter is divided into three main parts. The first (section 2) relates the interactionist account of adaptive behavior to the topics of scalar organization and self-organizing systems. Behavior is described as a multiply scaled, self-organizing phenomenon. Section 3 extends this picture by drawing an analogy with morphogenesis. Morphogenesis is the process in which a germ cell develops into a full-grown adult organism. I will argue that a conceptual framework, now being developed for morphogenesis, provides a way to extend the behavioral systems idea in a way that makes it capable of dealing with anticipatory behavior. Section 4 sketches the general characteristics and some implications of the proposed extended form of BST (eBST). In the final section, I will address the issue whether the internal states figuring in eBST are to be interpreted as a form of representation.

2 Adaptive behavior consists of coordinations between differently scaled dynamics

The conceptual framework of BST interprets behavior as a result of interactions between a neural system, a specific sensory-musculo-skeletal embodiment, and the environment in which the embodied system is situated. Behavior is the result of the interactions between the preexisting order in these systems, and consists of the mutual modulation of neural, bodily, and environmental dynamics.

In this section, I will link the interactionist account of behavior explicitly to the topic of scale relations. The coordinations between the neural and sensory-musculo-skeletal systems and the environment are to be understood as relations between several differently-scaled dynamics. Neural happenings take place at a smaller scale than movements, which are, in turn, on a smaller scale than the environmental effects that result from them. Scale relations provide a good theoretical basis for understanding adaptive behavior and a starting-point for dealing with anticipatory behavior.

2.1 The multiple scales of behavioral organization

Philip and Phylis Morrison's picture-book *Powers of Ten* provides a well-known and evocative impression of scale. It consists of a sequence of pictures. The book starts with a picture of the universe at a scale of approximately 1 billion light-years. Each next picture portrays a part of the previous one, magnified by a power of ten. Going from one picture to the next, at first nothing changes very much. You see only white dots on a black ground. Then galaxies appear. Zooming in on our own galaxy, again only white dots are visible until, finally, earth appears. Here we see a few familiar scenes—a view of North America, Chicago, a picnic on a lakeside, and a hand. As the scale continues to decrease, increasingly more microscopic structure is depicted: a lymphocyte, DNA, atoms, and, finally, an impression of quarks. *Powers of Ten* shows very convincingly the following: (a) The scale on which observations are made makes a huge difference for what is conceived of as being there. (b) These scales correspond to multiple levels of organization which are hierarchically configured, ranging from very big to very small. Many scales have their own descriptions and ontology, such as molecules, cells, tissues, planets, or galaxies (Bechtel and Richardson, 1993). (c) Human observers have good differentiating powers at scales with which they are familiar on a day-to-day basis, but much less so at bigger and smaller scales. What remains outside the book is (d): these effects of changes in scale are typically related to changes in temporal scale (Allen and Starr, 1982). Larger-scaled events usually exist on a longer time scale than smaller-scaled events.

The message that 'what is there' actually consists of many different things—depending on how you focus—has often been difficult to digest. The common response is to ask which of the possible descriptions is the 'real' or 'fundamental' one. Heider once said: "The fact of multiple focus furnishes philosophy with many of its classical problems. Multiple focus is distasteful to thinking. . . . It is as if it were possible to read the same book in two ways; once by organizing the letter configurations into English sentences, and then again by organizing them into German sentences" (1959, p. 64). This distaste also shows in the strong appeal of physical reductionism. According to this view there are no real levels. Each level is no more than the sum of its parts, and ultimately a single dynamics should suffice to describe everything. Strictly, this would amount to the claim that nothing 'really' happens except for the most basic physical happenings, quantum events. This is a very high price to pay for a nonambiguous way of carving up the world. Nowadays, for all practical and scientific purposes it is generally accepted that the world clusters into multiple levels of organization, without each level being a linear derivative of the preceding level (Anderson,

1972; Bechtel and Richardson, 1993; Weiss, 1971; Yates, 1993). This means that there is a scalar hierarchy of natural phenomena in which it does not make much sense to ask which one is more 'real' or fundamental than the other (Bechtel, 1994).

It is one thing to acknowledge that the world is organized along multiple levels. It is quite another thing to address the implications of this general organization. Dividing the world in levels is an accepted and necessary way to divide scientific labor. It allows scientists to investigate isolated, specialized topics. However, as will be discussed below, a multiply scaled organization is itself a topic worth of serious research. This latter aspect of the multi-level world has only fairly recently been turned to. It offers a number of interesting explanatory notions that can be used for behavior.

An analysis in terms of multiple scales of organization applies well to behavioral phenomena. Behavior involves processes that extend over a wide range of spatio-temporal scales, ranging from molecular and cellular happenings within the nervous system, to muscle contractions, to relatively small-scaled simple behavior, and on to actions which consist of increasingly large spatio-temporal patterns, such as the yearly migration of knots which breed on the arctic tundra and spend the rest of the season in coastal intertidal areas on the other side of the earth. The interpretation of this kind of migrating bird's behavior at any particular time is scale-dependant. The knot's behavior can be described as flapping its wings, flying, flying north, or flying toward Lapland. The multiplicity of behavioral interpretations is even greater for humans. Take, for example, a person sitting in front of a computer, typing. What is he doing?

> Is he alternatively tensing and relaxing muscles in his arms? Yes. Is he moving his fingers up and down? Yes. Is he typing strings of symbols? Yes. Is he adding a return instruction that he forgot at the end of a subroutine? Yes. Is he writing a program for plotting stock market prices? Yes. Is he making a little extra money for a vacation? Yes. Is he justifying his hobby to his family? Yes. (Powers, 1979, p. 134)

Each of these descriptions forms an equally acceptable description of the 'same' behavior. The same typing movements can be related to diverging sets of environmental happenings. Selling a computer program involves a different set of consequent environmental happenings compared to those of the vacation which is paid for by the program. These environmental happenings can also vary a great deal in the time and space that they involve.

For example, moving a finger takes much less time and space then justifying a hobby to your family, which involves first making money and subsequently spending it on a vacation-trip.

Behavior thus involves many different scales. Yet, conceptually, its organization across those multiple spatio-temporal scales has not been well explored. One reason might be the general aversion to multiply scaled explanations, mentioned above. A more specific reason comes from the tendency to use a personal-level language to describe what agents do. At a personal level, an agent has intentions which can be described in a symbolical form. Being symbolical, the issue of relating small processes to large processes does not arise and even sounds silly. It is weird to inquire after the size of thoughts, intentions, or representations. Even when the discussion turns to symbolical expressions—which do have a size—the size of an expression is not related to the size of the entity referred to. The word 'universe' takes as much space as the word 'molecule'.

The beliefs and desires that are ascribed to an agent at a personal-level description of behavior—or action, rather, to abide by the terminology introduced in chapter 1—are perfectly neutral with respect to spatio-temporal scale. As a consequence, the general idea of translating thought into action is not at all interpreted as a scale-related phenomenon. This personal-level state of affairs is readily transferred to the subpersonal situation by AT. AT's representation-oriented preconceptions do not explicitly deal with scale-relations. The fact that representational specifications—as neurally instantiated entities—are much smaller than the outward behavior that they are supposed to instruct remains unaddressed and is even taken to be beside the point.

This book is about subpersonal explanations of the generation of behavior where the scale-independent intentional vocabulary does not apply. As the subpersonal use of the intentional vocabulary (AT) is also rejected on the basis of the arguments presented in chapter 3, the traditional intentional interpretation of behavior disappears. Without the intentional interpretation of the organism, the topic of relating processes at many different spatio-temporal scales comes to the fore immediately.

The biological context of behavior provides ample evidence of the importance of spatio-temporal scale. Growing bigger is one of the major evolutionary trends and is closely associated with increased complexity (Bonner,

1988, 1993). Living organizations started out as complex, autocatalytic sets of biochemical processes (Maynard-Smith and Szatmáry, 1995), which gave rise to cellular life at least 3.5 billion years ago (Gould, 1994). The fundamental interactions between a living organization and its environment thus occur at the molecular and cellular scales. Only much later, about 530 million years ago, the famous Cambrian explosion took place. In a mere 5 million years all but one modern phylum of animal life made their first appearance in the fossil record (ibid.). These multi-cellular organisms extended the range of organism-environment interactions to the much larger spatio-temporal scales with which we are familiar from everyday life—roughly the range between millimeters and kilometers.

The new scales of interaction opened up a whole new range of potential interactions (Breland and Breland, 1966; Maturana and Varela, 1988). A multi-cellular organization is not a simple magnification of an unicellular organism, which would look like an amorphous blob of living tissue. Instead, new, large-scale structures are generated to exploit the possibilities of this new, large-scale level for the benefit of the cellular basis of life. The structure of plants is one example. Plants grow stalks which lift light-catching leafs above potential obstructions and grow roots which reach underground reservoirs of water. Plant structure exploits the large-scale environmental characteristics in which light comes from above while water can be found underground.

Additionally, a living organization can come to interact with its environment at the scale of its multi-cellular body by self-initiated, reversible movement, without addition in tissue. Reversible movement offers a way to manipulate large-scaled environmental events, otherwise left to chance alone, in a way which is less costly and much faster than growth. Here, adaptive behavior has its origins. Compared to the plant strategy of building 'permanent' structures, the ingenuity of even the most simple of behaviors is remarkable. When environmental circumstances become less agreeable, an organism does not have to stick it out or die. It can move away, or even change the disagreeable circumstances into something more congenial. By means of reversible movement, an organism can influence environmental happenings at scales far larger than its own body: Food is sought and found over wide areas and subsequently ingested, the body's integrity is maintained by avoiding harmful situations and so on. The capacity for behavior—which is the result of these reversible movements—is an extraordinary feat for what is initially a clumping of cells.

Motor capacities and a nervous system play the key roles in extending the scale of interaction. Specialized cells capable of contracting make it possible for the multi-cellular organism to move as a whole. A nervous system, made up from cells which send activation to one another at relatively large speeds, makes it possible to coordinate the capacity for self-initiated movement across the scale of the whole body in a fast way, compared to normal inter-cellular influences. The capacity for coordinated motion at the bodily scale can, in turn, be modulated by specific sensory cues, and ultimately by very sophisticated sensory processes, which make possible the coordinated manipulation of the large-scale environment. Neural, bodily, and large-scale environmental dynamics become linked to one another. Behavior, interpreted as a subpersonal process, thus involves a spatio-temporal structure extending over multiple scales of organization. Somehow, the large-scale dynamics have to be harnessed to benefit the small-scale dynamics of the living organization. A way to come to grips with these properties is by turning to the theory of self-organizing systems.

2.2 Self-organization: dynamical relations between scalar levels

The idea of multiple levels of organization implies that a distinction has to be made between happenings within one scalar level and relations between different scalar levels of organization. A simple metaphor can be enlightening here. The traditional image of basic happenings is that of simple elements, endlessly moving and colliding with one another. Once the position, direction and force of each element is exactly known, dynamical laws allow the exact prediction of all future and—because of the time symmetry here—past states of the system. The elements within such a system can be said to traverse exactly specifiable 'Newtonian trajectories' (Yates, 1993). The description of simple colliding elements can be applied to different levels of organization. Depending on the focus used, a described trajectory could be either that of a molecule in a gas or of a billiard-ball on a pool table. This raises the question of how to describe the relation between the molecules, which make up the billiard-ball, and the billiard-ball as a whole. The Newtonian picture does not deal with these relations between different ontologies. Molecules do not collide with billiard-balls, they collide with other molecules, those which make up the billiard-ball. In principle, the Newtonian view treats the larger-scaled phenomenon in a reductive way. The billiard-ball is just a large collection of molecules. In practice, this view treats the separate dynamics independently from one another. In both cases, relations *between* differently scaled dynamics are left out of the picture.

Accepting the multiple scales of natural organization as a fact, how should the dynamical relations between those scales be described? A standard answer here is that there are (almost) no such dynamical relations. Different scalar levels arise and can be treated as independent systems because the interactions with different levels are severely restricted (Simon, 1973; Salthe, 1985). If there were close dynamical interactions, the processes making up the different levels would not be dissociated from one another. With a change of scale the average rate with which processes take place changes as well. These rate differences restrict dynamical interactions between differently scaled events. For example, the dynamical changes within a single molecule are so fast compared to the dynamics of the billiard-ball that the latter does not change at all within the molecular time frame. Given a focal scale $S(n)$, dynamical changes at a scale $S(n + 1)$ are so slow that, compared to processes happening at $S(n)$, they do not change at all. Changes at $S(n - 1)$ on the other hand happen so fast that they do not occur as individual events at $S(n)$. Happenings at $S(n - 1)$ have to be averaged to describe their influence on $S(n)$. As a result, both figure as (different) constants in the equations describing focal level dynamics (Salthe, 1985). The isolated dynamics cluster into separate levels which together make up a scalar hierarchy.

Nevertheless, while scalar levels may be independent of one another in general, there are many exceptions to this rule. In particular when living systems are concerned, processes happening at different scales can be closely connected. There is also a straightforward explanation for such coordinations between differently scaled dynamics. Given a clustering into separate levels as a consequence of rate differences, manipulating the rate changes at a specific scale would enable dynamical interactions between differently scaled dynamics. The different scales would no longer be independent under such circumstances. This type of speeding up and slowing down definitely occurs. The rate at which chemical reactions take place, for instance, is not only sensitive to the large-scale boundary conditions (temperature) but also to the presence of catalysts which operate within the same scalar level. The rate of change is thus variable at a specific scale, and different scales can dynamically interact.

The study of self-organizing systems addresses the relations between differently scaled, so-called microscopic and macroscopic, events. As pointed out above, in the original Newtonian view on dynamics there were no different levels. The development of thermodynamics in the nineteenth century changed the picture in so far that it now made sense to talk about the collective properties of many parts in terms of simple, large-scaled variables like heat and pressure. However, the second law of thermodynamics, then formulated, states that natural systems tend toward a state of thermal equilibrium where disorder is maximal. There did not seem to be many possibilities for the generation of large-scale *order* as a collective property of many interacting parts. Only fairly recently has it been established that under specific circumstances—in systems pumped with energy and thus far from thermal equilibrium—large-scale order does result from the interactions of small scaled parts (Prigogine and Stengers, 1984; Gleick, 1987; Haken, 1987). One impressive early example that helped to bring this message home consists of a chemical reaction discovered by Belousov and Zhabotinskii in the fifties. Some chemicals diffusing in a solution in a shallow glass dish produce concentric circles and spiral waves across the solution's surface (Goodwin, 1994). Since then, the occurrence of large-scale, or macroscopic, patterns from small-scale, or microscopic, interactions have become a widely established phenomenon.

I will introduce two concepts which have been developed in the study of self-organizing systems—the order parameter and the control parameter (Haken, 1987)—by looking at a system of coupled oscillators (Strogatz and Stewart, 1993; Matthews and Strogatz, 1990; Stewart and Golubitsky, 1992). An oscillator is any system which executes periodic behavior, for example, a clock, a flashing firefly, a neural rhythm, or a dripping faucet. When an oscillator has a stable—that is perturbation resistant—frequency and amplitude it is called a limit-cycle oscillator. A limit-cycle oscillator has a dissipative mechanism to damp oscillations that grow too large and a source of energy to pump up those that become too small. The paradigmatic example is the pendulum clock. Such clocks also illustrate the coupling or entrainment of oscillators. Christiaan Huygens discovered in 1665 that two pendulum clocks, hanging on a common support, tend to synchronize (Strogatz and Stewart, 1993). When hung more widely apart, the clocks lose this perfect synchrony. This mutual influence of two separate oscillators is called *coupling*. In this case only two oscillators were present, but it is also possible to have a large group of coupled oscillators, such as a swarm of fireflies or a collection of neural elements which show individual oscillatory activity. In a large system of coupled oscillators interesting things can happen. Because of the mutual influence of the individual oscillators, global synchronization can occur at a much larger temporal scale than the cycles of the individual oscillators. The system as a whole can show large-scale order, even when the individual oscillators diverge in their amplitude and their individual frequency. The large-scale order of the system can then be described by a simple *order parameter* or *collective variable* (Haken, 1987; Kelso, 1995).

Haken first developed his order parameter concept when working on the laser. This concept is based on a so-called linear stability analysis: An initial random starting pattern can be described as the superposition of many different vibratory modes. A system of coupled oscillators slightly out of phase and frequency would be an example. Given random initial conditions, some, or even most, of these different modes will be damped out. At the same time, others will expand across the system. The mode or pattern with the biggest rate of increase will eventually dominate the total system. The order parameter describes the resulting, large-scale coherent pattern which exhibits its own large-scale characteristics. Haken describes the mutual influence between the macroscopic order parameter and the microscopic oscillations as *circular causality* (Kelso, 1995; Haken, 1995). The large-scale order parameter acts as an independent entity which constrains—Haken says enslaves—the activity of the small-scale individual oscillators. At the same time, the small-scale individual oscillators together generate a large-scale order parameter. The influence is mutual, neither is primary to the other one.

The second important concept is that of a *control parameter*. This is usually an experimentally manipulatable parameter to which the collective behavior of the system is sensitive. When a control parameter is changed, the system of coupled oscillators may start to exhibit different order parameters. In this case, the system undergoes a so-called phase shift. So far, for reasons of mathematical tractability, primarily systems in which each oscillator is coupled equally to each of the others have been investigated (Matthews and Strogatz, 1990). Under these circumstances, changing the coupling strength by which each oscillator influences the other ones or the spread of the individual oscillator frequencies results in typical macroscopic behaviors, for example locking, incoherence and amplitude death (ibid.). In these cases, the density of interaction can thus be used as a control parameter to modulate large-scale phase shifts of the macroscopic order parameter.

The word 'control parameter' is a bit unfortunate, as it invokes associations with control theory and a controller. However, the control parameter does not 'control' the system in any conventional sense. The order comes from the system itself. The control parameter does not prescribe what the system should do. This parameter is an externally modifiable variable that pushes the system into different forms of self-organized order. It is a mere nonspecific trigger with respect to the changed dynamics of the self-organizing system. The nonspecific control parameter concept is a very powerful challenge to the accepted machine and computer metaphors of biological order (Thelen and Smith, 1994, p. 62), and will play a prominent role when discussing anticipatory behavior.

2.3 Coordinations between neural, bodily and environmental dynamics

The self-organization of systems of coupled oscillators offers a new way to understand the operation of a nervous system (Alexander and Globus, 1996; Bickhard and Terveen, 1995; see also Kortmulder, 1994; Kortmulder and Feuth-de Bruijn, 1993). In behavioral explanations based on representational specification the activity of neurons is interpreted as an input-output device which receives and sends information. However, neurons can also easily be interpreted as oscillatory units (Alexander and Globus, 1996). Given this interpretation, the total nervous system forms a larger oscillatory network, the behavior of which depends on the characteristics of its components and their connections. As the nervous system is an organ that extends itself over the scale of the total body of an organism, and because the connections between neurons allow very swift interactions across this network, it forms a means for dynamical patterns to organize themselves very fast (starting at tens of milliseconds) at the bodily scale. In turn, the neural dynamics is tied to a musculo-skeletal system capable of initiating environmental changes at the bodily scale. The bodily dynamics in turn influences dynamical relations within the environment.

This multiply scaled conceptualization of adaptive behavior is a good way to describe the behavioral systems approach to behavior. For example, Beer's insect can be interpreted in this way. The neural network generates rhythms that are taken over by the legs, the rhythmic movement of which, in turn, can influence the network. Work done by Taga on bipedal locomotion provides an example which is explicitly formulated as the coordination of several differently scaled dynamics (Taga, 1994; Taga, Yamaguchi, and Shimizu, 1991). The model consists of a rhythm generating neural network, a musculo-skeletal system and an environment (figure 5.1).

These act in parallel as three dynamical systems which mutually entrain one another and therefore become and remain coordinated. The total result is bipedal locomotion which remains stable when perturbed. The neural rhythm generator generates spatio-temporal patterns of activity without any external input. These patterns provide the motor signals which set the

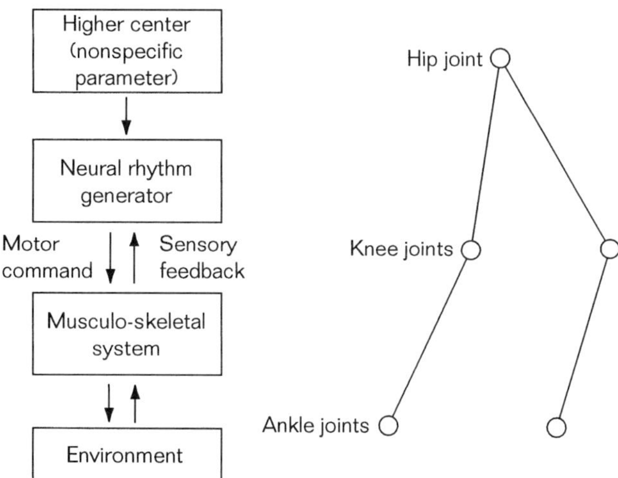

Figure 5.1
Taga's general model for control of the locomotor system (left). Model of the musculo-skeletal system (right). (Redrawn from Taga, Yamaguchi, and Shimizu, 1991.)

musculo-skeletal system into motion. The latter consists of two legs, each composed of a hip-, knee-, and ankle joint and a thigh and shank. The legs are connected together at the hip joint. The musculo-skeletal system moves according to its own dynamics, given the constraints of the environment and the motor signals. It can be thought of as a swing which has its own momentum while it is kept in motion by someone who pushes it at the right moments. Sensory signals which indicate the current state of the musculo-skeletal system and the environment are sent to the neural rhythm generator. These signals in turn entrain the centrally generated neural rhythm and allow it to adapt to the limbs' actual rhythm. The total neuro-musculo-skeletal system is situated on a stable limit cycle in the system's state space. Unpredictable environmental influences on the system, for instance changes in the profile of the ground which disturb the limbs' rhythm, are neutralized by the orbital stability of the limit cycle. Changes in the gait patterns are produced by bifurcations of the limit cycle. The whole system in turn is influenced by a central control parameter which changes the level of activity of the neural rhythm generator. Changes in this parameter induce changes in speed as well as changes in the gait between walking and running.

Similar models of the mutually flexible entraining between neural rhythm generators and the rhythm of the musculo-skeletal are also employed in neuroethology. Camhi, for example, describes how locust flight involves the coaction of oscillators at two different scales. A neural oscillator tends to impose a steady rhythm on the wings, while the wing's actual oscillations are used to modulate the neural oscillator so that the locust can react flexibly to differing environmental circumstances (Camhi, 1984, p. 353). A similar interaction between neural and bodily oscillations has been established for leech swimming (Cohen, Rossignol, and Grillner, 1988).

A scalar interpretation in which several dynamical levels of organization are coupled and generate the spatio-temporal patterns of behavior in a self-organizing process agrees very well with actual models of adaptive behavior in artificial and real agents. The behavior which such models can generate remains limited, however: It consists of short-term repeatable behavior which is well adapted to the local, so-called proximal, environment. Adaptive longer-term behavioral sequences are not accounted for.

It is self-evident that, given time, the continuous locomotion generated by a model such as that of Taga will allow a behaving system to travel large distances. However, for biological organisms long-distance movement is usually oriented toward specific places, objects, or events which have to be reached or achieved. Such a large-scale, or *distal* orientation of behavior is often maintained despite many intervening environmental disturbances. Taga's model, for example, has no such capacity. It only counteracts environmental disturbances on the walking movement itself, and is not a goal-achieving mechanism at all when it comes to reaching specific places.

The obvious solution is to use sensory signals to trigger, steer, and modulate behavior. This allows a behaving system to maintain an interaction with the environment which is goal-achieving on a larger scale. For example, a behaving system might steer toward a directed source of sensory stimulation by maintaining an even input at two frontally placed sensors (Loeb, 1918; Braitenberg, 1984). In this way a distal goal can be reached despite intervening disturbances. Enriching such sensory capabilities allows increasingly complex behavior to be guided in this way, making up the reactive behavior of BST. However, anticipatory behavior consists of behavior in which a sequence of ongoing sensor states does not suffice to explain observed goal-achievement. For example, the lion goes in search of a prey; it does not wait till it sees, smells, or hears one.

Here we enter the next stage in the comparative evaluation of AT and BST. BST provides a good conceptual framework for reactive behavior which is under immediate environmental guidance. Given that anticipatory behavior goes beyond this sensory guidance, how can a BST conceptual framework account for this phenomenon?

3 Applying a morphogenetic conceptual framework to anticipatory behavior

Adaptive behavior has been interpreted as a macroscopic structure that emerges from the self-organizing interplay between micro- and macroscopic processes. To deal with specific *anticipatory* behavior it will be necessary to extend our thinking in terms of micro-macro interactions. A BST conceptual framework is required which is able to deal with distal goal-achievement. More specifically, the conceptual framework should explain how specific long-term spatio-temporal structure arises (distally oriented behavior) of which the short-term constituents can be interpreted as arising 'in order to' achieve the distal goal.

The new territory for thinking in terms of micro-macro interactions consists of the multiple scales of behavior itself. The relations between smaller- (e.g., movements) and larger-scaled behavior (e.g., functional goal-achievements) are to be interpreted as a coordination between micro- and macroscopic events.

3.1 Similarities between morphogenesis and behavior

The first step toward an extended BST conceptual framework—or eBST for short—consists of drawing an analogy between anticipatory behavior and morphogenesis. Morphogenesis is the process by which a single germ cell grows into a highly complex and differentiated multicellular organization. How this comes about has been a long-standing problem in biology and forms the topic of embryology or, to use the more modern expression, developmental biology. How, for example, after a number of cell-divisions, does a cell 'know' that it has to turn into epidermis while its neighbor becomes part of the nervous system? Important constitutive principles at a microscopic scale, like cell movements, cell death, and cell differentiation (Edelman, 1988), all happen in real time in order to generate a particular multicellular structure on a larger time scale. The process of morphogenesis leads consistently and (particularly for big and highly differentiated organisms) in nonstereotypical ways to a highly specific goal state: a multicellular body with the right parts in the right place. As in the case of behavior, disturbances of the normal course of events can be counteracted up to a point. If they are not, specific deformations occur.

There are several reasons why someone interested in behavior might take a closer look at morphogenesis. For one, the structure of a nervous system is itself a result of morphogenetic processes. These processes are thus directly relevant for the construction of one of the most important factors in behavioral organization. Foremost, however, I want to stress the conceptual similarity of morphogenesis and behavior, a similarity already noticed by Lashley (1951; see also Kelso, 1995; Keijzer and De Graaf, 1994). Both processes can be described as goal oriented, regularly resulting in a well-formed adult body and an achieved act respectively. In both cases, this anticipatory character tends to be explained by representational specifications, localized either in the genes or in the brain (Pattee, 1977, 1987).

An important difference between morphogenesis and behavior consists of the detailed knowledge of the processes involved in morphogenesis. In the case of morphogenesis, both the material substrates of the microscopic 'symbolical description' and the macroscopic form are known. Genes, encoded in DNA, provide a concrete embodiment of the 'symbolical description', while it is not established which feature of a nervous system would be its behavioral equivalent. The same goes for the large-scale, behavioral equivalent of bodily form. Behavior is in large part a temporal structure, consisting of patterns in time (Eibl-Eibesfeld, 1970). It is not naturally fixated in matter, such as body tissues. Behavior's fleeting structure requires recording techniques such as video or abstract notations to fixate the temporal pattern in a spatial form that can be studied at leisure (Berridge, 1990; Fentress, 1990; Jacobs, et al. 1988). The systematic and particularly the detailed study of behavioral form has consequently had a late start compared to the study of bodily form. Even now there is no generally accepted way of encoding behavioral structure and a lot of work is still based on highly intuitive notions (Jacobs et al., 1988). Embryology is thus a field which addresses a problem very similar to behavior, but with much more background knowledge of the concrete details involved. Its way of conceptualizing and modeling the relation between 'symbolical descriptions' and macroscopic form is highly corroborated by a relatively detailed knowledge of the actual processes happening in between. An account of behavior could benefit greatly from the ideas and models developed here.

Both morphogenesis and behavior have given rise to the idea of representational specifications. How this is thought to work for behavior has been discussed above, but the case of morphogenesis deserves attention here. The idea that a genetic program specifies body form implies a separation of the genetic information and the process by which this information is turned into a multi-cellular organism. This separation is reflected in the distinction between the biological fields of genetics and embryology. Embryology is mainly concerned with the developmental process within the individual. The embryologist's question is "How does a germ cell develop into a multicellular organism?" In the nineteenth century and in the first half of the twentieth century, the study of morphogenesis turned from a mainly descriptive into a real experimental science. Many details of the developmental process, as well as ways to manipulate it experimentally, were discovered, for instance by grafting cells taken from one place on another part of the embryo, adding chemicals, and so on (Gilbert, 1991; Gottlieb, 1992). The embryologist's focus was thus on the intricacies of the developmental processes which happen within the cellular cytoplasm and on the interactions between cells.

However, starting in the 1920s, embryology as a front-line science was largely overtaken by developments within the new and vigorous field of genetics. In the 1930s, Mendelian genetics and Darwin's model of variation and selection had just been welded together to form the 'modern synthesis' or 'neo-darwinism' (Depew and Weber, 1995; Gottlieb, 1992). The modern synthesis brought biology what it did not have before—a coherent theoretical basis: Life on earth was the result of genetic variation and consequent selection. In contrast to embryology's interest in the cytoplasmic processes leading up to a grown individual organism, the new view stressed the importance of the genetic program to a very high degree. Interest became much more explicitly and exclusively focused on the contingency of evolutionary processes, in contrast to the search for general principles underlying individual development (Resnik, 1994; Gottlieb, 1992). Genes were the entities that could vary and were transmitted from one generation to the next. These were the entities that mattered for evolution theory and it was thought that gene action alone could explain everything that a biologist might be interested in. The embryological questions became viewed as less relevant than questions relating to shifts in gene frequencies: "the great bulk . . . of the protoplasm [is], after all, only a by-product of the action of the gene material" (Muller, 1926, quoted in Keller, 1995, p. 8). American geneticists in the twenties started to talk about gene action as if it was self-evident what that meant. The embryologist's question "How does a germ cell develop into a multicellular organism?" was replaced by another: "How do genes produce their effects?" What happened in between was not conceived of as an interesting topic in its own right but was seen as a "chain of reactions" leading from the gene to the gene's effect.

This was the context in which genes could be interpreted as the 'brain' of a cell (Keller, 1995). The cell's nucleus (and in particular its DNA) became the initiator of intelligent action which instructed the cell's cytoplasm to do what was necessary to achieve the cell's goals. As far as the genesis of multi-cellular structure is concerned, these ideas led to a conceptual schema in which genes are the symbolical encodings of large-scale traits, to which they are connected by a causal chain. This can be envisioned in the same way as the relation between representational specifications and the resulting behavior (see figure 3.1). The conceptual overlap between anticipatory behavior and morphogenesis should be clear by now. But what relevance does it have for an interactionist account of behavior? So far, morphogenesis is just another explanation in terms of representational specifications.

3.2 Genes do not specify traits; they act in mutual interaction with the cytoplasm

The geneticists ignored the cytoplasmic complexities of morphogenesis and searched instead for simple relations between genes and traits. This approach turned out to be extremely productive. In 1940 Beadle and Tatum proposed an explanation of how genes produce their effects in a form that came to be known as the 'one gene-one enzyme' hypothesis (Keller, 1995, p. 17). The most important success was, of course, Crick and Watson's discovery of the structure of DNA as the molecular basis of genes in 1953. The long and variable sequences of base pairs making up the DNA molecules gave material evidence of entities which were previously theoretical. DNA sequences explained how the reproduction of genetic traits takes place across generations. They also offered a 'code-book' for prescribing the composition of proteins which could act as enzymes. Gene action could now be understood as DNA coding for specific enzymes. These basic insights led to the subsequent rise of molecular biology and an explosion of insight into the details of molecular interactions within and between cells.

Ironically, as a result of the increasingly detailed knowledge of the molecular operation of genes, somehow the experimental frame of reference changed. It became more and more clear that genes were not the sole, or even the major, locus of control. They did not, in a uni-directional way, instigate protein building and subsequently macroscopic structure. Instead, the genetic code is part of an intricate, parallel, and reciprocal interaction with cytoplasmic processes, which are at least as much in control as the genetic material (Nijhout, 1990). Talk about 'gene action' was replaced by 'gene activation' (Keller, 1995, p. 26). DNA is not directly transcribed into proteins, but first into nuclear RNA (in multi-cellular organisms at least), then into messenger RNA, and only then into proteins. All these steps are modulated by cytoplasmic processes and can even lead to one gene coding for more than one protein (Kauffman, 1993, p. 416). Another thing that has become clear is that many genes do not code for proteins at all. These genes are not 'structural genes' but 'regulatory' ones. Regulatory genes influence the transcription of structural genes in direct or indirect ways. For example, *promoters* are DNA sites situated near a structural gene. When the promoter is bound by (reacts with) a specific molecular 'key', transcription takes place—unless, of course, an *operator* site, situated between the promoter and the structural site, blocks transcription. This happens when the operator is bound by the presence of its own molecular key. In turn, the operator's block can be removed again by the presence of yet another molecular key. Together all these interacting factors form an extensive system of interlocking feedback loops—providing multiple checks and balances—that has become known as a genetic regulatory network (Kauffman, 1993; McAdams and Arkin, 1999). This is not a static array but a dynamical organization "made up of all the complex feedback webs and cycles of control acting at all these levels" (Kauffman, 1993, p. 417). Again, this network is not only genetic. Cytoplasmic factors are important in initiating and maintaining proper regulation. The mutually influencing genetic, cytoplasmic, and larger-scaled factors make up a very complex regulative network, in which no single entity forms *the* locus of control. This is a large step away from the initial thought that genes direct the cytoplasm and so determine bodily form.

The drift away from the idea of any direct gene action becomes even greater when considering the relation between genes which do code for proteins and larger-scaled processes, such as cell differentiation and tissue formation. Gene products change the direction in which specific cells or tissues develop, but not by directly specifying the proper end result. Instead, the embryological frame of reference has again come to the fore: Gene products tend to direct the developing organism into specific epigenetic pathways. An epigenetic pathway (Waddington, 1975) can be visualized as floating downstream into a river delta. An undifferentiated germ cell starts at the undivided point and subsequently choices have to be made between successive right and left turns. The consecutive choices decide which branch of the river—or, correspondingly, which multi-cellular structure—is reached. Gene products can initiate choices, whether to go 'right' or 'left', at particular turns within this epigenetic landscape. On the other hand, genes do not direct the layout of the epigenetic landscape. Their activity depends on and is limited by the features of the landscape which it confronts. The landscape itself is a cumulative result of all the variables which influence morphogenesis on all relevant scales. The developing embryo is an unstable dynamical system which has many time- and space-dependent dispositions for further development. Gene products can trigger such propensities, but so can many other nonspecific 'signals' in an experimental setup when the system is situated at a branching point.

A concrete example will make more clear what genes do and what they do not do. Take the process of neurulation, the beginning of the formation of the nervous system in vertebrates. After a previous developmental stage called gastrulation, the embryo consists of three basic germ layers; the most inward is called the endoderm, the middle is the mesoderm, and the most outward is the ectoderm. The endoderm is destined to become the gut and related structures. The mesoderm turns into skeleton, connective tissues, and muscles. The ectoderm becomes epidermis and the nervous system. At some point in development, the ectoderm must thus differentiate into the nervous system on the one hand, and epidermis on the other. This happens when on the dorsal side—the embryo's 'back'—the part of the ectoderm layer which will become nervous system folds inward to form an elongated groove. This inward folding of ectodermal cells continues until a separated, closed neural tube is formed. This tube is situated underneath the remaining ectoderm which closes above it and develops further into epidermis (Gilbert, 1994). The neural tube differentiates further to form the nervous system. The process of neurulation is triggered by chemical "inducing factors" originating in the underlying mesoderm.

What is surprising here is that the inducing factor is very unspecific, no more than a trigger which initiates the process of neurulation. Once set in motion, the rather complex set of happenings runs its own course. This was already discovered in the 1930s when it was shown that ectoderm could be turned into neural tissue by introducing many different and nonspecific factors into a cell culture, such as alcohol and even distilled water (Holtfreter, 1991, p. 121). Thus "it became clear that the ectoderm was delicately balanced between epidermal and neural pathways and that a variety of stimuli could tip the balance one way or the other" (Slack, 1991, p. 106). The increased insight into molecular biology allows the revindication of these old findings in the context of genetic functioning.

One of the most significant discoveries that served to bring home the importance of genetic regulatory circuits is the unraveling of the functioning of homeotic genes (Gehring, 1998). These genes are recognizable by a specific DNA sequence called the homeobox. Homeotic genes instigate the organization along the anterior-posterior axis of a developing embryo and regulate, for example, the identity and placement of body segments and appendages such as antennas, wings, eyes, and legs. The operation of homeotic genes first was first investigated in fruitflies where bizarre mutations were produced with legs growing where antenna should have been or flies with an extra pair of wings. However, soon after, it was discovered that the homeobox sequence was also present in mice and there also regulated the embryo's organization along the anterior-posterior axis. This was the case even though mice and flies differ greatly in the anatomical details of the diverse body-organs. For example, the expression of the *Pax*-6 gene instigates the development of both the insect as well as the vertebrate eye despite huge anatomical differences (Gilbert, Opitz, and Raff, 1996). Nowadays, the homeobox cluster has been identified in all major phyla of the animal kingdom, presumably functioning there in a similar way (Valentine, Erwin, and Jablonski, 1996).

The widespread and possibly universal operation of homeotic genes in the animal kingdom gives an important indication of the power and flexibility of genetic regulatory circuits. Genetic regulatory circuits can be used and then re-used for a different function later on in development, they can become duplicated in evolution and acquire new functions enabling increased complexity of the organism. They are very general processes that form robust developmental building blocks that are used over and over again across all species. Major biological structures are not painstakingly assembled genetic piece by genetic piece, but the result of the differential recruitment of whole groups of gene circuits that allow the rapid development of structural novelties.

Kauffman summarizes the new view on morphogenesis as follows: "Morphogenesis is not just the genome's 'doing'; rather, it is the consequence in time and space of the structural and catalytic properties of proteins encoded in time and space by the genome, acting in concert with nonprotein materials and with physical and chemical forces to yield reliable forms" (1993, p. 410). Genes do not instruct the cytoplasm, they rely on the intrinsic disposition of cytoplasmic processes to generate spatial and temporal structure. As Gottlieb puts it, genes are a part of a complex but highly coordinated system of regulatory dynamics that operate simultaneously at multiple scales, extending from genes to chromosomes, to the cell's nucleus, cytoplasm, tissues and up to the whole organism (Gottlieb, 1992, p. 142).

3.3 A dynamical interpretation: genes act as internal control parameters

Molecular biology is primarily concerned with unraveling the specific details of the molecular interactions within living organisms. A more theoretical approach is now proposed by, for example, Stuart Kauffman (1993) and Brian Goodwin (1984, 1994; Goodwin, Kauffman, and Murray, 1993; see also Boyd and Noble, 1993; Sachs, 1994). Kauffman and Goodwin try to give a more general, and a more abstracted, understanding of the minute molecular interactions. They search for general principles characterizing these interactions. They stress the self-organizing properties of the living organization. Many small-scale interactions in the living organization give rise to order at a larger scale and these, in turn, on still larger scales. The topic of self-organization has already been discussed above. The new thing here is the implication of the genome.[3] When genes are no longer to be seen as specifying what the cell has to do, then what do genes do? Goodwin and Kauffman argue that the order exhibited by living organisms is largely the result of inherent, dynamical ordering principles which are a general feature of all of nature. In this respect they hark back to the rational morphologists of the nineteenth century who sought general organizing principles in living nature and eschewed the selectionist ideas of Darwin because these would make living systems a hodgepodge of independent traits which could either be present or not (Resnik, 1994).

The general picture sketched by people like Kauffman and Goodwin is as follows. Self-organizing systems produce macroscopic order. This order is not the result from genetic instructions, but results from the intrinsic dispositions of dynamical, nonequilibrium systems. Such systems conform to a macroscopic order parameter when certain boundary conditions are met. This order is highly specific and arises predictably when, and as long as, the proper control parameters are present. When the control parameters change, a different order parameter can occur or order can disappear. Ordinarily, the presence of control parameters is a matter of chance. Either there is a heat gradient or an enzyme present, or not. However, if things are not left to chance, then the manipulation of control parameters offers a means to influence the order parameter in predictable and repeatable ways. If a self-organizing system were to be exposed to specific sets, sequences, and distributions of control parameters, this could lead to a highly specific and intricate macroscopic structure which would never occur when left to chance (Pattee, 1987). The whole process would be even more geared to generate specific macroscopic order when the control parameters could be turned on and off by the same self-organizing process in an appropriate way. The notion of a genetic regulatory network offers a way in which this switching could take place.

It is easy to see how the gene-cytoplasm relations could be interpreted as such a self-modulating, self-organizing system. Processes occurring within the cytoplasm and between cells exhibit self-organizing properties which, under the influence of specific gene products, could be guided over longer time scales to develop an appropriate multi-cellular structure (Goodwin, 1994, p. 97; see also Kelso, 1995, p. 140). Genes can then be interpreted as control parameters which are internal to the system, *Internal Control Parameters* (ICP) for short (Meijer and Bongaardt, 1996). This interpretation offers a more general, theoretical understanding of the role played by genes in the self-organizing cytoplasmic processes resulting in the formation of specific macroscopic structures. Of course, it is an idealization which glosses over all the actual molecular, cellular, and intercellular intricacies involved (Slack, 1991; Edelman, 1988). On the other hand, it is just the sort of idealization which is needed: It gives a general conceptual framework which allows a global understanding of the production of an extended and highly specific macroscopic order by a microscopic organization. It provides a conceptual alternative to the similarly general idea of the genetic specification of extended macroscopic order. I will apply the new conceptual framework in order to make sense of anticipatory behavior, without representational specification.

Before turning to behavior it will be useful to introduce some terminology to accompany the interpretation given here to gene-trait relations. It has been argued that genes do not specify macroscopic order. This order is inherent in the self-organizing system. Nevertheless, when genes act as internal control parameters, there will be a connection between genes and traits on a large scale. There should be, of course, as there is ample empirical evidence relating specific genes to specific macroscopic traits. Consequently, when a coarse enough focus is maintained, genes can still be said to specify traits (Thelen and Smith, 1994). There are two problems with this loose usage of 'specification'. The first problem is that it is very unclear. Whether or not a gene specifies a trait depends on the scalar focus used and can thus be considered to be both true and false, depending on the scale of observation used. Natural language does not usually keep track of the scale at which a statement applies, and talking about 'specification' does not do much to remedy this. The second problem has to do with the implied directness and directedness of the word 'specify'. It neglects the intervening, self-organizing processes and the mutual influencing which goes in both directions. It highlights only the genetic code and the encoded trait and puts them in an unidirectional relation: the code specifies the trait.

In contrast, when genes are interpreted as ICPs, the very existence of the large-scale relations depends on the always slightly divergent and non-repeatable happenings in between code and trait. Two technical terms will be introduced to stress this point: appropriateness and sufficiency. Both terms relate to the intermediate scale relations and stress the historical, contingent nature of the relations between microscopy and macroscopy.

Genes are importantly related to macroscopic structure because they modulate and are modulated by the living organization which ultimately comes to exhibit a macroscopic structure, or not. Genes will be said to be *appropriate* or not, on the basis of their relevance for generating happenings at larger scales. Genes are appropriate when their presence is a condition for the occurrence of a macroscopic form. But appropriateness only applies within the context of the living organization in which they take part. There is no meaning or symbolism intrinsic to genes outside of this context. Within this context they are only entities with the propensity to help attain macroscopic orderings which are suitable to maintain the living system's integrity. This is basically an arbitrary connection.

Sufficiency replaces the other side of the seeming specificity of large-scale gene-trait relations. Macroscopic traits are *sufficient* or not, depending whether they suffice to fulfill the requirements posed by the microscopic living organization. There is of course a degree of specificity present. For instance, for a leopard it is important for it to have four legs, one tail, one head, and so on. The point here, however, is that next to such general specificity there is a lot of room for individual variation. In that sense, the large-scale structure does not have to be a specific one at all. It only has to fulfill certain standards of sufficiency. To return to the leopard, it tends to have spots, but how these are distributed across its pelt varies. Thus, while 'specificity' is conceptually connected to a precise and exact macroscopic structure, 'sufficiency' focuses our attention on the variability and contingency of the macroscopy. The underlying microscopic processes do not have to converge on one specific point, but on anything which falls within a much wider area of acceptable macroscopic structures.

3.4 Can anticipatory behavior be guided by internal control parameters?

Genetic functioning is no longer interpreted in terms of a simple specification model. The latter only applies within a coarse-grained analysis of gene-trait relations. It is time to turn around the old analogy in which genes are envisioned as the 'brain of a cell' and the image of an 'intelligent and knowledgeable brain' is used to understand gene action. Instead, I will use the modern interpretation of genetic activation to make sense of the relation between the nervous system and anticipatory behavior.

The big picture of the morphogenetic conceptual framework consists of a cellular microscopy which succeeds in generating a sufficient order at increasingly large spatio-temporal scales. The following features appear to be crucial for this phenomenon: (a) There is a self-organizing, dynamical organization in which reciprocal relations between the macroscopic dynamics at $S(n)$ and microscopic dynamics at $S(n-1)$ produce macroscopic orderings at $S(n)$. (b) The microscopy contains selected variables which—in specific time windows and under appropriate boundary conditions—can act as internal control parameters. (c) The internal control parameters are part of a regulatory network at $S(n-1)$ which modulates the timing of their activation. (d) Under the influence of the modulated timing of the internal control parameters an epigenetic pathway is traversed which results in an ordering at the larger scale of $S(n)$). (e) Success or failure of generating order at $S(n)$ must eventually feed back to the regulatory network at $S(n-1)$, either by learning, sensing, or selection.

To apply the morphogenetic conceptual framework to behavior, these features will have to be present in the behavioral context. The task at hand is to argue that this is a plausible assumption. This task is both simple and complex. It is simple because these features often almost self-evidently apply to neural and behavioral phenomena. There are many obvious correspondences. What makes it complex is to establish how deep such correspondences run. Offering detailed accounts of the neural, musculo-skeletal, and environmental equivalents of these features would be a huge enterprise, one which would occupy the agenda of complete research institutions for extended periods. However, the immediate goal is limited to establishing that the morphogenetic framework is at least consistent with the behavioral facts. So, what I will do is point out the most conspicuous correspondences and hint at some of the details which could actually implement the morphogenetic conceptual framework.

In section 2, behavior was conceptualized as the mutual coupling between the differently scaled dynamics of the neural system, the musculo-skeletal system, and the environment. This dynamical organization provides an obvious candidate to play the role of feature (a). The initial condition for applying the morphogenetic conceptual framework to behavior is thus fulfilled. In accordance with feature (d), it was also argued in section 2 that regular, behavioral trajectories emerge at a larger spatio-temporal scale than more basic organism-environment couplings. After all, this correspondence drew out the conceptual link with morphogenesis in the first place. The remaining features are more specific and arguing for their presence is more speculative. Nevertheless, it is clearly possible that the neural system, the musculo-skeletal system and the environment have the required features.

First, it is very probable that the nervous system is capable of providing internal control parameters for behavior (b). Maybe the most convincing argument in favor of this possibility is the sheer complexity of the nervous system. Anything could happen there. Providing ICPs should not be a problem.

Several general features point in this direction. The brain shows many mappings in which environmental features map onto specific neural structures. These could play a role in the longer-term guidance of behavior. It is also evident that the nervous system operates on multiple time-scales. Humans exhibit fast reflexes as well as slow, reflective actions. Berridge (1990) compared the grooming behavior of several rodent species and found that the large scale structure of grooming was more stable across species than were the component actions. Fentress (1990, 1991) mentions research on rats in which striatal lesions had minimal effects upon movement form but disrupted the integrity of behavioral sequences and made the animals hypersensitive to environmental disturbances. All this points to a dissociation of the neural involvement in behavioral organization at different time-scales. Can these generally supportive properties be interpreted in a way which is coherent with a morphogenetic conceptual framework? Work now being done on reinterpreting neural functioning in terms of coupled oscillators is an approach which is congenial to the one advocated here (Alexander and Globus, 1996). A specific argument for the existence of behavioral ICPs comes from Scott Kelso (1995). Kelso's famous 'finger-experiments' demonstrated that simple finger-movements exhibit properties indicative of dynamical self-organization. These self-organizing movement properties are under the influence of nonspecific control parameters such as the frequency of the movement. However, when dealing with issues of learning and intentionality, Kelso states: "I argue that it is necessary to incorporate another kind of forcing, namely, that of *specific parametric influences*. . . . Instead of frequency moving the fingers through different phasing patterns, the fingers are instead required to produce a *specific* phasing pattern" (Kelso, 1995, p. 138). Kelso argues that a dynamical self-organizing behavioral process can be guided in specific directions by appropriate control parameters, originating within the brain (p. 140). This fits the bill well enough.[4]

Another requirement is that behavioral ICPs are part of a regulatory network which modulates the timing of their activation. Well, the nervous system is more or less the prototype for thinking in terms of regulatory networks. While in morphogenesis the network is the abstract part of the system—a set of modulatory influences between different processes—and the produced form the tangible end-result, in the case of the neural system matters are reversed. The nervous system is physically a network. In addition, in case of the human nervous system most of the network is not directly connected to sensory or motor surfaces. Maturana and Varela (1988) mention a ratio of 10:100,000:1 respectively for sensory-, inter-, and motor neurons. A very large part of the nervous system thus seems to have some regulatory function. Bickhard and Terveen (1995, pp. 310–314) discuss recent work in neuroscience centering on modulatory processes of endogenous oscillatory activity. This research stresses the variation in volume and temporal modulatory relationships which permeates the whole brain. "The larger volume effects are clearly also longer time scale modulations. In the brain, such slower and larger volume modulations can constitute modulations of the already ongoing modulations among neural oscillations and within neural networks" (p. 312). There are clear empirical possibilities for the requisite regulatory network.

Finally, the consequences of large-scale, behavioral order will have to feed back to the regulatory network at the scale of the neural modulations (e). As anticipatory behavior operates on relatively long time scales, this feedback arrives rather slowly, and takes the form of selection or a sensory signal that can be used for learning. The latter is the more interesting case. This looks like a simple requirement—learning definitely occurs—but when considering plausible mechanisms which could accomplish appropriate feedback relations, things become remarkably complex. General ideas about how the neural system can change appropriately so that large-scale order arises, have been provided by, for example, Edelman (1987) and Purves (1988). To make successful feedback possible, specific structures at the neural scale are necessary. For instance, learning by reinforcement requires a value system within the neural system to distinguish appropriate and inappropriate actions (Friston et al., 1994). Specific neural pathways that signal positive and negative outcomes of behavior (pain and pleasure) could provide this value. However, for anticipatory behavior, the feedback should apply to large spatio-temporal behavioral structures, not just the last molecular action. Not only the ingestion of food is to be evaluated as good, but also the behavioral sequence which led to having a meal. The complication here—in comparison with representational specification models—is that ICPs do not form a model which *re*presents environmental structure. The appropriate ICP structure cannot be copied from the environment by a perceptual process. As in the case of genes, the environment does not have the power to *instruct* appropriate codings. There has to be a different way to acquire an appropriate ICP structure. How this works is unclear for now, but there are clearly possible solutions to this problem. To offer just one example, in work on reinforcement learning with artificial agents it is now well established that learning can be greatly improved by predicting future reinforcements and comparing the results with the actual reinforcements (Sutton and Barto, 1998). This allows the system to take into account a larger time frame in which its actions are evaluated and changes in ICPs could be realized.

There do not seem to be any intrinsic obstructions to applying the morphogenetic conceptual framework to behavior. The latter can be explained as a dynamical organization which expands its self-organized order over increasingly large spatio-temporal scales by incorporating regulatory networks which modulate and are modulated by 'stored' internal control parameters.

However, all this attention for the possible implementation of this interpretation entails the risk of neglecting the general picture. Superficially it might even seem that there are only slight changes with respect to the AT story. Neural ICPs could be interpreted as representations. As they are also taken to be a highly relevant factor for accomplishing anticipatory behavior, the outward similarity with AT's view on behavior could lull one into thinking that there are no fundamental differences. This is a mistake. Anticipatory behavior is no longer interpreted as the execution of preconceived plans. The ICPs do not constitute a 'program' in any conventional, computer sense. The similarity exists at one specific, large-scale organizational level. The scale-oriented, dynamical view stresses that the interactions between dynamical processes happening at multiple spatio-temporal scales are essential for building up and maintaining this large-scale coordination on which the very idea of representational specification is based. In section 5, I will return to the issue of whether ICPs are 'a form of representation'. First, I will be more specific about what it *means* to say that anticipatory behavior consists of a structure extending over multiple, increasingly large, spatio-temporal scales.

3.5 Anticipatory behavior as a self-organized regular trajectory

When the morphogenetic framework is used to interpret behavioral phenomena, anticipatory behavior turns out to be a developmental process. This is a claim about behavior itself. It does not mean that behavior is the result of developmental processes, which produce a nervous system capable of instigating anticipatory behavior. The claim is that every action itself is *literally* a developmental process, played out on a comparatively short time scale—usually ranging from tens of milliseconds to seconds and minutes, but sometimes extending over hours, days, or even longer. Anticipatory behavior is a macroscopic spatio-temporal form which is each time self-assembled anew from dynamical, self-organizing interactions between multiple scales of organizations. Thelen and Smith say the following in this respect: "Each act is a new behavioral form: stable and predictable in some of its features, but variable, flexible, and adaptive in each instantiation" (1994, p. 73). A behavioral process, from its beginning to its end, traverses an epigenetic pathway, that is, it proceeds in a historical and contingent fashion (ibid., p. 142). Following Yates (1993), I will call such a self-organized trajectory a "regular trajectory."

Yates contrasts the concept of a regular trajectory with 'Newtonian trajectories' (see section 2.2). A Newtonian trajectory is characterized by a precisely defined change in a set of variables which describe a system of interest. This trajectory is, in principle, endlessly repeatable by returning the system to the same initial state and applying the same set of changes. Industrial robots provide a good example of this 'Newtonian' approach. These robots perform relatively complex tasks by being very precisely instructed at a microscopic scale. The instructions sent to the motors set the total macroscopic system in motion. Because of the robot's rigid make up—the motors initiate very precise changes in the joints, the arms are made of stiff materials and securely fastened to a firm support—these signals reliably initiate the *specific* and endlessly repeatable macroscopic movements which are so useful in the factory.

There are two kinds of problems with this approach. First, many, very precise instructions are needed to generate the specific macroscopic effects. All the large-scale order has to be present in the initial description, which must rigidly control subsequent happenings. It is a bit like building a house by gluing together grains of sand, instead of using large pre-fab elements in which a lot of the intermediate structure is present in the building material itself. It is difficult to maintain the necessary control when the number of elements becomes large. The other problem is related to the first one. How can disturbances of the linear translation of microscopic instructions into macroscopic movement be dealt with? The large-scale dynamics of a robot's structure tends to interfere with the translation of the microscopic instructions into exact large-scale movements. A robotic arm might be too flexible, in which case the instruction to put the joints in a particular position will not lead to the end of the arm being at the required place, at least temporally. If the robot arm is made stiffer, and so more massive, to prevent these disturbances, it will more readily show slippage. After performing the same movement many times the robot will wrench itself loose from its support. Such disturbances will result in a scattering around the intended movement result, a scattering which will have to be counteracted by keeping the robot and its environment as tightly constrained as possible. For these robots to work, a highly restricted and stereotypical environment is necessary, together with endless calibration of the machine by human engineers to keep it that way. It is not an attractive setup for dealing with real world environments in which disturbances of 'normal' functioning are the rule rather than the exception.

In contrast, a self-organized, regular trajectory takes the existence of order at multiple scales as its starting-point. A regular trajectory, spanning several scales of organization, emerges when the dynamics at multiple scales become coupled to one another. The neural system modulates short-term organism-environment interactions. These short-term interactions in turn modulate happenings in the environment on a longer time-scale, and so on. Large-scale order results from intrinsic self-organizing tendencies at that scale. This order is manipulated by changing control parameters within the microscopy. It is not specified beforehand within the microscopy. The makeup of the intervening levels of organization ensures a *sufficient* result (section 3.3), not the specificity of the precisely instructed and tightly constrained Newtonian trajectory. The microscopy 'uses' the intrinsic order at larger scales to generate the trajectory. This order (or the disturbances for a Newtonian trajectory) need or, even stronger, should not be suppressed or minimized. What is needed at smaller scales is a regulatory network which plays these self-ordering tendencies. When this works appropriately, regular trajectories take form. In contrast to the Newtonian ones, they are never exactly the same, never exactly repeatable. Each one is a historical, contingent event.

A way to visualize this is by thinking of circles in circles (Fentress, 1991). The dynamics belonging to a particular scale $S(n)$ can be represented by a circle. This circle is in turn surrounded by a larger circle representing the dynamics of $S(n + 1)$, and so on (see figure 5.2). The arrows represent the reciprocal relations between different scales. The total picture gives the image of an expanding, reciprocal influence of an initially small organization which subsequently manages to draw increasingly large-scaled dynamics into its influence. At the same time this picture can still accommodate the traditional image of representational specification, which turns up as a coarse view on the nested set of dynamical structures. When all the details of the mediating processes are kept out of view, a seemingly direct link between factors at the neural scale and macroscopic events will be seen.

Despite their outward resemblance, a Newtonian and a regular trajectory are very different. The first is a precisely defined change in a set of variables over time. The second consists of a change in a set of variables at $S(n - 1)$ which act as control parameters that modulate and change the dynamics of a set of variables at $S(n)$, which in turn do the same for the

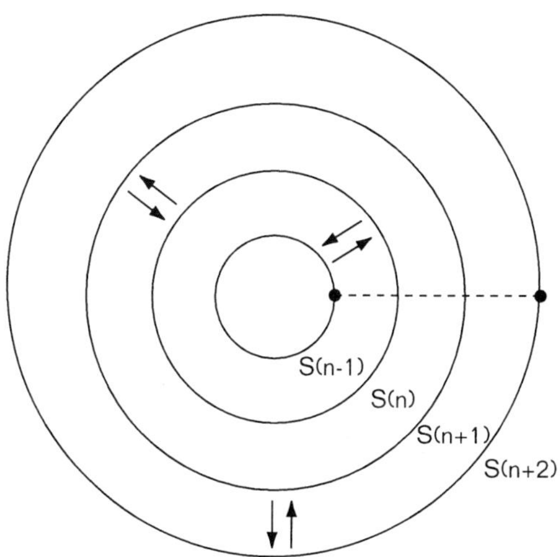

Figure 5.2
The multiply focused model of behavioral organization. Circles represent separate dynamics. The dotted line portrays a self-organized regular trajectory.

dynamics at a scale $S(n + 1)$, and so on. Several sets of descriptions are needed simultaneously to keep track of this organization. One implication, for example, is that the seemingly similar movements, performed by industrial robots on the one hand, and humans and animals on the other, reflect very different organizational principles. Consequently, behavioral research should become much more sensitive to the organizing principles behind behavioral phenomena, instead of focusing on the outward movements themselves.

Interpreting anticipatory behavior as a regular trajectory has also implications for the relation between the neural factors—which might act as ICPs—and achieved goals. In a model based on representational specifications the relation between a relevant neural factor and a related external macroscopic state is seen as fairly direct. Both are seen as being specific to one another. The relation between ICPs and macroscopic structure is better characterized in terms of appropriateness and sufficiency. This relation is much less direct, does not draw on an abstract isomorphism between internal and external processes, and stresses the importance of the self-organizing processes which are needed to generate large-scale order. Talking about a *specific* goal to be achieved generates the impression of a tightly constrained end-result. Using the concept of *sufficiency* changes this picture. The trajectory, as well as the goal itself, is now much less pinned down. In the Newtonian case, an obvious strategy would be to define the goal-state and backtrack from there until a route to the goal is found. On the other hand, in the case of real behavior it is normally not necessary at all to reach a very specific goal. A broad range of states will do, as long as they fall within a certain range. Going out for pizza does not imply that there is only one 'good' outcome for this behavior, namely eating the piece of pizza which you actually ate. Innumerable slices of pizza of sufficient quality, and served within a reasonable time frame, would have been equally acceptable. There is only specificity after the fact. Afterward is it a historical truth that a particular piece was eaten.

Again, a comparison with AT-based robotics is enlightening. Robots are built to perform tasks for human users. These users do have very specific goals in mind for their expensive robots. These tasks are often thought to be relatively simple, such as housecleaning or making a tuna sandwich.

Given the analysis of behavior presented here, performing such specific tasks at a specific time would be at the upper end of behavioral complexity. These are not simple tasks at all. Behavior is rather a general manipulation of large-scale dynamics in ways which over many trials tends to be successful often enough to enhance the continuing existence of living organizations. All animals would have extreme difficulties with the tasks envisioned by the average roboticist. As a way of modeling behavior, roboticists seem to be held hostage to the commercial demands for useful robots without a sufficiently clear appreciation of the real problems surrounding adaptive and anticipatory behavior.

In summary, anticipatory behavior occurs when a behavioral system is capable of generating regular trajectories, which lead to a sufficient macroscopic order. Given a capacity for self-organized behavioral regularities at a short time-scale, a regulatory network which modulates a set of control parameters will be able to guide this process over longer time-scales in a way that makes it relatively independent of the immediate environment. It will enable the system to achieve long-term goals. An extended interactionist account of adaptive behavior can thus deal with problems which formerly necessitated representational specifications.

The eBST conceptual framework, with its ideas imported from modern views on morphogenesis, expands the interactionist account of behavior in a way which enables it to explain the occurrence of anticipatory behavior—at least, in theory. The thing being offered so far is, of course, only an idea, an alternative, very general conceptual structure for thinking about the organizing principles behind adaptive and anticipatory behavior. Its validity will depend on its usefulness as a source for more concrete ideas concerning the origins of behavior. Empirical research and the development of more elaborate and concrete models of behavior will have to decide on that. Still, the intrinsically good thing about this framework, come what may, is that it focuses attention where it should be: onto the mediating processes which actually generate behavior. Morphogenesis is a phenomenon where a lot of solid facts concerning its biochemical, genetic, cellular, and topological organization eventually led to a more general understanding of this process. The promise is that it offers a theoretical lead to direct our attention to those facts which are central to the organization of behavior.

4 Behavioral Systems Theory: the extended version

At the beginning of chapter 4, BST was characterized by two central commitments, a positive and a negative one:

a. The behavior of organisms (as well as of BST-based models) results from multiple, dynamical, reciprocal interactions between a neural system (or another control structure when it comes to the models), a sensory-musculo-skeletal system (or just embodiment in the robotic case), and an interaction space (the environment incorporated in the behavioral regularities).
b. The postulation and use of subpersonal representations (interpreted as an internal structure isomorphic to the behaviorally relevant environment) to instruct behavior is rejected.

In what way do the ideas of scale-relations and morphogenesis bear on these two commitments? In the following, I will discuss the links with the first, positive, commitment. In section 5, I will turn to the negative one, the rejection of representations.

As a general comment, I think that BST acquires a more robust and specific theoretical background when behavioral systems are interpreted as a multiply scaled organization consisting of several—usually isolated but now coupled—differently scaled dynamical systems. Compared to the work discussed in chapter 4, eBST is a more concrete elaboration of ideas derived from Maturana and Varela. It adds a more theoretical understanding of organism-environment interaction to the practices of AAR. It also provides extra backing for interpreting behavioral phenomena in terms of coupled dynamical systems. The topic of scale and the genetic regulatory circuits in which ICPs play their role provides a view on the concrete physical systems involved in behavior that leads in a natural way to an interpretation in terms of dynamicals systems and self-organization.

In the next two sections, some of the consequences of the proposed extension of BST will be discussed. First, I will sketch some theoretical advantages of eBST. In the second section, the relation between eBST and empirical research will be discussed.

4.1 Theoretical advantages of extended BST: a definition of behavior and a picture for the mind

Besides the advantages of eBST in making the idea of behavioral systems more specific, I see two more general conceptual advantages arising from the theoretical background provided by a multiply scaled interpretation of behavioral systems. (a) Interpreting behavior as self-organized regular trajectories makes the phenomenon of behavior itself more specific. Extended BST demands a certain, complex organization to be present before we can speak about behavior. (b) The scale-related view provides a view on behavior which allows us to remove ourselves from personal-level interpretations of action when we are investigating the subpersonal generation of behavior. I will discuss these two points in turn.

Awareness and use of the scale-relations involved in behavior provides BST with more specific ideas concerning the nature of behavior. In chapter 1, I noted that behavior to a large extent is an intuitive notion with no clear and universally accepted criteria to mark its borders. Because of this, I focused in this book only on prototypical behavior, the self-initiated, purposive movements of humans and other animals, explicitly excluding the doings of robots. To provide a vocabulary for the possibility that robots do not behave whereas humans and other animals do, I distinguished movement and behavior. Robots definitely move and possibly behave, while animals and humans definitely do both. To back up the possibility that robots might not behave, I argued that behavior is not necessarily delineated by functional criteria alone, such as being goal-achieving, but also by structural criteria that derive from the processes constitutive of behavior.

Now it is time to return to this distinction between movement and behavior and see whether robots can be said to behave after all or not. Or in terms of the earlier used example, does a human welding two pipes together constitute an example of behavior while a robot performing the same task does not?

Extended BST posits that (human and animal) behavior consists of self-organized regular trajectories, involving coordinations between multiple scales of dynamical organization. Extended BST also claims that this organizational form is necessary to produce reliable distally oriented behavior that can overcome a wide variety of proximal happenings. Being constituted by self-organized regular trajectories can then be used as a defining characteristic of behavior. What counts is not only the outward appearance of behavior, the executed macroscopic movements and the achieved goal, but also the proper organization which ensures that these movements arise on many different occasions and under always variable circumstances leading to consistent goal achievement. Behavior, thus interpreted, is never simply movement. It is a large-scale order that arises in a reciprocal interaction with lower-level processes. In this definition, behavior becomes dissociated from purposive movements that arise from mechanisms not exhibiting the required multiply scaled dynamical organization. That is, movements produced by robots build upon the principle of Newtonian trajectories. Once the proposed definition is accepted, behavior becomes a more specific and less intuitive phenomenon.

Making a difference here on the basis of structural criteria might offset those people who are used to interpreting behavior in a strict functional way. However, as discussed in chapter 3 (section 2.2), the proposed structural criterion of being constituted by regular trajectories is intimately connected to a functional criterion, the requirement of functional robustness. When it comes to consistent goal-achievement under many different circumstances, the human and the robot welder do not perform the same task. Their performance differs in the perturbation resistance of their welding. Given that they both achieve a sufficient weld in condition A, the human, but not the robot welder, is likely to achieve sufficient welds in many other conditions. Having this robustness or flexibility is a marked functional criterion of behavior, and robots, so far, definitely do not score well on this criterion. To conclude, the verdict is that the human welder does and the robot welder does not behave. Of course, future robots may come to behave whenever they incorporate the capacity to initiate and maintain regular trajectories. The movement-behavior distinction is definitely not one between metal and flesh.

Ironically, when this demarcation of behavior is accepted, it turns out that AT's solution to the generation of behavior would turn animal and human behavior into something that is not behavior any longer—according to the new criterion. The new criterion also implies that models of behavior that are based on AT—such as the Ambler—are no models of behavior after all; they are machines that only move about.

The eBST framework, of course, is at the moment only a proposal and the same goes for the definition of behavior proposed here. Before this definition can be accepted, it will have to operationalized and its usefulness evaluated in an empirical context. However, whatever the long-term verdict, the proposed definition of behavior helps to set up behavior as a better-conceptualized phenomenon.

The eBST framework has another important theoretical benefit: It provides a lucid image for the mind which makes intuitive sense, without being a disguised version of a personal-level description of behavior. Extended BST offers a way to think about behavior which is imaginable—something that we can see before our mind's eye—and which nevertheless departs from AT.

An important reason for the seeming inevitability of an explanation along the lines of AT consists of the intuitive strength and plausibility of our personal-level view on behavior: there is an environment to be perceived by an agent who subsequently instigates actions (whether these are based on instincts, learned reflexes, or deliberate thought does not matter here) that are appropriate to the external situation. Instead of importing this personal-level image into the subpersonal level, eBST offers an image in which there isn't any agent who perceives, and in which there is no ready-made environment to be acted on by the agent. Instead, there are differently scaled dynamics that can be made to move together under certain circumstances. The nervous system is not interpreted as a materialized mind, but as a modulator of dynamical patterns on several spatio-temporal scales. The body is not an arbitrary conveyer of the commands initiated by a mind-brain, but an important contributor to the dynamical patterns of behavior. The environment is not a set stage, interpreted at a particular scale which defines beforehand what is supposed to be 'out there' (e.g. rocks and trees rather than grains of sand and algal filaments). In the image of eBST there exist many differently scaled environmental dynamics, some of whom can be modulated by the behaving system and so become a part of the behavioral system.

Understanding behavior as a regular trajectory across multiple spatio-temporal scales provides an image that can stand up to the one presented by AT: an entity manipulating representations and so initiating and guiding outward behavior. The image provided by eBST makes sense as a global story about how behavior might be generated. This global story is extremely important, as it liberates our thinking about behavior from the constraints of AT. It gives evidence that all the options that are available for explaining the generation of behavior have not yet been explored, and that something radically different is possible. Even when the eBST picture has to be rejected, its very existence shows that it is not necessary to look at behavior through the eyes of AT.

4.2 The empirical grounding of extended BST

The presentation of the conceptual framework of eBST has so far been fairly abstract and relatively unconnected to behavioral research. Being abstract is of course what eBST is meant to be. Like AT, eBST is a *conceptual* framework that helps us to order our thoughts about the generation of behavior at a very general level. Still, to be of use, eBST must link up with empirical research on behavior and make a difference there. In what way does eBST bear on empirical behavioral research?

Extended BST is too general to be directly translated into a separate and highly specific research agenda, and any influence on empirical research will be indirect. Still, this indirect influence can be considerable. Passing by old mind-based divisions, eBST instigates a close conceptual connection between psychological research and developments in fields like neurobiology, neuroethology, animal behavior, developmental biology, behavioral genetics, and, more generally, molecular biology. I will call this the genetic-neuro-behavioral setting of (extended) BST. The difference in conceptual setting, compared to AT, has many implications for psychological research into behavior.

The influence goes two ways. Starting out from eBST, its assessment of the psychological core issues leads to a particular selection and prioritization of possible lines of behavioral research. Compared to AT, eBST does not emphasize specifically human and cognitive abilities. Extended BST posits the coupling between neural, bodily, and environmental dynamics as an issue of central importance for psychology. Psychology should give high priority to any attempt to understand this basic coupling process, which occurs in humans and other animals alike. With such an understanding, it will become easier to comprehend the ways in which this coupling process becomes increasingly extended in more complex organisms until it eventually constitutes what we call cognitive behavior. Of course this does not imply any *ban* on attempts to understand cognitive functioning more directly. However, understanding the latter is, in the view of eBST, something that will be helped a great deal by having a lot more experience with, and insight in, simpler forms of neuro-behavioral coupling.

Starting out from the research side, eBST provides a favorable and encouraging conceptual context for research that addresses the issue of neuro-behavioral coupling but that does not bear directly on human cognition. AT's inherent dualism and exclusive focus on cognitive factors shielded psychology from neuro-behavioral research that did not specifically address human's cognitive behavior. Extended BST's stress on neurobehavioral couplings turns the presence or absence of recognizable cognitive factors into a nonissue when it comes to having relevance for psychology.

Putting psychology in the middle of a conceptual genetic-neuro-behavioral setting provides some general empirical links that strengthen eBST's interpretation of behavior as a short-term morphogenetic process. For example, when the fossil record is taken into consideration, there is from the start a close link between bodily morphology and behavioral morphology. Not only bodily tissues fossilize, but also the behavioral patterns of animals (Seilacher, 1967). In particular, the burrowing of worm-like animals has been preserved as trace-patterns that provide some of the earliest evidence of the presence of animal life (Seilacher, Bose, and Pflüger, 1998). The earliest trace-patterns consist of simple "scribbling" but later in the fossil record they become intricate meandering patterns and three-dimensional shapes which are increasingly adapted to the local circumstances (Seilacher, 1967). The claim that behavior is a dynamical morphology becomes very tangible here.

This evolutionary setting furthers the close connection between morphogenesis and behavior as it puts them both in the empirical context of genetic regulatory circuits. The evolutionary development of increasingly complex animal body forms goes hand in hand with that of increasingly complex behavior (as witnessed in trace fossils). Both are now seen as resulting from the development of genetic regulatory circuits which allowed the development of complex multicellular bodies, nervous systems, and behavior (Kauffman, 1993; Greenspan and Tully, 1994; Miklos, Campbell, and Kankel, 1994; Raff, 1996). And just to remind, these genetic circuits are not only genetic, but include their interactions with the spatially extended molecular interactions in the cytoplasm and between cells, as has been discussed above.

The awareness of the importance of genetic regulatory circuits has inspired a strong genetics-based approach in which the experimental investigation of genetic, neural, and behavioral relations becomes highly integrated. Miklos's plea for a highly integrated approach gives a good impression of the practical and theoretical concerns raised by such an outlook on behavior

(Miklos, 1993). He presents an overview of possible ways to uncover the interplay that connects molecular biological functioning all the way to behavior. He pleads for an experimental approach where transgenic technologies are used to investigate the behavioral outputs that are possible from an organism. He discusses the relative benefits and shortcomings of possible model systems (organisms) for this purpose on the basis of the possibilities for embryological, genetic, molecular biological, neural, and behavioral study. He considers questions about the levels at which findings from particular model systems may generalize and the levels at which they may not. Provoked by the existence of extremely miniaturized parasitic wasps, he raises the issue about the minimal neural circuitry necessary for behavioral functioning. Miklos's ambitious proposal perfectly gives the feel of a radically nontraditional, yet experimentally oriented attempt to understand the generation of behavior within a genetic-neurobehavioral context.

Miklos's vision serves as a general sketch of the conceptual habitat in which eBST operates. However, he still sees basic behavior as simple and robotic, a view that does no credit to its actual complexity and does not combine well with eBST. In this respect, a better and more specific empirical back up for eBST can be found by turning to more specialized neurobehavioral research which does address the intricacies of behavior.

A good place to start here consists of fine-grained neuroethological studies which try to relate neural functioning to behavioral patterns in animals (Camhi, 1984; Simmons and Young, 1999). When eBST is loosely described as the general idea that behavior arises as the result of the mutual influencing of dynamical processes happening at different levels of organization, then neuroethology abounds with examples of eBST. Neuroethology focuses on the relations between the molecular build up of neurons, the neuron level, the level of neural circuits, and the level of behavior. An important concept to describe the relation between these multiple levels in neuroethology is the concept of *modulation* (Harris-Warrick and Marder, 1991; Meyrand, Simmers, and Moulins, 1994). Modulation occurs when a signal or state parameter influences the normal operation of a system—be it a neuron, a neural circuit, the interactions between several neural circuits, or muscle properties. For example, by being modulated, a muscle can come to respond to an identical motor neuron discharge with quite variable movements (Harris-Warrick and Marder, 1991). Another example of modulation is its influence on neural circuits. The pattern of activity of neural circuits was originally thought to result essentially from its synaptic wiring which is anatomically fixed on the short term and thus a stable property. However, it has become clear that cellular and synaptic properties also play a major role in organizing circuit output. These modulating properties, in turn, are themselves continuously varying on numerous time-scales under the influence of extrinsic modulatory influences (Harris-Warrick and Marder, 1991; Marder, 1998).

An example that shows the force of modulation particularly well is a finding of Meyrand, Simmers, and Moulin (1991, 1994; see also Simmons and Young, 1999). They studied the stomatogastric ganglion in lobsters. This ganglion is important for regulating the activity in the lobster's foregut. The muscle contractions here show complex, regularly repeating patterns comparable to those used for moving limbs. Under normal circumstances, the activity of the stomatogastric ganglion is divided into three neural circuits, each linked to specific parts and functions of the foregut: first, the esophageal circuit, linked to the foregut region where the food enters; second, a circuit linked to the gastric mill where food is cut and ground by three teeth, and third, a circuit linked with the pyloric region where the resulting food particles are squeezed and mixed. Muscles of the gastric mill are activated in a rhythm that cycles every 5 to 10 seconds, those of the pyloric region cycle in 0.5 to 2 seconds.

This subdivision disappears when two pyloric suppressor neurons, projecting into the stomatogastric ganglion, become active. The separate rhythms of the pyloric and gastric mill region stop and some of the neurons involved in the three separate circuits now become enrolled in a newly arising, larger circuit with its own rhythmic activity. This new circuit probably is for swallowing, an activity which involves the global coordination of the whole foregut. When the pyloric suppressor neurons stop firing, the new circuit persists for several tens of seconds before the three smaller circuits reestablish themselves. The new circuit is thus not directly driven by the pyloric suppressor neurons. The circuits within the ganglion itself are reconfigured under the influence of the firing of these neurons. Here then is a case where the functional division of a ganglion becomes reconfigured in a dramatic way by an extrinsic modulatory influence.

Thus, modulation in a neuro-behavioral setting lets the behavior of a neuro-behavioral system at a certain level be influenced by signals or system states arising at different levels. I think that this kind of modulation forms a good example of the operation of ICPs as postulated by eBST.

4.3 Modulation: anticipatory behavior and self-organization

Having made the claim that the neuroethological notion of modulation provides an example of the working of ICPs as postulated by eBST, I find that two immediate concerns deserve attention. (a) Is there any anticipatory behavior present when such modulation occurs? (b) What is the relation between modulation and self-organization?

In chapter 1, anticipatory behavior has been described as behavior that requires internal states, which are usually interpreted as representations. It is the kind of behavior where cognition is usually thought to enter the scene and which is considered to form a problem for BST. As ICPs are specifically introduced to account for this kind of behavior, how can the low-level, noncognitive process of modulation be considered an example of the very concept that is supposed to lift BST up to the level of anticipatory behavior? The answer ought to be predictable by now: Anticipatory behavior is not restricted to an obvious cognitive context and is a much wider occurring phenomenon. To put the case even more strongly and more explicitly, *all behavior is anticipatory behavior*. If there is cognition involved here, then it is a form of cognition shared by humans and other animals alike.

Of course, within the AT framework the claim that basic behavior is always anticipatory ought to be undisputed. In the discussion of AT in chapter 2, it became clear that walking over rough terrain requires ample modeling and planning capacities. However, as discussed in chapter 4, within the BST framework the necessity of internal states (interpreted as representations) for all behavior is specifically opposed. At this point, eBST differs from more regular forms of BST.

Why hold that all basic behavior is anticipatory? According to eBST, all behavior requires a sufficiently complex sensory-musculo-skeletal system to achieve a robust functionality. This is the core issue behind the behavior-movement distinction and the definition of behavior as self-organized regular trajectories (section 4.1). In addition, all behavior that involves a sufficiently complex sensory-musculo-skeletal system requires internal states to organize and coordinate this bodily system. The sheer complexity of any biological sensory-musculo-skeletal system requires neural functioning at multiple time scales—making all sorts of internal preparatory adjustments—in order to accomplish fluent behavior (Hasan and Stuart, 1988). Current sensor states do not suffice to trigger and time all these continuously ongoing adjustments. Just thinking of the essential and universal role played by central pattern generators should impress the importance of internal states for all behavior (Marder and Calabrese, 1996).

Given this wide reading of anticipatory behavior, how does this reflect on the models discussed in chapter 4, such as Brooks's insect robots? These BST models are held in opposition to anticipatory behavior, as the immediate coupling between an organism or robot and its environment is said to suffice for generating behavior. When all behavior now turns out to be anticipatory, why doesn't this wreak havoc among the earlier ideas concerning BST?

For a start, eBST severs the link between anticipatory behavior and problems for BST. This kind of behavior is accommodated within a BST-styled framework without invoking the representations of AT. In addition, eBST forms a conceptual framework that is built up around the coupling idea, just like classic BST. However, eBST also draws this coupling inward, for example as genetic and neural regulatory circuits modulating ICPs, and outward, drawing in increasingly long-term and far off characteristics of the environment. With this extension of BST the discussion with AT changes. The work discussed in chapter 4 was formulated in a situation where the choice is between holding that the immediate short-term coupling between a behaving system and its environment suffices for behavior, or to succumb to AT's representationalism. In this context the distinction between reactive and anticipatory behavior is a sensible one and the same goes for the claim that most or even all behavior is reactive and not anticipatory. However, keeping representational explanations at bay thus came at the cost of acknowledging only a limited means for explaining behavior: the immediate short-term organism-environment coupling. AAR and DST showed that even this limited use of organism-environment coupling went a long way in making successful behaving systems, but it was not successful enough to still the tendency to return to representational explanations (see the discussion in the sections 3.3 and 4.3 of chapter 4). With eBST, the limited short-term coupling between a behaving system and environment can be added to without getting involved in AT's representations. Consequently, this defensive argument for maintaining the sufficiency of short-term coupling for all behavior loses its force.

To conclude, when it comes to the sufficiency of short-term organism-environment coupling, eBST certainly differs from the AAR and DST interpretation as presented in chapter 4. According to eBST such short-term coupling alone does not suffice for explaining the generation of behavior. However, this conclusion adds to, rather than detracts from, the earlier AAR and DST views on coupling and also solves the problem of the seeming need to combine BST ideas with AT.

A second concern that stems from taking the neuroethological notion of modulation as an example of the working of ICPs consists of the relation between modulation and self-organization. Self-organization has been introduced as a mathematically sophisticated dynamical description of how happenings at a particular spatio-temporal scale $S(n)$ give rise to the emergence of new orderings at a larger spatio-temporal scale $S(n + 1)$. The concepts of order and control parameters have been developed in this context (Haken, 1987, 1995; Kelso, 1995). The notion of modulation derives from a different context, the empirical study of behavioral systems. How well do the two fit?

Intuitively, the concept of self-organization seems to apply well to the effects of modulation. Changes in a single variable induce extensive reorderings of the neural systems functional operation. This picture is strengthened when it is set in the larger context of genetic regulatory circuits where similar regulative factors, such as the homeotic genes, have been used in evolution over and over again with a multitude of large-scale structures as a result. There must be robust and general pattern formation processes at work here. It is tempting to suppose that in all these cases the same principle is tapped to produce large-scale, long-term structure. It is even more tempting to suppose that this principle consists of dynamical self-organization. However, this interpretation is at present only a seductive and promising idea. It needs to be fleshed out in such a way that physical detail meets the mathematical descriptions of dynamical self-organizing processes.

Neuroethology focuses on the anatomical and physiological details of the nervous system involved in the generation of behavior. The dynamics of self-organization consists of a more abstracted description of the dynamical pattern-forming properties implemented by all this detail. How are the two to be brought together? Apart from the sheer complexity of nervous systems, an additional difficulty is that it remains unclear which characteristics of a nervous system are important for the dynamical—or computational—processes underlying behavior, and consequently need to brought into a more abstract characterization of a nervous system (Marder, 1998). The occurrence and extent of modulation, for example, challenges the adequacy of connectionism's abstract neural nets where synaptic connectivity and the slow change of synaptic weights are the sole factors determining network behavior. Important features are missed in these abstractions. To arrive at better dynamical abstractions, the anatomical connectivity of a nervous system will have to be distinguished from its functional, or behaviorally relevant connectivity, which is dependent on all kinds of modulatory influences that need to be specified (Marder, 1994). There is a double bind then. Specifying modulatory influences will be greatly helped with clear ideas about the general dynamical principles implemented by the biological details, while at the same time arriving at these general dynamical principles is severely hampered by the confusing details of any biological system.

At this point, AAR and DST approaches of BST return as promising generators of ideas concerning possible general principles involved in behavior generation. Working with artificial systems makes for simpler systems compared to the biological ones, while a dedication to modeling behavior keeps the work focused on behavioral explanation. A good example is provided by recent work of Chiel, Beer, and Gallagher (Chiel, Beer, and Gallagher, 1999; Beer, Chiel, and Gallagher, 1999). In two connected papers they address the problem of developing an abstract description of the dynamics of central pattern generators (CPGs). Because of the enormous complexity and variability of biological CPGs they analyzed artificially evolved CPGs for an artificial insect (see the discussion of Beer's work in chapter 4). In these papers they introduce a concept of *dynamical modules* as the basis for an abstract description of a model CPG. By using this concept, they were capable of analyzing the evolved CPGs in a way that allowed them to make not only qualitative statements about the operation of the model CPG, but also quantitative predictions. They could predict the robustness of the motor pattern to parameter variations, some of the constraints on the neural architecture, and the duration of transitions, a key issue when it comes to movement control. It also allowed them to formulate a number of general principles at a high level of abstraction while at lower levels of abstraction there was only a tremendous variability.

The work by Chiel, Beer, and Gallagher provides a good example of what the empirical agenda stemming from eBST might look like and how progress can be made with the topics on this agenda. The use of a dynamical analysis of artificial behavioral systems seems a good way to advance the formulation of general dynamical principles that are predicted to be at work within the multitude of variable anatomical and physiological detail. It does not yet prove that dynamical self-organization is an actual fact in behavioral systems, nor that modulation in a nervous system can be understood as the operation of ICPs, but it is on the right track of finding out whether these ideas are real enough or not.

This work also provides an indication of the general direction that AAR and a DST approach might take in the future, as hinted at by eBST. Extended BST stresses the importance of finding proper conceptual tools to deal with the coupling involved in basic behavior. Extended BST also stresses the need for a sufficiently complex sensory-musculo-skeletal system and the differentiation between movement and behavior. The suggestion that stems from this view then that it is worthwhile to focus on functionally robust, basic behavior, staying close to the biological examples, while striving at the same time to find good abstractions that allow one to shed as much of the biological detail as possible. Chiel and Beer (1997, p. 556) distinguished three broad approaches that emphasize different sides of these opposing tendencies. (a) One can build biologically realistic models, motivated by experimental questions. These models require much experimental work to set up, are complex and difficult to analyze, but allow quantitative, experimentally testable predictions. (b) One can construct more abstract models on the basis of specific theoretical questions. These models do not lead to quantitative testable predictions. They do however highlight key features of a problem, have few parameters to set, and are easier to analyze. (c) One can create physical models that exhibit properties of the system under study. Building an actual device is difficult, slow, and expensive. On the other hand, it provides the ultimate test whether one's ideas concerning the generation of behavior can be implemented in such a way that a real artificial behavioral system results. All three approaches have their own strengths and weaknesses and none is to be preferred at the expense of the others. A mutually enriching reciprocal influence, leading to a theoretical co-evolution of these different approaches seems to be the best bet for the future development of BST.

One last point, in the discussion above, the focus has been consistently on very basic behavior without any mention of the particulars of human behavior. I have given many theoretical reasons for making this choice, most importantly the almost universal deemphasizing of basic behavior as an important topic for understanding the human case. While no one blinks at the idea that the fruitfly has taught us a lot about human genetics, the tendency is to balk at the idea that organisms like fruitflies can teach us a lot about human behavior as well. Basic behavior simply needs all the scientific attention it can get. At the same time, stressing the importance of basic behavior does not imply the downplaying of the study of human cognitive behavior. Of course, the study of human cognition is of extreme importance; it just doesn't need the kind of promotion that basic behavior requires. Extended BST can also be pursued in a human context. For example, Thelen, Smith, and their co-workers have developed a dynamical model in which an internal dynamic field plays an important role in influencing the dynamics of reaching movements. This internal dynamical field, plausibly interpreted as a kind of ICP, is used in an argument in favor of a dynamical embodied explanation for a classic problem in developmental psychology, rather than a cognitive one (Thelen et al., in press; Smith et al., 1999). Thus, eBST is not restricted to low-level stuff, but only emphasizes its importance. Our best hopes for developing BST lie with a multipronged attack on high and low-level behavior in which, again, multiple approaches mutually influence and strengthen one another in a process of theoretical co-evolution. Still, for such co-evolution to get started, the importance of some of the players will have to be more generally recognized.

To conclude, eBST fits in a general genetic-neuro-behavioral setting and ICPs can be plausibly cast as modulatory factors in a nervous system. Saying more in this respect involves finding out more about the dynamical characteristics of behavioral systems and developing ways to make these characteristics understandable and tractable. All of this supports the general idea that psychology in the (extended) BST perspective is to turn explicitly to a subpersonal level of explanation and to theory building which doesn't bear any obvious relation to the macroscopic psychological phenomena. In some ways it is like the relation between macroscopic biology, dealing with life forms, and molecular biology, dealing with the processes making up and maintaining those life forms. Up to now, psychological theorizing tended to remain close to the surface characteristics of psychological phenomena and tended to interpret lower-level research such as going on in neuroscience in these surface terms. "Where in the brain does visual perception take place?" is a question that exemplifies this way of thinking. Extended BST is a conceptual backup of the empirical tendency to move away from surface theories and into a new unexplored realm of subpersonal processes making up our psychological functioning.

5 Where goes representation?

It is time to return to the central question of this book: What place, if any, should representations occupy in an explanation of the generation of behavior? The discussion has come a long way by now. It started with the debate between cognitivists and interactionists about the use of representations within cognitive science. This discussion became very fierce because the notion of representation is at the heart of cognitive science and the philosophy of mind serving many different functions. Questioning the use and even the presence of representations in a general way touches so many of these different functions that the critique of representations tended to be met with ridicule rather than serious attention.

I have tried to clean up the discussion by interpreting representations, as used in cognitive science, as an element in an explanation of the generation of behavior. There are two important consequences of this interpretation. First, the discussion becomes explicitly a discussion about subpersonal representations, leaving open the possibility and usefulness of personal-level representations. Second, these subpersonal representations are most plausibly constructed as representations that derive their representationality from a modeling capacity. The presence of an inner state bearing information about an external state is not sufficient to conceptualize this inner state as a representation. The critique on the use of representations in cognitive science thus targets a specific form of representation and does not touch the representations of our daily use, nor the idea of a correlation between inner neural events and external environmental events.

Consequently, the discussion about representations was cast as a discussion about conceptual frameworks that explained behavior with (AT) and without (BST) these modeling, subpersonal representations. I argued against AT and in favor of BST, which itself, however, came to incorporate theoretical entities that might be interpreted as some form of representation. The central question can now be rephrased as: What place, if any, should representations occupy in the conceptual framework provided by eBST?

To accommodate anticipatory behavior within BST a morphogenetic conceptual framework was introduced. The internal control parameters, or ICPs, which figure in this story can easily be interpreted as representations. Several observations point in this direction. (1) Like the genetic code, behavior-related ICPs are definite theoretical entities which stand out from the short-term operation of the nervous system. (2) They also function to guide long-term behavior, just as representations do in specification accounts. (3) In the case of morphogenesis the genetic factor was also interpreted as a set of instructions which already embodied the macroscopic form. Since this resulted in a very successful research-program, why not maintain a representational interpretation for behavior-related ICPs?

On the other hand, the arguments against interpreting ICPs as representations are very strong. The conceptual difference between the traditional concept of 'representation' and ICPs is huge: A representational interpretation is limited to one particular perspective on a multiply scaled organization. Behavioral ICPs are explicitly defined within the context of multiple scales of organization. To deem the two equivalent is putting too much value on one particular perspective on behavior. Representation is, literally, a *coarse* view. In contrast to representations ICPs are intrinsically connected to a regulatory network of which they are a part. Also, ICPs do not consist of models of the external circumstances. Such an interpretation goes right against the grain of the idea of a regular trajectory. The macroscopic order is newly generated; it is not already encoded within the organism's ICPs.

In addition, a representational interpretation could easily interfere with the morphogenetic conceptual framework. Equating ICPs with representations amounts to the injection of a particular set of thought habits into a tentative and still fragile, interactionist account of behavior. Representations are firmly associated with personal-level concepts such as intentionality and the mental frame of reference in general. Interpreting ICPs as representations brings in a lot of conceptual ballast to an otherwise nonencrusted concept. Without it there is much more freedom to develop new ideas and explanations, as is now being done in embryology (see, e.g., Nijhout, 1990). It will be easier to wrestle behavioral explanation free from AT's old Cartesian picture without interpreting ICPs as representations.

In this context one should also place Wheeler and Clark's plea to interpret ICP-like factors as 'genic representations' (Wheeler and Clark, 1999). Wheeler and Clark make a difference between causal spread and explanatory spread. Causal spread is, roughly, the BST idea that the relevant causal factors in behavior are spread out over happenings in the neural system, the body, and the environment. Explanatory spread is the idea that to explain behavior and cognition one should take into account all these causally spread processes. Their idea is to dissociate these two spreads. They acknowledge the importance of causal spread but are unwilling to accept the accompanying explanatory spread. They are particularly reluctant to give up the notion of representation, which in their view provides a unitary explanatory handhold that is not to be given up lightly for an explanatory spread account.

Indeed, if the choice is to hang on to representations or to give up hope of finding any transparent explanation for the causal spread of BST, then this would be a very strong incentive to hang on to representations. But, we do not face this choice at all. The concept of representation is not the only option to provide explanatory grip on the causal spread—I prefer causal mesh—of BST. With BST there comes a new and nearly uncharted territory to the attention of psychology and cognitive science. It goes without saying that explanatory instruments or concepts are needed to give shape to this territory. The theory of dynamical systems has brought a first sprinkling of the kind of concepts and theories that are necessary to get a grip on BST's mesh-like structure, but there is of course a long way to go.

What does the notion of representation add to this ongoing explanatory development? I don't see any explanatory benefits in keeping this mind-based concept around in this project. If representation is read in its older interpretation of an internal model, then it is just the wrong kind of concept to fit into the eBST conceptual framework. And when representations are reinterpreted as ICPs—genic representations in Wheeler and Clark's terminology—they acquire a different meaning and it becomes unclear what the extra representational interpretation adds to the explanation, except obscuring that psychology has moved into a new territory where our traditional mind-based conceptualizations are inappropriate.

This shift in the explanatory basis that accompanies the move from AT to BST must not be forgotten. Representation is not a self-evident and necessary concept in the context of a subpersonal BST. The sheer *possibility* of a representational interpretation should not be taken as a compelling reason to actually interpret ICPs as representations. Being able to establish a reliable relation between an environmental state and an ICP, or some neural state in general, does not imply that the latter is necessarily some kind of representation. Noticing that a tree rises from the ground up to a noticeable height does not make it a tower. Trees and towers are different things, even though they share certain properties. Consequently, why couldn't we discriminate representation-like entities from representations?

Somehow, there seems to be a strong reluctance to abandon the notion of representation as a suitable concept for explaining behavior. Instead, there is a tendency to *search* for entities that can bear the burden of being interpreted as representations (Clark, 1997a, 1997b; Wheeler and Clark, 1999). We would do well here to remember that the current aim is to formulate an account of the generation of behavior at a subpersonal level of description (see chapter 1). Any claims made here do not directly bear on the use of representations in descriptions that apply to complete, acting agents. And while it looks like that the notion of representation serves well enough in that personal-level context, its appearance as a subpersonal concept remains so unspecific and chameleon-like—so ad hoc—that I would like to ask the rhetorical question: "Why bother?"

Notes

Chapter 1

1. I chose 'psychology' instead of 'cognitive science' as a general label for the work that will be discussed. The term 'cognitive science' would have been a more modern and more common label. However, there are good reasons for choosing 'psychology' nevertheless: Given a long-term, historical view on the topics discussed, the label 'psychology' is most appropriate. Psychology has always been the study of human (and animal) mind and behavior. The fact that, in practice, psychology nowadays consists of a collection of narrow subdisciplines (clinical psychology, social psychology, developmental psychology, and experimental psychology) should not be used as an argument that this is what psychology *ought* to be. The label 'psychology' is used to signal what psychology should be in principle, rather than what it has become in practice. Another reason for being dissatisfied with 'cognitive science' as a label comes from the topic that will be discussed. That topic is behavior, and even though most of the work discussed will conventionally be called cognitive science, as a label for a study of behavior it strikes me as descriptively inadequate and misleading. Therefore 'psychology' it is, although at some places, where psychology would sound very awkward, I fall back on 'cognitive science'.

2. In my use, the term 'cognitivist psychology' is not the same as cognitive psychology, but a general label for a strong cognition oriented approach to the explanation of behavior.

3. I owe the neutral term 'internal state' to Bram Bakker, who pointed out to me that there is a similarity here with the distinction between Markovian and non-Markovian learning tasks (Sutton and Barto, 1998). Both tasks are formulated as the problem of finding, by the use of reinforcement learning, a specific output given an environmental state. In the Markovian case the current sensory state suffices for choosing the proper output, so that the learning problem becomes one of finding the direct input-output mappings. In addition to the current sensory states, non-Markovian tasks require internal states to choose the proper output at each moment in time. The requirement of internal states makes the latter similar to anticipatory behavior. Anticipatory behavior and non-Markovian tasks differ however in that the former is a phenomenon and the latter a formal description of a learning task that

might or might not apply to this phenomenon. Anticipatory behavior might require internal states for practical reasons (e.g. speed of learning) even while the task is Markovian (Bakker and Van der Voort van der Kleij, 2000). In addition, the conceptualization of behavior as 'choosing an output' will be criticized in the next chapters, which drives a further wedge between the two.

4. The interpretation of what psychological explanation amounts to is very similar to that of Cummins (1983), except for terminology. Cummins calls regular deductive-nomological descriptions 'transition theories' and contrasts them with property theories. I use the term 'transition' to refer to what has to be explained by Cummins' property theories.

5. These authors (Beer and Smithers) do not make a distinction between personal and subpersonal levels of description. They use 'agent' where I would use 'behaving system'.

Chapter 2

1. For example, Braitenberg (1984), Lloyd (1989), Dennett (1996), and Dretske (1988) all start out by considering (simple) behavior and then move onward to the mind-related topics as soon as possible.

2. The proximal-distal distinction should not be mixed up with the one mentioned earlier: Mayr's distinction between ultimate and proximate causation in biology. Ultimate causes are concerned with the evolutionary 'why' of biological phenomena, proximate causes with how these phenomena work. The proximal-distal distinction is made within the context of proximate causation, as a part of a story that aims to answer Mayr's 'how' question. Distal oriented behavior has definitely functional characteristics, but these relate to the 'why' for individual organism, not to the evolutionary 'why'.

3. Heider and Brunswik are only concerned with the environment as it bears on behavior. For example, the immediate presence of sufficient oxygen is essential for the continuing existence of an organism. But it does not require behavior, except for the initiation of airflow in larger animals. Oxygen is present all of the time.

4. Gibson's ecological approach was influenced by Heider's ideas (Gibson, 1966; Looren de Jong, 1995). However, according to Heider, as well as Brunswik, the relation between the proximal and distal environment is not one to one. This is in direct contradiction with Gibson's theory in which perception became direct and unmediated. Gibson's ecological approach should not be construed as the logical consequence of Heider's and Brunswik's theoretical ideas. The latter are perfectly congenial to a cognitivist approach.

5. Jackendoff (1987) calls this subpersonal organization the computational mind and sets it apart from the phenomenological mind, creating the mind-mind (in contrast to the mind-body) problem in the process. I think it is less confusing to talk about subpersonal mechanisms in this context, rather than postulating several forms of 'mind', some of which do not have its traditional—intentional, phenomenolog-

ical—characteristics (Searle, 1992). However, this issue is about choosing adequate labels, not about the contents of what is labeled. 'Subpersonal mechanism' and 'computational mind' refer to the same way of cognitive modeling.

6. The authors acknowledge that stereo vision techniques for planetary rovers have become much more feasible since they decided to use a laser rangefinder in 1987 (Krotkov and Simmons, 1996, p. 160).

7. It should be noted that the word 'implementation' refers here not to the relation between a computational level and its neural implementation. Rather, it refers to the relation between an AT-styled SMPA architecture and the concrete, detailed implementation of this architecture by classical computational means (including its neural implementation), or by a connectionist network.

8. Connectionism has also been the starting point for more alternative approaches to intelligence. Some of these developments will be discussed in later chapters.

9. Dennett also mentions *Gregorian creatures* (after Richard Gregory) whose "inner environments are informed by the *designed* portions of the outer environment" (1996, p. 99). Gregorian creatures are too fancy for my present exposition and I will ignore them here.

10. The difference between content and target is similar, but not identical, to the sense-reference distinction. Content cannot specify its target, whereas sense does specify its referent (Cummins, 1996, p. 19).

Chapter 3

1. See chapter 1, section 4.1.

2. A list of references can be found in chapter 1, section 4.1.

3. This section is partly based on Keijzer (1995).

4. I have taken great liberties here. The ideas discussed can be traced to Clancey, but they do not give a strict replication of his ideas. Clancey makes many points and talks about "frame of reference problems" (1989, p. 107). The discussion here focuses on a small subpart of his ideas, and though, I think, Clancey does hold the opinion ascribed to him here, he has many more which are not touched upon. In a sense I hijack his term "frame of reference problem" and use it for my own purposes, giving it a twist that Clancey himself might not be willing to make.

5. First-person cannot be taken as referring to *our* own perspective on ourselves, in contrast to the third-person perspective from the outside. In this book, I am concerned with a subpersonal level of description, so the subjective looking at ourselves does not apply. What applies is a metaphorical 'looking' at itself of the subpersonal neural-body-environment system. The epilogue in Clark (1997a) illustrates the difference between the brain's view and the person's view very nicely.

6. Von Uexküll (1980) is a compilation of the various theoretical writings of Jacob von Uexküll edited and commented on by his son. Most references are to Von Uexküll (1921), but the relevant passages can also be found in the newer work. See especially chapter 3, "Der Funktionskreis" (pp. 226–290).

Chapter 4

1. I am indebted to Tim Smithers for the term 'interaction space.'

2. For example Beer (1990, 1995a), Smithers (1994), and Winograd and Flores (1986).

3. Their book *The Tree of Knowledge* is a good introduction. It provides a highly didactical overview of their major ideas. An even more accessible set of introductory texts consists of Mingers (1989, 1990, 1991), but these miss the flavor and many of the nuances of the original work.

4. This section and the next are based on Keijzer and Bem (1996).

5. These and other seminal papers by Brooks on AAR are now collected in Brooks (1999). This collection does however not incorporate any papers about the Cog project, the current attempt of Brooks and his associates to build a humanoid robot (Brooks and Stein, 1993; see also Dennett, 1994).

6. A background complication must be mentioned. I hold that the distinction between AT and BST as explanations of behavior is orthogonal with respect to a computation-dynamics distinction. The former and not the latter distinction is the one that matters. In contrast, Van Gelder makes the computation-dynamics distinction the core issue that sets AT and BST (as I use the terms) apart (1995, 1998). Fitting Van Gelder's dynamical approach to cognition into BST does not imply an agreement with the centrality of the computation-dynamics distinction.

As to the source of this difference of opinion, Van Gelder holds that his defense of the dynamical approach to cognition is much broader than the idea of dynamical coupling alone (Van Gelder, 1998), and that many aspects of BST fall within his own broad view of a dynamical approach to cognition. He is right that this is a possible way to carve up the territory. I have two reasons for making different cuts (see also Keijzer, Bem , and Van der Heijden, 1998). First, a hard computation-dynamics distinction is controversial (see the commentaries to Van Gelder 1998). BST avoids this problem of demarcation, while maintaining a close association with dynamical theories and models as the natural choice for developing BST. Second, dynamics can be tied down to become a 'dynamical approach to cognition' but at its heart it remains a thoroughly general way of conceptualizing dynamical systems in general, and not of cognition and behavior in particular. I prefer to build up the conceptual framework around the phenomena that need to be explained rather than around the method and models that seem so promising at present.

Chapter 5

1. Parts of this chapter are based on Keijzer (1998a).

2. As said before, only the outward characteristics of anticipatory behavior are addressed in this definition. Anticipatory behavior is often interpreted as involving a subjective sense of anticipating a future result, or intentions to achieve some goal. These personal-level issues are beyond the scope of this discussion.

3. There is a tendency to put the so-called 'developmental tradition' (Resnik, 1994; Griffiths, 1996), sketched here, in opposition to the neo-Darwinian position (Dennett, 1995). The developmentalists argue that not all order which is present in living nature is the result of selection. For example, Kauffman remarks that lipid membranes, which provide such useful cell boundaries, do not originate in genetic instructions. Lipid membranes are a physical phenomenon and they come for free under the proper circumstances (Kauffman, 1993). However, acknowledging the importance of self-ordering principles in living nature does not in any way detract from the importance of selection as a crucial factor in generating order (ibid.). I would like to follow Depew and Weber's (1995) lead and hold that the dynamical view could form a refinement and extension of Darwinian ideas, similarly to how Mendelian genetics and the statistical approach to population genetics formed the 'modern synthesis' of neo-darwinism. There is no reason to posit any deep disagreement with basic Darwinian insights.

4. Kelso gives an intentional interpretation to these parametric influences and uses the word 'specific' in this context. For Kelso this is a way to combine self-organizing systems with intentionality. In the preceding chapters, it has been argued, however, that intentions apply at a higher level of organization and that they form a part of the explanandum. Intentions should not play a role in a subpersonal account of the generation of behavior. Intentions can thus not be used to make the parametric influences specific; the specificity, or rather the appropriateness of internal control parameters derives from the set up of the system.

References

Abraham, R. H., and Shaw, C. D. (1987). Dynamics: a visual introduction. In F. E. Yates (ed.), *Self-organizing systems: the emergence of order* (pp. 543–597). New York: Plenum Press.

Abraham, R. H., and Shaw, C. D. (1992). *Dynamics: the geometry of behavior* (2nd ed.). Redwood City, Calif.: Addison-Wesley.

Alcock, J. (1989). *Animal behavior: an evolutionary approach* (4th ed.). Sunderland, Mass.: Sinauer Associates.

Alexander, D. M., and Globus G. G. (1996). Edge-of-chaos dynamics in recursively organized neural systems. In E. MacCormac and M. Stamenov (eds.), *The secret symmetry: fractals of brain, mind, and consciousness*. Amsterdam: John Benjamin.

Allen, T. F. H., and Starr, T. B. (1982). *Hierarchy: perspectives for ecological complexity*. Chicago: University of Chicago Press.

Amsel, A. (1989). *Behaviorism, neobehaviorism, and cognitivism in learning theory*. Hillsdale, N.J.: Erlbaum.

Anderson, J. A. (1991). On what building a Martian three-wheeled iguana tells us about complex minds. *Behavior and Philosophy, 19*, 91–102.

Anderson, P. (1972). More is different. *Science, 177*, 393–396.

Arbib, M. A. (1975). Cybernetics after 25 years: a personal view of systems theory and brain theory. *IEEE Transactions on Systems, Man, and Cybernetics*, May, 359–363.

Ashby, W. R. (1956). *An introduction to cybernetics*. London: Methuen.

Ashby, W. R. (1960). *Design for a brain: the origin of adaptive behaviour* (2nd ed.). London: Chapman and Hall.

Baker, L. R. (1987). *Saving belief: a critique of physicalism*. Princeton, N.J.: Princeton University Press.

Bakker, B., and Van der Voort van der Kleij, G. (2000). Trading off perceptions with internal state: reinforcement learning and analysis of Q-Elman networks in a Markovian task. In *Proceedings of the International Joint Conference on Neural Networks, IJCNN 2000*.

Barwise, J. (1987). Unburdening the language of thought. *Mind and Language, 2*, 82–96.

Bechtel, W. (1988). *Philosophy of science: an overview for cognitive science.* Hillsdale, N.J.: Erlbaum.

Bechtel, W. (1994). Biological and social constraints on cognitive processes: the need for dynamical interactions between levels of inquiry. *Canadian Journal of Philosophy, suppl. vol. 20*, 133–164.

Bechtel, W. (1998). Representations and cognitive explanations: assessing the dynamicist's challenge in cognitive science. *Cognitive Science, 22*, 295–318.

Bechtel, W., and Richardson, R. C. (1993). *Decomposition and localization as strategies in scientific research*. Princeton, N.J.: Princeton University Press.

Beckermann, A. (1988). Why tropistic systems are not genuine intentional systems. *Erkenntnis, 29*, 125–142.

Beer, R. D. (1990). *Intelligence as adaptive behavior: an experiment in computational neuroethology*. San Diego: Academic Press.

Beer, R. D. (1995a). A dynamical systems perspective on agent-environment interaction. *Artificial Intelligence, 72*, 173–215.

Beer, R. D. (1995b). Computational and dynamical languages for autonomous agents. In R. E. Port and T. van Gelder (eds.), *Mind as motion: explorations in the dynamics of cognition* (pp. 121–147). Cambridge, Mass.: MIT Press.

Beer, R. D., Chiel, H. J., and Gallagher, J. C. (1999). Evolution and analysis of model CPGs for walking. II: General principles and individual variability. *Journal of Computational Neuroscience, 7*, 119–147.

Bem, S. (1989). *Denken om te doen: een studie over cognitie en werkelijkheid.* Unpublished doctoral thesis, Leiden University.

Bem, S., and Keijzer, F. A. (1996). Recent changes in the concept of cognition. *Theory and Psychology, 6*, 449–469.

Berridge, K. C. (1990). Comparative fine structure of action: rules of form and sequence in the grooming patterns of six rodent species. *Behaviour, 113* (1–2), 21–56.

Bickhard, M. H. (1993). Representational content in humans and machines. *Journal of Experimental and Theoretical Artificial Intelligence, 5*, 285–333.

Bickhard, M. H., and Terveen, L. (1995). *Foundational issues in artificial intelligence and cognitive science: impasse and solution.* Amsterdam: Elsevier.

Boden, M. (1972). *Purposive explanation in psychology.* Cambridge, Mass.: Harvard University Press.

Bonasso, R. P., Kortenkamp, D., and Murphy, R. (1998). Mobile robots: a proving ground for artificial intelligence. In D. Kortenkamp, R. P. Bonasso, and R. Murphy (eds.), *Artificial intelligence and mobile robots: case studies of successful robot systems* (pp. 3–18). Cambridge, Mass.: MIT Press.

Bongaardt, R. (1996). *Shifting focus: the Bernstein tradition in movement science.* Unpublished doctoral thesis, Vrije Universiteit, Amsterdam.

Bonner, J. T. (1988). *The evolution of complexity by means of natural selection.* Princeton, N.J.: Princeton University Press.

Bonner, J. T. (1993). *Life cycles.* Princeton, N.J.: Princeton University Press.

Boorse, C. (1976). Wright on functions. *Philosophical Review, 85,* 70–86.

Boring, E. G. (1929). *A history of experimental psychology.* New York: Appleton-Century Company.

Boyd, C. A. R., and Noble, D. (1993). *The logic of life: the challenge of integrative physiology.* Oxford: Oxford University Press.

Braitenberg, V. (1984). *Vehicles.* Cambridge, Mass.: MIT Press.

Breland, K., and Breland, M. (1966). *Animal behavior.* New York: Macmillan Company.

Brooks, R. A. (1986). A robust layered control system for a mobile robot. *IEEE Journal of Robotics and Automation, 1,* 14–23.

Brooks, R. A. (1989). A robot that walks: emergent behaviors from a carefully evolved network. *Neural Computation, 1,* 253–262.

Brooks, R. A. (1991a). Intelligence without representation. *Artificial Intelligence,* 47, 139–159.

Brooks, R. A. (1991b). Intelligence without reason. In *Proceedings of the International Joint Conference on Artificial Intelligence* (pp. 569–595). San Mateo: Morgan-Kaufman.

Brooks, R. A. (1991c). New approaches to robotics. *Science, 253,* 1227–1232.

Brooks, R. A. (1999). *Cambrian intelligence.* Cambridge, Mass.: MIT Press.

Brooks, R. A., and Stein, L. A. (1993). Building brains for bodies. Memo 1439, MIT Artificial Intelligence Lab, Cambridge, Mass.

Brunswik, E. (1952). *The conceptual framework of psychology.* Chicago: University of Chicago Press.

Brusca, R. C., and Brusca, G. J. (1990). *Invertebrates.* Sunderland, Mass.: Sinauer.

Camhi, J. M. (1984). *Neuroethology.* Sunderland, Mass.: Sinauer.

Campbell, D. T. (1966). Pattern matching as an essential in distal knowing. In K. R. Hammond (ed.), *The psychology of Egon Brunswik* (pp. 81–106). New York: Holt, Rinehart, and Winston.

Campbell, D. T. (1973). Evolutionary epistemology. In P. Schilpp (ed.), *The philosophy of Karl Popper* (vol. 1, pp. 413–463). La Salle: Open Court.

Carello, C., Turvey, M. T., Kugler, P. N., and Shaw, R. E. (1984). Inadequacies of the computer metaphor. In M. S. Gazzaniga (ed.), *Handbook of cognitive neuroscience* (pp. 229–248). New York: Plenum.

Chiel. H. J., and Beer, R. D. (1997). The brain has a body. *Trends in Neuroscience, 20* (12), 553–557.

Chiel, H. J., Beer, R. D., and Gallagher, J. C. (1999). Evolution and analysis of model CPGs for walking. I: Dynamical modules. *Journal of Computational Neuroscience,* 7, 99–118.

Chomsky, N. (1959). Review of Skinner's *Verbal Behavior. Language, 35*, 26–58.

Churchland, P. M. (1989). *A neurocomputational perspective: the nature of mind and the structure of science.* Cambridge, Mass.: MIT Press.

Churchland, P. M. (1990). On the nature of explanation: a PDP approach. *Physica D, 42*, 281–292.

Churchland, P. M. (1995). *The engine of reason, the seat of the soul.* Cambridge, Mass.: MIT Press.

Churchland, P. S. (1986). *Neurophilosophy: toward a unified science of the mind-brain.* Cambridge, Mass.: MIT Press.

Churchland, P. S., and Churchland, P. M. (1983). Stalking the wild epistemic engine. *Noûs, 17*, 5–18.

Churchland, P. S., and Sejnowsky, T. J. (1990). Neural representation and neural computation. In J. Tomberlin (ed.), *Action theory and philosophy of mind* (pp. 343–382). Atascadero, Calif.: Ridgeview.

Clancey, W. J. (1989). The frame of reference problem in cognitive modeling. In *Proceedings of the Annual Conference of the Cognitive Science Society* (pp. 107–114). Hillsdale, N.J.: Erlbaum.

Clancey, W. J. (1993). Situated action: a neuropsychological interpretation. Response to Vera and Simon. *Cognitive Science, 17*, 87–116.

Clark, A. (1994). Autonomous agents and real-time success: some foundational issues. In T. Smithers (ed.), *Proceedings of the Third International Workshop on Artificial Life and Artificial Intelligence* (pp. 19–22). San Sebastian, Spain: Universidad del País Vasco.

Clark, A. (1997a). *Being there: putting brain, body, and world together again.* Cambridge, Mass.: MIT Press

Clark, A. (1997b). The dynamical challenge. *Cognitive Science, 21*, 461–481.

Clark, A., and Toribio, J. (1994). Doing without representing? *Synthese, 101*, 401–431.

Cohen, A. H., Rossignol, S., and Grillner, S. (eds.), (1988). *Neural control of rhythmic movements in vertebrates.* New York: Wiley.

Cordeschi, R. (1991). The discovery of the artificial: some protocybernetic developments, 1930–1940. *AI and Society, 5*, 218–238.

Craik, K. (1943). *The nature of explanation.* Cambridge: Cambridge University Press.

Cummins, R. (1983). *The nature of psychological explanation.* Cambridge, Mass.: MIT Press.

Cummins, R. (1989). *Meaning and mental representation.* Cambridge, Mass.: MIT Press.

Cummins, R. (1991). The role of representation in connectionist explanations of cognitive capacities. In W. Ramsey, S. P. Stich, and D. E. Rumelhart (eds.), *Philosophy and Connectionist Theory* (pp. 91–114). Hillsdale, N.J.: Erlbaum.

Cummins, R. (1996). *Representations, targets, and attitudes*. Cambridge, Mass.: MIT Press.

De Graaf, J. W. (1999). *Relating new to old: a classical controversy in developmental psychology*. Unpublished doctoral thesis, University of Groningen.

Dennett, D. C. (1978). *Brainstorms*. Brighton: Harvester Press.

Dennett, D. C. (1987a). *The intentional stance*. Cambridge, Mass.: MIT Press.

Dennett, D. C. (1987b). Eliminate the middletoad! *Behavioral and Brain Sciences, 10*, 372–373.

Dennett, D. C. (1987c). Cognitive wheels: the frame problem of AI. In Z. Pylyshyn (ed.), *The robot's dilemma: the frame problem in artificial intelligence* (pp. 41–64). Norwood, N.J.: Ablex.

Dennett, D. C. (1994). The practical requirements for making a conscious robot. *Philosophical Transactions of the Royal Society, A349*, 133–146.

Dennett, D. C. (1995). *Darwin's dangerous idea*. New York: Simon and Schuster.

Dennett, D. C. (1996). *Kinds of minds: towards an understanding of consciousness*. London: Weidenfeld and Nicolson.

Depew, D. J., and Weber, B. H. (1995). *Darwinism evolving: systems dynamics and the genealogy of natural selection*. Cambridge, Mass.: MIT Press.

Dewey, J. (1896). The reflex arc concept in psychology. *Psychological Review, 3*, 357–370.

Dijksterhuis, E. J. (1950). *De mechanisering van het wereldbeeld*. Amsterdam: Meulenhof.

Dretske, F. I. (1983). Précis of knowledge and the flow of information. *Behavioral and Brain Sciences, 6*, 55–90.

Dretske, F. I. (1988). *Explaining behavior*. Cambridge, Mass.: MIT Press.

Dreyfus, H. (1972). *What computers can't do: a critique of artificial reason*. New York: Harper and Row.

Edelman, G. M. (1987). *Neural Darwinism: the theory of neural group selection*. New York: Basic Books.

Edelman, G. M. (1988). *Topobiology: an introduction to molecular embryology*. New York: Basic Books.

Edelman, G. M. (1992). *Bright air, brilliant fire*. London: Penguin.

Eibl-Eibesfeldt, I. (1970). *Ethology: the biology of behavior*. New York: Holt, Rinehart, and Winston.

Ekeland, I. (1988). *Mathematics and the Unexpected*. Chicago: University of Chicago Press.

Elman, J. L. (1990). Finding structure in time. *Cognitive Science, 14*, 179–211.

Fentress, J. C. (1990). Organizational patterns in action: local and global issues in action pattern formation. In G. Edelman, W. Gall, and W. Cowan (eds.), *Signal and sense: local and global order in perceptual maps* (pp. 357–382). New York: Wiley.

Fentress, J. C. (1991). The role of timing in motor development. In J. Fagard and P. H. Wolff (eds.), *The development of timing control in coordinated action* (pp. 341–366). Amsterdam: Elsevier Science Publishers.

Fodor, J. A. (1975). *The language of thought*. New York: Thomas Crowell.

Fodor, J. A. (1981). *Representations*. Brighton: Harvester Press.

Fodor, J. A. (1986a). Why paramecia don't have mental representations. *Midwest Studies in Philosophy, 10*, 3–23.

Fodor, J. A. (1986b). Discussion. In Z. Pylyshyn and W. Demopoulos (eds.), *Meaning and cognitive structure*. Norwood, N.J.: Ablex.

Fodor, J. A. (1987). *Psychosemantics*. Cambridge, Mass.: MIT Press.

Fodor, J. A., and McLaughlin, B. P. (1990). Connectionism and the problem of systematicity. *Cognition, 35*, 183–204.

Fodor, J. A., and Pylyshyn, Z. W. (1981). How direct is visual perception? Some reflections on Gibson's *Ecological approach*. *Cognition, 9*, 139–196.

Fodor, J. A., and Pylyshyn, Z. W. (1988). Connectionism and cognitive architecture: a critical analysis. *Cognition, 28*, 3–71.

Ford, K. M., and Hayes, P. J. (eds.), (1991). *Reasoning agents in a dynamic world: the frame problem*. Greenwich, Conn.: JAI Press.

Franklin, S. (1995). *Artificial minds*. Cambridge, Mass.: MIT Press.

Friston, K. J., Tononi, G., Reeke, G. N., Sporns, O., and Edelman, G. M. (1994). Value-dependent selection in the brain: simulation in a synthetic neural model. *Neuroscience, 59*, 229–243.

Gallistel, C. R. (1989). Animal cognition: the representation of space, time, and number. *Annual Review of Psychology, 40*, 155–189.

Gallistel, C. R. (1990a). *The organization of learning*. Cambridge, Mass.: MIT Press.

Gallistel, C. R. (1990b). Representations in animal cognition. *Cognition, 37*, 1–22.

Gardner, H. (1985). *The mind's new science*. New York: Basic Books.

Garfinkel, A. (1991). Reductionism. In R. Boyd, P. Gasper, and J. Trout (eds.), *The philosophy of science* (pp. 443–459). Cambridge, Mass.: MIT Press.

Gat, E. (1998). Three-layer architectures. In D. Kortenkamp, R. P. Bonasso, and R. Murphy (eds.), *Artificial intelligence and mobile robots: case studies of successful robot systems* (pp. 195–210). Cambridge, Mass.: MIT Press.

Gehring, W. J. (1998). *Master control genes in development and evolution*. New Haven: Yale University Press.

Gibson, J. J. (1966). *The senses considered as perceptual systems*. Boston: Houghton Mifflin.

Gibson, J. J. (1979). *The ecological approach to visual perception*. Boston: Houghton Mifflin.

Gilbert, S. F. (ed.), (1991). *A conceptual history of modern embryology*. Baltimore, Md.: Johns Hopkins University Press.

Gilbert, S. F. (1994). *Developmental biology* (4th ed.). Sunderland, Mass.: Sinauer.

Gilbert, S. F., Opitz, J. M., and Raff, R. A. (1996). Resynthesizing evolutionary and developmental biology. *Developmental Biology, 173*, 357–372.

Gleick, J. (1987). *Chaos: making a new science*. London: Cardinal.

Globus, G. G. (1992). Toward a noncomputational cognitive neuroscience. *Journal of Cognitive Neuroscience, 4*, 299–310.

Golani, I. (1976). Homeostatic motor processes in mammalian interactions: a choreography of display. In P. P. G. Bateson and P. F. Klopfer (eds.), *Perspectives in ethology* (vol. 2). New York: Plenum Press.

Goodwin, B. (1984). A relational or field theory of reproduction and its evolutionary implications. In M.-W. Ho and P. Saunders (eds.), *Beyond neo-Darwinism*. London: Academic Press.

Goodwin, B. C. (1994). *How the leopard changed its spots: the evolution of complexity*. New York: Scribner's Sons.

Goodwin, B. C., Kauffman, S. A., and Murray, J. D. (1993). Is morphogenesis an intrinsically robust process? *Journal of Theoretical Biology, 163*, 135–144.

Gottlieb, G. (1992). *Individual development and evolution*. New York: Oxford University Press.

Gould, S. J. (1994). The evolution of life on the earth. *Scientific American, 271* (October), 62–69.

Greenspan, R. J., and Tully, T. (1994). Group report: how do genes set up behavior? In R. J. Greenspan and C. P. Kyriacou (eds.), *Flexibility and constraint in behavioral systems* (pp. 65–80). Chichester: Wiley.

Griffiths, P. E. (1996). Chaotic futures. *Nature, 373*, 208.

Grobstein, C. (1973). Hierarchical order and neogenesis. In H. H. Pattee (ed.), *Hierarchy theory* (pp. 29–47). New York: George Braziller.

Guttenplan, S. (1994a). An essay on mind. In S. Guttenplan (ed.), *A companion to the philosophy of mind* (pp. 1–107). Oxford: Blackwell.

Guttenplan, S. (1994b). Naturalism. In S. Guttenplan (ed.), *A companion to the philosophy of mind* (p. 449). Oxford: Blackwell.

Haken, H. (1987). Synergetics: an approach to self-organization. In F. E. Yates (ed.), *Self-organizing systems: the emergence of order* (pp. 417–437). New York: Plenum Press.

Haken, H. (1995). Some basic concepts of synergetics with respect to multistability in perception, phase transitions, and formation of meaning. In M. Stadler and P. Kruse (eds.), *Ambiguity in mind and nature*. Berlin: Springer Verlag.

Hall, S. S. (1992). *Mapping the next millennium*. New York: Random House.

Hardin, C. L. (1988). *Color for philosophers*. Indianapolis: Hackett Publishing Company.

Harnad, S. (1990). The symbol grounding problem. *Physica D, 42*, 335–346.

Harris-Warrick, R. M., and Marder, E. (1991). Modulation of neural networks for behavior. *Annual Review of Neuroscience, 14*, 39–57.

Harvey, I. (1992). Untimed and misrepresented: connectionism and the computer metaphor. Cognitive Science Research Paper 245, University of Sussex.

Harvey, I., Husbands, P., and Cliff, D. (1993). Issues in evolutionary robotics. In J.-A. Meyer, H. Roitblat and S. Wilson (eds.), *From animals to animats 2*. Cambridge, Mass.: MIT Press.

Hasan, Z., and Stuart, D. G. (1988). Animal solutions to problems of movement control: the role of proprioceptors. *Annual Review of Neuroscience, 11*, 199–223.

Haselager, W. F. G. (1997). *Cognitive science and folk psychology: the right frame of mind*. London: Sage.

Haugeland, J. (1985). *Artificial intelligence: the very idea*. Cambridge, Mass.: MIT Press.

Haugeland, J. (1987). An overview of the frame problem. In Z. Pylyshyn (ed.), *The robot's dilemma: the frame problem in artificial intelligence* (pp. 77–93). Norwood, N.J.: Ablex.

Hebb, D. O. (1982). Alice in wonderland, or psychology among the biological sciences. In H. B. Buchtel (ed.), *The conceptual nervous system* (pp. 42–52). Oxford: Pergamon.

Heider, F. (1959). On perception and event structure and the psychological environment. *Psychological Issues, 1* (4), 1–123.

Heims, S. J. (1980). *John von Neumann and Norbert Wiener: from mathematics to the science of life and death*. Cambridge, Mass.: MIT Press.

Heims, S. J. (1991). *The cybernetics group*. Cambridge, Mass.: MIT Press.

Hendriks-Jansen, H. (1996). *Catching ourselves in the act: situated activity, interactive emergence, evolution, and human thought*. Cambridge, Mass.: MIT Press.

Herrnstein, R. J. (1967). Introduction. In J. B. Watson, *Behavior: an introduction to comparative psychology* (pp. xi–xxxi). New York: Holt, Rinehart, and Winston.

Hilgard, E. R. (1987). *Psychology in America: a historical survey*. San Diego: Harcourt Brace Jovanovich.

Hinton, G. E., McClelland, J. L., and Rumelhart, D. E. (1986). Distributed representations. In D. E. Rumelhart and J. L. McClelland (eds.), *Parallel distributed processing: explorations in the microstructure of cognition*. Vol. 1: *Foundations* (pp. 77–109). Cambridge, Mass.: MIT Press.

Hintzman, D. L. (1993). Twenty-five years of learning and memory: was the cognitive revolution a mistake? In D. E. Meyer and S. Kornblum (eds.), *Attention and performance XIV* (pp. 359–391). Cambridge, Mass.: MIT Press.

Hodgins, J. K., and Raibert, M. H. (1991). Adjusting step length for rough terrain locomotion. *IEEE Transactions on Robotics and Automation, 7*, 289–298.

Hofstadter, D. R. (1985). *Metamagical themas*. London: Penguin.

Hofstadter, D. R., and Dennett, D. C. (eds.), (1981). *The mind's I*. Toronto: Bantam Books.

Holtfreter, J. (1991). Reminiscences on the life and work of Johannes Holtfreter. In S. F. Gilbert (ed.), *A conceptual history of modern embryology* (pp. 109–127). Baltimore, Md.: Johns Hopkins University Press.

Horgan, T. (1993). From supervenience to superdupervenience: meeting the demands of a material world. *Mind, 102*, 555–586.

Hornsby, J. (1997). *Simple mindedness: in defense of naive naturalism in the philosophy of mind.* Cambridge, Mass.: Harvard University Press.

Hornsby, J. (2000). Personal and sub-personal: a defence of Dennett's early distinction. *Philosophical Explorations, 3*, 6–24.

Hurley, S. L. (1998). *Consciousness in action.* Cambridge, Mass.: Harvard University Press.

Jackendoff, R. (1987). *Consciousness and the computational mind.* Cambridge, Mass.: MIT Press.

Jacobs, W. J., et al. (1988). Observations. *Psychobiology, 16*, 3–19.

Janlert, L.-E. (1987). Modeling change—the frame problem. In Z. Pylyshyn (ed.), *The robot's dilemma: the frame problem in artificial intelligence* (pp. 1–40). Norwood, N.J.: Ablex.

Jeannerod, M. (1997). *The cognitive neuroscience of action.* Oxford: Blackwell.

Johnson-Laird, P. N. (1983). *Mental models.* Cambridge: Cambridge University Press.

Judson, H. F. (1979). *The eight day of creation: makers of the revolution in biology.* London: Penguin.

Kauffman, S. A. (1993). *The origins of order: self-organization and selection in evolution.* New York: Oxford University Press.

Kauffman, S. A. (1995). *At home in the universe.* London: Viking.

Keijzer, F. A. (1995). Hitchhiking in cognitive science. In I. Lubek, R. van Hezewijk, G. Pheterson, and C. Tolman (eds.), *Trends and issues in theoretical psychology* (pp. 246–252). New York: Springer.

Keijzer, F. A. (1998a). Doing without representations which specify what to do. *Philosophical Psychology, 11*, 269–302.

Keijzer, F. A. (1998b). Some armchair worries about wheeled behavior. In R. Pfeifer, B. Blumberg, J.-A. Meyer, and S. W. Wilson (eds.), *From animals to animats 5* (pp. 13–21). Cambridge, Mass.: MIT Press.

Keijzer, F. A., and Bem, S. (1996). Behavioral systems interpreted as autonomous agents and as coupled dynamical systems: a criticism. *Philosophical Psychology, 9*, 323–346.

Keijzer, F. A., Bem, S., and Van der Heijden, A. H. C. (1998). The dynamics of what? *Behavioral and Brain Sciences, 21*, 644–645.

Keijzer, F. A., and De Graaf, J. W. (1994). Agents have representations, but what about things? In T. Smithers (ed.), *Proceedings of the Workshop on the Role of Dynamics and Representation in Adaptive Behavior and Cognition* (pp. 174–176). San Sebastian, Spain: Universidad del País Vasco.

Keller, E. F. (1995). *Refiguring life: metaphors of twentieth-century biology*. New York: Columbia University Press.

Kelso, J. A. S. (1995). *Dynamic patterns: the self-organization of brain and behavior*. Cambridge, Mass.: MIT Press.

Kelso, J. A. S., and Tuller, B. (1984). A dynamical basis for action systems. In M. S. Gazzaniga (ed.), *Handbook of cognitive neuroscience* (pp. 321–356). New York: Plenum.

Kim, J. (1998). *Mind in a physical world*. Cambridge, Mass.: MIT Press.

Kirsh, D. (1991). Today the earwig, tomorrow man? *Artificial Intelligence, 47*, 161–184.

Kornblith, H. (ed.), (1985). *Naturalizing epistemology*. Cambridge, Mass.: MIT Press.

Kortmulder, K. (1994). Towards a field theory of behaviour. *Acta Biotheoretica, 42*, 281–293.

Kortmulder, K., and Feuth-de Bruijn, E. (1993). On some generative orders of behaviour. *Acta Biotheoretica, 41*, 329–344.

Krakauer, D. C. (1995). Simple connectionist models of spatial memory in bees. *Journal of Theoretical Biology, 172*, 149–160.

Krotkov, E. P., and Hoffman, R. (1994). Terrain mapping for a walking planetary rover. *IEEE Transactions on Robotics and Automation, 10*, 728–728.

Krotkov, E. P., and Simmons, R. G. (1996). Perception, planning, and control for autonomous walking with the Ambler planetary rover. *International Journal of Robotics Research, 15*, 155–180.

Krotkov, E. P., Simmons, R. G., and Whittaker, W. L. (1995). Ambler: performance of a six-legged planetary rover. *Acta Astronautica, 35*, 75–81.

Kugler, P. N., Shaw, R. E., Vincente, K. J., and Kinsella-Shaw, J. (1990). Inquiry into intentional systems. I: Issues in ecological physics. *Psychological Research, 52*, 98–121.

Kuhn, T. (1962). *The structure of scientific revolutions*. Chicago: University of Chicago Press.

Langton, C. G. (ed.), (1989). *Artificial life*. Redwood City: Addison-Wesley.

Lashley, K. S. (1951). The problem of serial order in behavior. In L. A. Jeffress (ed.), *Cerebral mechanisms in behavior* (pp. 112–146). New York: Wiley.

Latour, B. (1987). *Science in action*. Cambridge, Mass.: Harvard University Press.

Leahey, T. H. (1992). *A history of psychology* (3rd ed.). Englewoods Cliffs, N.J.: Prentice-Hall.

Lettvin, J. Y., Maturana, H. R., McCullogh, W., and Pitts, W. (1959). What the frog's eye tells the frog's brain. *Proceedings of the IRE, 47*, 1940–1951.

Levelt, W. J. M. (1989). *Speaking: from intention to articulation*. Cambridge, Mass.: MIT Press.

Libersat, F., Levy, A., and Camhi, J. M. (1989). Multiple feedback loops in the flying cockroach: excitation of the dorsal and inhibition of the ventral giant interneurons. *Journal of Comparative Physiology A, 165*, 651–668.

Lloyd, D. E. (1989). *Simple minds*. Cambridge, Mass.: MIT Press.

Lloyd Morgan, C. (1900). *Animal behaviour*. London: Arnold.

Loeb, J. (1918). *Forced movements, tropisms, and animal conduct*. Philadelphia: Lippincott Company.

Looren de Jong, H. (1995). Ecological psychology and naturalism: Heider, Gibson, and Marr. *Theory and Psychology, 5*, 251–269.

Lorenz, K. (1973). *Die Rückseite des Spiegels*. München: Piper.

MacDonald, G. (1989). Biology and representation. *Mind and Language, 4*, 186–200.

Marder, E. (1994). Polymorphic neural networks. *Current Biology, 4* (8), 752–754.

Marder, E. (1998). From biophysics to models of network function. *Annual Review of Neuroscience, 21*, 25–45.

Marder, E., and Calabrese, R. L. (1996). Principles of rhythmic motor pattern generation. *Physiological Reviews, 76*, 687–717.

Marr, D. (1982). *Vision*. New York: Freeman.

Matthews, P. C., and Strogatz, S. H. (1990). Phase diagram for the collective behavior of limit-cycle oscillators. *Physical Review Letters, 65*, 1701–1704.

Maturana, H. R., and Varela, F. J. (1980). *Autopoiesis and cognition: the realization of the living*. Dordrecht: Reidel.

Maturana, H. R., and Varela, F. J. (1988). *The tree of knowledge: the biological roots of human understanding*. Boston: New Science Library.

Maynard Smith, J. (1986). *The problems of biology*. Oxford: Oxford University Press.

Maynard Smith, J., and Szathmáry, E. (1995). *The major transitions in evolution*. Oxford: Freeman.

Mayr, E. (1961). Cause and effect in biology. *Science, 134*, 1501–1506.

McAdams, H. H., and Arkin, A (1999). It's a noisy business! genetic regulation at the nanomolar scale. *Trends in Genetics, 15*, 65–69.

McCarthy, J., and Hayes, P. (1969). Some philosophical problems from the standpoint of artificial intelligence. In B. Meltzer and D. Michie (eds.), *Machine intelligence 4* (pp. 463–502). Edinburgh: Edinburgh University Press.

McClelland, J. L., and Rumelhart, D. E. (ed.), (1986). *Parallel distributed processing: explorations in the microstructure of cognition*. Vol. 2: *Psychological and biological models*. Cambridge, Mass.: MIT Press.

McCullogh, W., and Pitts, W. (1943). A logical calculus of the ideas immanent in nervous activity. *Bulletin of Mathematical Biophysics, 5*, 115–133.

McDermott, D. (1987). We've been framed, or why AI is innocent of the frame problem. In Z. Pylyshyn (ed.), *The robot's dilemma: the frame problem in artificial intelligence* (pp. 113–123). Norwood, N.J.: Ablex.

McFarland, D. (1989). Goals, no-goals, and own goals. In A. Montefiori and D. Noble (eds.), *Goals, no-goals, and own goals: a debate on goal-directed and intentional behaviour* (pp. 39–57). London: Unwin Hyman.

McFarland, D., and Bösser, T. (1993). *Intelligent behavior in animals and robots.* Cambridge, Mass.: MIT Press.

Meijer, O. G. (1988). *The hierarchy debate: perspectives for a theory and history of movement science.* Amsterdam: Free University Press.

Meijer, O. G., and Bongaardt, R. (1996). The maizena argument: a reaction. *Journal for Ecological Psychology,* 7, 285–290.

Meijer, O. G., and Roth K. (eds.), (1988). *Complex movement behaviour: the motor-action controversy.* Amsterdam: North Holland.

Meyer, J.-A., and Wilson, S. W. (eds.), (1991). *From animals to animats.* Cambridge, Mass.: MIT Press.

Meyrand, P., Simmers, J., and Moulins, M. (1991). Construction of a pattern-generating circuit with neurons of different networks. *Nature, 351,* 60–63.

Meyrand, P., Simmers, J., and Moulins, M. (1994). Modulation and specification of behavior at the small circuit level. In R. J. Greenspan and C. P. Kyriacou (eds.), *Flexibility and constraint in behavioral systems* (pp. 165–176). Chichester: Wiley.

Midgley, M. (1995). *Beast and man: the roots of human nature* (2nd. ed.). London: Routledge.

Miklos, G. L. G. (1993). Molecules and cognition: the latterday lessons of levels, language, and *lac. Journal of Neurobiology, 24* (6), 842–890.

Miklos, G. L. G., Campbell, K. S. W., and Kankel, D. R. (1994). The rapid emergence of bio-electronic novelty, neural architecture, and behavioral performance. In R. J. Greenspan and C. P. Kyriacou (eds.), *Flexibility and constraint in behavioral systems* (pp. 269–293). Chichester: Wiley.

Miller, G. A., Galanter, E., and Pribram, K. H. (1960). *Plans and the structure of behavior.* New York: Holt, Rinehart, and Winston.

Miller, G. F., and Freyd, J. J. (1993). Dynamic mental representations of animate motion: the interplay among evolutionary, cognitive, and behavioral dynamics. Cognitive Science Research Paper 290, University of Sussex.

Mingers, J. (1989). An introduction to autopoiesis—implications and applications. *Systems Practice,* 2, 159–180.

Mingers, J. (1990). The philosophical implications of Maturana's cognitive theories. *Systems Practice, 3,* 569–584.

Mingers, J. (1991). The cognitive theories of Maturana and Varela. *Systems Practice,* 4, 319–328.

Mondada, F., and Verschure, P. (1993). Modeling system-environment interaction: the complementary roles of simulations and real world artifacts. Unpublished manuscript.

Moravec, H. (1999). Rise of the robots. *Scientific American, 281* (6), 86–93.

Morrison, P., and Morrison, P. (1982). *Powers of ten.* New York: Scientific American Books.

Moser, P. K. (1994). Naturalism and psychological explanation. *Philosophical Psychology,* 7, 63–84.

Moya, C. J. (1990). *The philosophy of action.* Cambridge: Polity Press.

Müller, J. (1848). Specific energy of nerves. In W. S. Sahakian (ed.), *History of psychology: a source book in systematic psychology* (pp. 115–121). Itasca, Ill.: Peacock Publishers, 1981.

Nijhout, H. F. (1990). Metaphors and the role of genes in development. *BioEssays, 12* (9), 441–446.

Nitzan, D. (1992). Robotics. In S. C. Shapiro (ed.), *Encyclopedia of artificial intelligence* (2nd ed.), (pp. 1375–1398). New York: Wiley.

Nussbaum, M. C. (1978). *Aristotle's De motu animalium.* Princeton, N.J.: Princeton University Press.

Palmer, S. E. (1978). Fundamental aspects of cognitive representation. In E. Rosch and B. B. Lloyd (eds.), *Cognition and categorization* (pp. 259–303). Hillsdale, N.J.: Erlbaum.

Papineau, D. (1993). *Philosophical naturalism.* Oxford: Blackwell.

Pasteur, G. (1994). Jean Henri Fabre. *Scientific American, 271* (1), 58–64.

Pattee, H. H. (1977). Dynamic and linguistic modes of complex systems. *International Journal of General Systems, 3*, 259–266.

Pattee, H. H. (1987). Instabilities and information in biological self-organization. In F. A. Yates (ed.), *Self-organizing systems* (pp. 325–338). New York: Plenum Press.

Pfeifer, R., and Verschure, P. (1992). Beyond rationalism: symbols, patterns, and behavior. *Connection Science*, *4*, 313–325.

Plotkin, H. C. (1994). *The nature of knowledge: concerning adaptations, instinct, and the evolution of intelligence.* London: Penguin Books.

Pollack, J. B. (1990). Recursive distributed representations. *Artificial Intelligence, 46*, 77–105.

Port, R. F., and Van Gelder, T. (eds.), (1995). *Mind as motion: explorations in the dynamics of cognition.* Cambridge, Mass.: MIT Press.

Powers, W. T. (1979). The nature of robots. Part 1: Defining behavior. *Byte, 4* (6), 132–144.

Pribram, K. H., and Robinson, D. N. (1985). Biological contributions to the development of psychology. In C. E. Buxton (ed.), *Points of view in the modern history of psychology* (pp. 345–381). Orlando: Academic Press.

Prigogine, I., and Stengers, I. (1984). *Order out of chaos.* London: Fontana Paperbacks.

Purves, D. (1988). *Body and brain: a trophic theory of neural connections.* Cambridge, Mass.: Harvard University Press.

Putnam, H. (1987). *The many faces of realism.* LaSalle, Ill.: Open Court.

Putnam, H. (1988). *Representation and reality.* Cambridge, Mass.: MIT Press.

Pylyshyn, Z. W. (1984). *Computation and cognition: towards a foundation for cognitive science.* Cambridge, Mass.: MIT Press.

Pylyshyn, Z. W. (ed.), (1987). *The robot's dilemma.* Norwood, N.J.: Ablex.

Quine. W. V. O. (1969). Epistemology naturalized. In *Ontological relativity and other essays* (pp. 69–90). New York: Columbia University Press.

Rachlin, H. (1994). *Behavior and mind: the roots of modern psychology.* New York: Oxford University Press.

Raff, R. A. (1996). *The shape of life: genes, development, and the evolution of animal form.* Chicago: Chicago University Press.

Raibert, M. H. (1986). *Legged robots that balance.* Cambridge, Mass.: MIT Press.

Raibert, M. H. (1990). Trotting, pacing, and bounding by a quadruped robot. *Journal of Biomechanics, 23*, suppl. 1, 79–98.

Raibert, M. H., and Hodgins, J. K. (1993). Legged robots. In R. D. Beer, R. E. Ritzmann, and T. McKenna (eds.), *Biological neural networks in invertebrate neuroethology and robotics* (pp. 319–354). San Diego, Calif.: Academic Press.

Ramsey, W., Stich, S. P., and Garon, J. (1991). Connectionism, eliminativism, and the future of folk psychology. In W. Ramsey, S. P. Stich, and D. E. Rumelhart (eds.), *Philosophy and connectionist theory* (pp. 199–228). Hillsdale, N.J.: Erlbaum.

Reed, E. S. (1982). An outline of a theory of action systems. *Journal of Motor Behavior, 14*, 98–134.

Reed, E. S. (1987). Why ideas are not in the mind: an introduction to ecological epistemology. In A. Shimony and D. Nails (eds.), *Naturalistic epistemology* (pp. 215–229). Dordrecht: Reidel.

Resnik, D. (1994). The rebirth of rational morphology: process structuralism's philosophy of biology. *Acta Biotheoretica, 42*, 1–14.

Roitblat, H. L. (1982). The meaning of representation in animal memory. *Behavioral and Brain Sciences, 5*, 353–406.

Roland, P. E. (1994). Obstacles on the road towards a neuroscientific theory of mind. *Journal of Theoretical Biology, 171*, 19–28.

Rorty, R. (1979). *Philosophy and the mirror of nature.* Princeton, N.J.: Princeton University Press.

Rosen, R. (1979). Anticipatory systems in retrospect and prospect. *General Systems Yearbook, 24*, 11–23.

Rosen, R. (1987). On complex systems. *European Journal of Operational Research, 30*, 129–134.

Rosenberg, A. (1978). The supervenience of biological concepts. *Philosophy of Science, 45*, 368–386.

Rosenberg, C., and Sejnowski, T. J. (1987). Parallel networks that learn to pronounce English text. *Complex Systems, 1*, 145–168.

Rosenblueth, A., Wiener, N., and Bigelow, J. (1943). Behavior, purpose, and teleology. *Philosophy of Science, 10*, 18–24.

Rumelhart, D. E., Hinton, G. E., and Williams, R. J. (1986). Learning internal representations by error propagation. In D. E. Rumelhart and J. L. McClelland (eds.),

Parallel distributed processing: explorations in the microstructure of cognition. Vol. 1: *Foundations* (pp. 318–362). Cambridge, Mass.: MIT Press.

Rumelhart, D. E., and McClelland, J. L. (eds.), (1986). *Parallel distributed processing: explorations in the microstructure of cognition*. Vol. 1: *Foundations*. Cambridge, Mass.: MIT Press.

Rutkowska, J. (1994). Emergent functionality in human infants, In D. Cliff, P. Husbands, J.-A. Meyer, and S. W. Wilson (eds.), *From animals to animats 3* (pp. 179–188). Cambridge, Mass.: MIT Press.

Sachs, T. (1994). Variable development as a basis for robust pattern formation. *Journal of Theoretical Biology, 170*, 423–425.

Salthe, S. N. (1985). *Evolving hierarchical systems*. New York: Columbia University Press.

Searle, J. R. (1980). Minds, brains, and programs. *Behavioral and Brain Sciences*, 3, 417–457.

Searle, J. R. (1992). *The rediscovery of the mind*. Cambridge, Mass.: MIT Press.

Seilacher, A. (1967). Fossil behavior. *Scientific American, 217*, 72–80.

Seilacher, A., Bose, P., and Pflüger, F. (1998). Triploblastic animals more than 1 billion years ago: trace fossil evidence from India. *Science, 282*, 80–83.

Shanon, B. (1993). *The representational and the presentational*. New York: Harvester Wheatsheaf.

Shastri, L., and Ajjanagadde, V. (1993). From simple associations to systematic reasoning: a connectionist representation of rules, variables, and dynamic bindings using temporal synchrony. *Behavioral and Brain Sciences, 16*, 417–494.

Sheets-Johnstone, M. (1999). *The primacy of movement*. Amsterdam: John Benjamins.

Selverston, A. I. (1980). Are central pattern generators understandable? *Behavioral and Brain Sciences, 3*, 535–571.

Simmons, P., and Young, D. (1999). *Nerve cells and animal behaviour* (2nd ed.). Cambridge: Cambridge University Press.

Simmons, R., and Krotkov, E. (1991). An integrated walking system for the Ambler planetary rover. In *Proceedings of the IEEE International Conference on Robotics and Automation* (pp. 2086–2091). Sacramento, Calif.

Simon, H. A. (1973). The organization of complex systems. In H. H. Pattee (ed.), *Hierarchy theory: the challenge of complex systems* (pp. 1–27). New York: Braziller.

Skarda, C. A. (1986). Explaining behavior: bringing the brain back in. *Inquiry, 29*, 187–202.

Skarda, C. A., and Freeman, W. J. (1987). How brains make chaos in order to make sense of the world. *Behavioral and Brain Sciences, 10*, 161–195.

Slack, J. M. W. (1991). *From egg to embryo: regional specification in early development* (2nd ed.). Cambridge: Cambridge University Press.

Sluga, H. D. (1980). *Gottlob Frege*. London: Routledge and Kegan Paul.

Smith, L. B., Thelen, E., Titzer, R., and McLin, D. (1999). Knowing in the context of acting: the task dynamics of the A-not-B error. *Psychological Review, 106*, 235–260.

Smithers, T. (1994). What the dynamics of adaptive behaviour and cognition might look like in agent-environment interaction systems. In T. Smithers (ed.), *Proceedings of the Workshop on the Role of Dynamics and Representation in Adaptive Behavior and Cognition* (pp. 134–153). San Sebastian, Spain: Universidad del País Vasco.

Smolensky, P. (1988). On the proper treatment of connectionism. *Behavioral and Brain Sciences, 11*, 1–73.

Steels, L. (1991). Towards a theory of emergent functionality. In J.-A. Meyer and S. W. Wilson (eds.), *From animals to animats*. Cambridge, Mass.: MIT Press.

Stefik, M., and Bobrow D. (1994). Review of T. Winograd and F. Flores's *On understanding computers and cognition: a new foundation for design*. In W. Clancey, S. Smoliar, and M. Stefik (eds.), *Contemplating minds* (pp. 180–186). Cambridge, Mass.: MIT Press.

Stewart, I., and Cohen, J. (1997). *Figments of reality*. Cambridge: Cambridge University Press.

Stewart, I., and Golubitsky, M. (1992). *Fearful symmetry: is God a geometer?* London: Penguin Books.

Stich, S. P. (1983). *From folk psychology to cognitive science: the case against belief*. Cambridge, Mass.: MIT Press.

Stich, S. P. (1994). What is a theory of mental representation? In S. P. Stich and T. A. Warfield (eds.), *Mental representations: a reader* (pp. 347–375). Oxford: Blackwell.

Strogatz, S. H., and Stewart, I. (1993). Coupled oscillators and biological synchronization. *Scientific American, 269* (6), 68–75.

Sutton, R. S., and Barto, A. G. (1998). *Reinforcement learning: an introduction*. Cambridge, Mass.: MIT Press.

Taga, G. (1994). Emergence of bipedal locomotion through entrainment among the neuro-musculo-skeletal system and the environment. *Physica D, 75*, 190–208.

Taga, G., Yamaguchi, Y., and Shimizu, H. (1991). Self-organized control of bipedal locomotion by neural oscillators in unpredictable environment. *Biological Cybernetics, 65*, 147–159.

Thelen, E., Schöner, G., Scheier, C., and Smith, L. B. (in press). The dynamics of embodiment: a field theory of infant perseverative reaching. *Behavioral and Brain Sciences*.

Thelen, E., and Smith, L. B. (1994). *A dynamic systems approach to the development of cognition and action*. Cambridge, Mass.: MIT Press.

Thorpe, C. E. (1992). Robots, mobile. In S. C. Shapiro (ed.), *Encyclopedia of artificial intelligence* (2nd ed.), (pp. 1409–1416). New York: Wiley.

Tinbergen, N. (1951). *The study of instinct*. Oxford: Clarendon Press.

Tolman, E. C. (1939). Prediction of vicarious trial and error by means of the schematic sowbug. *Psychological Review, 46*, 318–336.

Tolman, E. C. (1948). Cognitive maps in rats and men. *Psychological Review, 55*, 189–208.

Tolman, E. C., and Brunswik, E. (1935). The organism and the causal texture of the environment. *Psychological Review, 42*, 43–77.

Touretzky, D. S., and Pomerleau, D. A. (1994). Reconstructing physical symbol systems. *Cognitive Science, 18*, 345–353.

Turing, A. M. (1937). On computable numbers, with an application to the Entscheidungsproblem. *Proceedings of the London Mathematical Society, 42*, 230–265.

Valentine, J. W., Erwin, D. H., and Jablonski, D. (1996). Developmental evolution of metazoan body plans: the fossil evidence. *Developmental Biology, 173*, 373–381.

Vallacher, R. R., and Nowak, A. (eds.), (1994). *Dynamical systems in social psychology.* San Diego, Calif.: Academic Press.

Van Brakel, J. (1992). The complete description of the frame problem: book review of Ford and Hayes on the frame problem. Psycholoquy.92.3.60.frame-problem.2.vanbrakel.

Van der Heijden, A. H. C. (1992). *Selective attention in vision.* London: Routledge.

Van der Maas, H. L. J., and Molenaar, P. C. M. (1992). Stagewise cognitive development: an application of catastrophe theory. *Psychological Review, 99*, 395–417.

Van Geert, P. (1991). A dynamic systems model of cognitive and language growth. *Psychological Review, 98*, 3–53.

Van Gelder, T. (1990). Compositionality: a connectionist variation on a classical theme. *Cognitive Science, 14*, 355–384.

Van Gelder, T. (1991). Connectionism and dynamical explanation. In *Proceedings of the Thirteenth Annual Conference of the Cognitive Science Society*. Hillsdale, N.J.: Erlbaum.

Van Gelder, T. (1995). What might cognition be if not computation? *Journal of Philosophy, 91*, 345–381.

Van Gelder, T. (1998). The dynamical hypothesis in cognitive science. *Behavioral and Brain Sciences, 21*, 615–665.

Van Gelder, T., and Port, R. F. (1995). It's about time: an overview of the dynamical approach to cognition. In R. F. Port and T. van Gelder (eds.), *Mind as motion: explorations in the dynamics of cognition* (pp. 1–43). Cambridge, Mass.: MIT Press.

Varela, F. J., Maturana, H. R., and Uribe, R. (1974). Autopoiesis: the organization of living systems, its characterization, and a model. *Biosystems, 5*, 187–196.

Varela, F. J., Thompson, J. E., and Rosch, E. (1991). *The embodied mind.* Cambridge, Mass.: MIT Press.

Vellino, A. (1994). Review of T. Winograd and F. Flores's *On understanding computers and cognition: a new foundation for design.* In W. Clancey, S. Smoliar and

M. Stefik (eds.), *Contemplating minds* (pp. 173–180). Cambridge, Mass.: MIT Press.

Vera, A. H., and Simon, H. A. (1993a). Situated action: a symbolic interpretation. *Cognitive Science, 17*, 7–48.

Vera, A. H., and Simon, H. A. (1993b). Situated action: reply to William Clancey. *Cognitive Science, 17*, 117–133.

Vera, A. H., and Simon, H. A. (1994). Reply to Touretzky and Pomerleau: reconstructing physical symbol systems. *Cognitive Science, 18*, 355–360.

Vere, S. (1992). Planning. In S. C. Shapiro (ed.), *Encyclopedia of artificial intelligence* (2nd ed.), (pp. 1159–1171). New York: Wiley.

Verschure, P. F. M. J. (1992). Modeling adaptive behavior: the dynamics of system-environment interaction. Unpublished doctoral thesis, University of Zürich.

Von Holst, E. (1980). On the nature of order in the central nervous system. In C. R. Gallistel, *The organization of action: a new synthesis* (pp. 81–107). Hillsdale, N.J.: Erlbaum.

Von Holst, E., and Mittelstaedt, H. (1980). The reafference principle. In C. R. Gallistel, *The organization of action: a new synthesis* (pp. 176–209). Hillsdale, N.J.: Erlbaum.

Von Uexküll, G. (1964). *Jakob von Uexküll: seine Welt und seine Umwelt.* Hamburg: Wegner Verlag

Von Uexküll, J. (1921). *Umwelt und Innenwelt der Tiere* (2. Aufl.). Berlin: Springer Verlag.

Von Uexküll, J. (1980). *Kompositionslehre der Natur*. Frankfurt am Main: Verlag Ullstein.

Vowles, D. M. (1970). Neuroethology, evolution, and grammar. In L. R. Aronson, D. S. Lehrman, and J. S. Rosenblatt (eds.), *Development and evolution of behavior* (pp. 194–215). San Francisco: Freeman.

Waddington, (1975). *The evolution of an evolutionist.* Edinburgh: Edinburgh University Press.

Waldrop, M. M. (1992). *Complexity: the emerging science at the edge of order and chaos*. London: Viking.

Walter, W. G. (1953). *The living brain*. London: Duckworth.

Warden, C. J. (1927). The historical development of comparative psychology. *Psychological Review, 34*, 57–85, 135–168.

Webb, B. (1994). Robotic experiments in cricket phonotaxis In D. Cliff, P. Husbands, J.-A. Meyer, and S. W. Wilson (eds.), *From animals to animats 3* (pp. 45–54). Cambridge, Mass.: MIT Press.

Weiss, P. A. (1971). The basic concept of hierarchic systems. In P. A. Weiss (ed.), *Hierarchically organized systems in theory and practice* (pp. 1–43). New York: Hafner.

Wheeler, M. (1994). Active perception in meaningful worlds. Cognitive Science Research Paper 327, University of Sussex.

Wheeler, M., and Clark, A. (1999). Genic representation: reconciling content and causal complexity. *British Journal for the Philosophy of Science, 50*, 103–135.

Wiener, N. (1948). *Cybernetics*. New York: Wiley.

Wilson, E. O. (1992). *The diversity of life*. London: Penguin Press.

Wilson, E. O. (1995). *Naturalist*. London: Penguin Press.

Winograd, T., and Flores, F. (1986). *Understanding computers and cognition: a new foundation for design*. Reading, Mass.: Addison Wesley.

Winograd, T., and Flores, F. (1994). On *Understanding computers and cognition: a new foundation for design*: a response to the reviews. In W. Clancey, S. Smoliar, and M. Stefik (eds.), *Contemplating minds* (pp. 210–221). Cambridge, Mass.: MIT Press.

Winston, P. H. (1977). *Artificial intelligence*. Reading, Mass.: Addison-Wesley.

Wooldridge, D. (1968). *The mechanical man: the physical basis of intelligent life*. New York: McGraw-Hill.

Wright, L. (1973). Functions. *Philosophical Review, 82*, 139–168.

Yates, F. E. (1993). Self-organizing systems. In C. A. R. Boyd and D. Noble (eds.), *The logic of life: the challenge of integrative physiology* (pp. 189–218). Oxford: Oxford University Press.

Young, R. M. (1970). *Mind, brain, and adaptation in the nineteenth century*. Oxford: Clarendon.

Zill, S. N., and Seyfarth, E.-A. (1996). Exoskeletal sensors for walking. *Scientific American, 275* (1), 70–74.

Index